# MURD

# BIRCH

# DRIVE

D0901462

## The True Story
## of the
## Michelle Young
## Murder Case

---

"A **compelling and accurate** description of a fascinating murder case, from the initial investigation through the twists and turns of two trials, and all the strategic decisions in between. **One of the best true crime books I have read.** Very entertaining."

—*David S. Rudolf, defense attorney for Michael Peterson, featured in the Netflix series* The Staircase

"**Psychological thriller meets true crime story at its best!** MURDER ON BIRCHLEAF DRIVE is a riveting account of what, at first blush, appears to be a boy-meets-girl romance but ends in bloody horror. Epstein brilliantly details the unraveling of the couple's relationship and eloquently captures the legal details, making the most complicated aspects of the murder case completely understandable. Prepare yourself for an **intense, heart-pounding** read!"

—*Dr. Jean G. Spaulding, Forensic Psychiatrist and Associate Consulting Professor of Psychiatry and Behavioral Sciences, Duke University*

"**An amazing first book** by a talented new author, MURDER ON BIRCHLEAF DRIVE drops the reader into the complex web and dark beauty of the criminal justice system. Epstein skillfully recounts a chilling tale of human emotion, betrayal, and calculated murder. **This story cannot be matched** by the best of crime fiction—its power unleashed by the haunting reality of truth. I hope this is the first book among many for this gifted author."

*— Joseph B. Cheshire, V, criminal defense attorney whose successful representation of Duke University lacrosse players falsely accused of sexual assault received national attention and acclaim*

"Steve Epstein's debut effort is **an outstanding achievement in true crime writing.** A seasoned trial attorney in his own right, he skillfully brings this heartbreaking case to life with a detailed accounting of both the crime and the complex legal battles that followed, while helping us get to know the many individuals impacted by the tragic murder of Michelle Fisher Young. This is a must-read for anyone interested in seeing our criminal justice system at work."

*— Hon. Barbara Jackson,*
*Associate Justice, North Carolina Supreme Court, 2011-2019;*
*Judge, North Carolina Court of Appeals, 2005-2011*

"This **fascinating and well-told** story of a North Carolina murder and the trials that followed has more twists and turns than the road to Murphy. Clear your schedule and settle down for a long evening with some of the state's best trial attorneys. I enjoyed the daylights out of it."

*— Hon. Robert H. Edmunds, Jr.,*
*Associate Justice, North Carolina Supreme Court, 2001-2017;*
*Judge, North Carolina Court of Appeals, 1999-2001;*
*U.S. Attorney, Middle District of North Carolina, 1986-1993*

# MURDER ON BIRCHLEAF DRIVE

## The True Story
## of the
## Michelle Young
## Murder Case

## STEVEN B. EPSTEIN

Black Lyon Publishing, LLC

Our books may be ordered through your local bookstore or by
visiting the publisher:

**www.BlackLyonPublishing.com**

Black Lyon Publishing, LLC
PO Box 567
Baker City, OR 97814

ISBN: 978-1-934912-86-7
Library of Congress Control Number: 2019936659

Published and printed in the United States of America.

---

# More praise for this book!

"MURDER ON BIRCHLEAF DRIVE is **a gripping story** that
captures the true essence of a bizarre 'who done it' murder
investigation and prosecution, with remarkable insights
and thoughtful analysis. The book provides an unvarnished
look behind the curtain at how the criminal justice system
really works. Epstein has skillfully fleshed out the characters
involved and courtroom theatrics. **A great read, and a must-
read**, for those who are fascinated with the drama of real life—
it's even better than fiction."

*—Colon Willoughby, District Attorney*
*of Wake County, North Carolina, 1987-2014*

"Some heinous crimes, like premeditated murder, are relatively easy to solve due to damning physical evidence and direct witness testimony. Others, like the one Steven B. Epstein details in his captivating book, MURDER ON BIRCHLEAF DRIVE, are **anything but simple**. The solution to such crimes, resulting in justice for the victim, comes only through unwavering witnesses, dedicated law enforcement efforts, and well-prepared prosecutors ... This book documents, accurately, the work it takes to make 'circumstantial evidence' persuasive. As such it should make the reader appreciate the tenacity those involved in criminal prosecution must display if justice is to truly be done on behalf of victims. **An excellent book**, and I recommend it highly."

*— Jerry Boyd, Coronado, California Police Chief (ret.);*
*author of multiple books including FIRESTONE PARK:*
*POLICING SOUTH-CENTRAL LOS ANGELES*
*and MY YEARS AS A CHIEF*

"Reading MURDER ON BIRCHLEAF DRIVE is **like being at the scene of the crime** and inside the well of the courtroom during every moment of one of North Carolina's most notorious murder trials. Epstein does an **exceptional** job with the challenging task of describing how it feels to be there as law enforcement cracks a case and when great lawyers go to battle."

*— Ripley Rand, U.S. Attorney,*
*Middle District of North Carolina, 2011-2017;*
*Superior Court Judge, 2002-2010*

"**There is no way to put down this book!** Once you begin, it draws you in right from the start. I felt as though Michelle Young could have been my very own sister. Many times I forgot I was reading a book; it is so difficult to fathom this being a true story."

*— Stacie Overman, co-star of SyFy's* Ghost Mine,
*author of ANGEL KISSES: NO MORE CANCER*

*In loving memory of Morris Goldstein—my "Papa"—
who instilled in me a passion for writing and who taught
me good writing is the result of hard work.
I hope the pages that follow live up to his example.*

# Part I
# Murder

# 1

The incessant ringing of her cell phone woke Meredith Fisher from a deep sleep. Slowly, she crawled out of bed and stumbled to the bathroom to brush her teeth. She set her phone on the counter and began listening to the voicemail, instantly recognizing the familiar voice of her brother-in-law, Jason Young.

"Strange," she thought. In the four years she had known her sister Michelle's impetuous husband, she couldn't recall a single time he had called her twice in a week, let alone on consecutive days.

Jason, who grew up in the North Carolina mountains, had been married to Michelle, a native New Yorker, for just over three years. She was a talented accountant and dedicated mother to the couple's two-year-old daughter, Cassidy. Though he was a relatively successful salesman and devoted father, Jason often drank and partied like an impulsive college student. That didn't sit particularly well with Michelle, a meticulous planner who charted out every aspect of her life.

Their roller-coaster relationship had turned especially sour over the last few months. Meredith, three years younger than Michelle and a manager at the Lucky 32 restaurant, knew the couple's differences well. After their most recent fight on November 1, Michelle had called her sister in frustration to tell her Jason had thrown a TV remote at her.

"I'm done. I just can't do this anymore," Michelle whimpered despondently.

Jason had left a voicemail for Meredith the following morning, after she had begun her shift at Lucky 32. He had overheard Michelle telling Meredith about the TV remote, he said. He vehemently denied her account, telling his sister-in-law Michelle was just being dramatic. He implored her to call him back.

For better or worse, Meredith had volunteered for this umpiring duty. With a degree in psychology and an interest in pursuing a master's degree in marriage counseling and social work, she had willingly accepted the role of mediating the all-too-frequent arguments between her sister and brother-in-law.

The prior Friday evening had turned into a marathon session in the den of Jason's and Michelle's Raleigh home, the two arguing over whether and how long Michelle and Meredith's mother, Linda Fisher—a blunt-spoken Long Islander for whom Jason had little tolerance—would stay at the couple's home over the Christmas holidays. Jason wanted her to stay at a hotel. Michelle couldn't dream of asking her mom to do that.

A related topic that caused a heated argument that night was what would happen after Cassidy's baby brother, Rylan, was born the following March. Linda had already been a frequent visitor to their home to assist with caring for her granddaughter. Michelle wanted to finish the third-floor attic to create a bedroom for her mother so that she could be Rylan's nanny. Jason was adamant that wasn't going to happen. The thought of seeing Linda Fisher in his home every day—and listening to her never-ending criticisms of his treatment of her daughter—was more than he could bear.

Meredith listened as her sister and brother-in-law bickered about sex and romance. To Jason, romance was asking his wife whether she wanted a "hot beef injection." Michelle enlisted Meredith to explain to Jason why his vulgar entreaties didn't make her feel attracted to him. She craved genuine romance. Jason just wanted more sex and was deeply frustrated Michelle wasn't complying.

"All of this would go away if you would just let me have a girl on the side," Jason blurted out as his final, parting shot.

Exasperated, Michelle rolled her eyes, responding, "Really, this whole discussion, and that's what you take away from it?"

That four-hour counseling session was still fresh on Meredith's mind when she returned Jason's call from her car after leaving work around 9:00 p.m. on November 2. Jason told his sister-in-law he was on his way to the Virginia mountains for a business trip and had stopped at a Cracker Barrel restaurant in Greensboro for dinner. He insisted he never threw a remote at Michelle. She was blowing things completely out of proportion, he protested.

Though Meredith wanted to call Michelle to get her take on Jason's portrayal of their fight, that conversation would have to wait. She had just pulled into the parking lot of the Carolina Ale House, already late for a nightcap with a friend. Meredith also knew her sister had her friend Shelly over that night to watch *Grey's Anatomy*, her favorite TV show. They could talk later, Meredith thought.

So as she brushed her teeth and listened to Jason's voicemail shortly after noon on November 3, Meredith fully expected his message to be a postscript on their discussion about the TV remote. But to her surprise, his message didn't mention that topic at all. Rather, Jason asked Meredith for a "huge favor" — to run by his and Michelle's house to pull some printouts of eBay Coach purse auctions off the printer in the second-floor office.

As he explained in his voicemail, "I kind of screwed up last night and I actually, when Shelly was over there at our house, I was printing up the Coach stuff that I was looking at on eBay for Michelle and they started coming up the stairs putting Cass to bed right before I left, and I stopped printing, but I thought I grabbed that stuff and put it in my bag to take with me, but I think it's sitting there on the printer. I talked to Michelle late last night. I don't think she's seen it, but I do want to still surprise her."

His voicemail continued, "I'm actually going to my parents'

house tonight because I'm so far west. I'm heading to their house right now. My phone is giving horrible reception—I haven't gotten any all morning. So, I was going to see if you would mind calling me or my mom … and letting her know if you're able to get that … because if not I'm going to have to think of something [to tell] Michelle in regards to what it is and why I'm printing it because I really do want to surprise her. I think that would be a nice thing and I think your mom would appreciate it that I'm getting leather for the third anniversary. Anyway, well you can certainly try calling me back, but my phone's been doing weird things. Talk to you later. Bye."

This was the second time her brother-in-law had mentioned to Meredith his idea of buying Michelle an expensive leather purse for their anniversary. He first broached that topic two weeks earlier when Meredith swung by the house to print out her work schedule while Michelle was away on a business trip.

As she arrived, Jason was backing out of the driveway in his white Ford Explorer with his old friend Carol Anne Sowerby in the passenger seat and Cassidy strapped in her car seat in the back. Jason stopped long enough to tell Meredith, through the open car window, he needed help choosing a leather purse for Michelle for their anniversary. She volunteered to go shopping with him and look through her sister's closet to get some ideas on color.

Something about that conversation—and Jason's voicemail—nagged at Meredith as she completed some chores around her house and drove the familiar fifteen-minute route from her Fuquay-Varina home to Jason's and Michelle's home in Raleigh. For starters, the couple's third wedding anniversary was on October 10—more than three weeks ago. It seemed a little late for Jason to be so worried about surprising his wife with a gift.

Secondly, not once since that chance driveway meeting had her brother-in-law mentioned anything about purchasing a leather purse for Michelle—not while she was there for the marathon counseling session nor during their phone conversation the prior evening. Not a single word.

Even more baffling, some seventeen hours had elapsed

since Jason left home without those printouts. Surely he would have discovered long before now they weren't in his bag? He knew full well Michelle would have walked within a few feet of their home office—and those printouts—on her way to the master bedroom to go to bed the prior evening and as she got Cassidy up and ready for daycare that morning. Why did he wait until after noon to call her?

It was about 1:15 p.m. when Meredith pulled into south Raleigh's Enchanted Oaks subdivision and turned into the driveway at 5108 Birchleaf Drive. Even though it was bright and sunny that afternoon, the lanterns atop the brick pillars at the driveway entrance were still lit.

"Odd," Meredith thought. She also noticed the gate to the backyard was open, which also seemed strange because the Youngs' dog—a black mixed lab named Mr. Garrison—would often be let out into the fenced-in backyard and allowed to roam free.

Meredith parked her Honda Accord by the front walkway and approached the front door, where she was able to hear Mr. Garrison whimpering from inside. She reached for the house key on her keychain, then remembered she had recently given it to a friend to feed the dog while she, Jason, Michelle, and Cassidy were in New York.

"Not a problem," she thought. She went to the back of the house where a door she thought might be open led into the garage. But when she tried to open the door, it was locked.

Meredith then recalled the electronic garage door opener wasn't working. She was able to manually lift the door just high enough to slip inside. She was surprised to see Michelle's silver Lexus SUV sitting in the garage—she was supposed to be at work.

"Weird," she thought, her concern beginning to grow.

As she walked through the unlocked kitchen door, Meredith spotted her sister's brown purse on the floor against the leg of a small desk at the far end of the kitchen.

"Michelle?" Meredith called out. "Michelle?"

No response. Something wasn't right.

She quickly climbed the stairs leading to the second-floor

bedrooms, her heart beginning to beat faster. As she neared the top of the staircase, out of the corner of her eye, Meredith could see dark red streaks in Cassidy's bathroom to the right of the upstairs landing. There were red stains on the bathroom floor too, as well as on the hallway carpeting. The more closely she looked at the stains, the more bewildered she became. They were actually tiny footprints—Cassidy's. Perhaps her little niece had gotten into Michelle's hair dye and made a mess, she speculated.

"Michelle must be pissed," she thought.

Meredith then turned to face the master bedroom, directly across from Cassidy's bathroom. On the left side of the room, bright red spots were splattered across the walls, all the way up to the ceiling.

"Oh my God!" she cried out. Near Jason's closet, a red liquid had soaked through the white comforter on Michelle's side of the bed. Red splotches dotted her pillow.

Alarm now reaching a fever pitch, Meredith glanced at the floor between the closet and the bed. There, below the most concentrated red spots on the wall, she was confronted with the most horrifying image of her entire life. Just to the left of the bed, facedown in a large pool of red, lay the lifeless body of her sister.

Frantically, Meredith reached for the cordless phone on the nightstand next to the other side of the bed. She had barely punched in the numbers 9-1-1 when something else startled her—a rustling from under the covers. To her astonishment, Cassidy wriggled out from beneath them and began staring at her intently. Amazingly, her niece appeared unharmed. She was wearing pink fleece pajamas with no socks, diaper, or underwear. In view of the tiny red footprints on her bathroom floor and hallway carpet, she appeared shockingly clean.

Cassidy lunged toward her aunt and hooked onto her hip like a Koala bear, as the 911 dispatcher came onto the line.

"I think my sister's dead!" Meredith exclaimed. "Oh my God!"

As she gave the dispatcher her name and sister's address— routine information gathered during all 911 calls—Meredith finally realized that the red streaks, spots, and footprints throughout the second floor weren't Michelle's hair dye after all. "Oh my God! There's blood everywhere!" she shrieked.

Was Michelle conscious, still breathing, the dispatcher asked.

"No, I don't think so. Should I try to help her?" Meredith answered in a panicked tone. In her shock, she hadn't checked for a pulse. She then touched Michelle and remarked, despondently, "She's cold."

"Did you see what happened?" the dispatcher inquired.

Meredith replied she didn't know, but there were "blood footprints all over the house from her daughter's little footprints ... I just came here on a fluke. I usually, you know, don't come here during the day. She shouldn't be home. She should be at work."

The dispatcher pushed Meredith for any details that could explain what had happened at the ghastly scene. "I don't know. I have no idea," Meredith said. "There's blood all over the place."

Cassidy, still clinging to her aunt—who she called "Emmy"—then chimed in, "Emmy, Emmy, there's blood ... Can you get a washcloth?"

Meredith interrupted. "Did you see what happened to Mommy? Did she fall?"

In her little voice, Cassidy explained the situation the only way she knew how: "She got boo boos *everywhere*."

Meredith took her niece to her room—as the dispatcher instructed—and told her to stay there. When she returned alone to her sister's side, the dispatcher asked her to try CPR. She was told to turn Michelle onto her back, but budging her sister's twisted, lifeless body proved impossible.

"She's so heavy. I really think she's dead," Meredith said after several failed attempts. "She's ice cold. Her body is stiff."

That chilling revelation prompted the dispatcher to halt any life-saving efforts.

"Oh my God, I don't know what happened to her," Meredith whimpered helplessly.

Was anything unusual, out of place, the dispatcher probed.

As Meredith surveyed the bedroom, she remarked, "This place does not look like what it normally looks like ... There's blood in the bed." Also, Mr. Garrison had been "freaking out" when she arrived, she noted. Another thing out of place, though Meredith didn't notice it at the time, was that the wedding and engagement rings Michelle always wore—no matter how much she and Jason argued and fought—were nowhere to be found.

An operator from the Sheriff's Office then joined the line. He had more questions.

Meredith told him she was at her sister's house and had found blood "everywhere." Turning her attention to Jason, she mentioned he traveled quite a bit. "I spoke with him last night. He's out of town. He's on his way to his parents' house."

"Normally my sister goes to work early and takes [Cassidy] to daycare," Meredith continued. "You know like today, something's not right." Cassidy was very smart for her age, she said, and seemed to be saying that someone had been in the house.

Still gathering basic information, the Sheriff's operator asked for Michelle's age.

"Twenty-nine," Meredith responded. Was Meredith aware of any personal problems Michelle might have been having? he asked. Meredith thought for a moment, then responded, "Um, not really. You know, her and her husband fight a little bit, but nothing too ridiculous."

It was at that point that another realization set in, this one hitting Meredith like a prize fighter's blow to the gut. Michelle wasn't the only victim of this savage attack.

"She's about four-and-a-half months pregnant," Meredith sobbed. "Oh my God. Oh my God ... I can't even believe that this is real. Like the two of them play jokes on each other, like my sister and her husband, like I almost thought it was a joke, that's how over the top it seems ... Something's not right."

# 2

This wasn't exactly how Michelle had imagined her third wedding anniversary. Yet here she was—alone with Cassidy—with her husband more than 1,500 miles away on business in Denver, Colorado. To make matters worse, Jason had been away from home since Saturday morning, when he flew off to Orlando to begin back-to-back business trips. The anniversary card he sent from Florida, along with $25 in Starbucks gift cards, hardly made up for his prolonged absence.

The only consolation for Michelle was her mother and grandmother were arriving that day from New York for a full ten days. The plan was for them to take care of Cassidy over the weekend while she and Jason were in Winston-Salem for the wedding of their close friends, Shelly Doub and Ryan Schaad.

Shelly and Michelle attended N.C. State together and were both members of the Alpha Delta Pi sorority—Michelle was Shelly's "big sister." They got along so well they ultimately became roommates and best friends. The two lived together for more than four years while Michelle completed her undergraduate education and master's degree in accounting. They ran together, had meals together, and tailgated at N.C. State football games together. Shelly was even with Michelle the night she and Jason first met.

Similarly, Ryan and Jason had been best friends for years

dating back to their time at N.C. State. They had attended a gazillion Wolfpack football and basketball games together—and tailgates—and began living in a townhome together shortly after Jason started dating Michelle. Jason and Ryan eventually invited her to move in with them.

Shelly and Ryan owed their relationship to Michelle and Jason. They introduced Ryan to Shelly at a Stanley Cup playoff game between the Carolina Hurricanes and Detroit Red Wings in June 2002. The foursome had been on many double-dates, and attended many N.C. State tailgates since then. Now it was Shelly's and Ryan's turn to get married.

Michelle had been looking forward to spending a belated anniversary weekend with Jason in the midst of their friends' marital bliss. Seeing them tie the knot within days of her own anniversary almost made up for Jason's extended absence. She envisioned a romantic time with her husband in between the bridal luncheon and rehearsal dinner that Friday and following the wedding on Saturday. The couple also had a belated anniversary dinner planned for Thursday evening, after Jason returned from Denver, at Bella Monica, their favorite Italian restaurant.

Linda drove her daughter to her office at Progress Energy in downtown Raleigh that Thursday morning so Jason could pick her up from work and escort her to their special dinner.

When Jason arrived that evening, however, he was on the phone. He told Michelle he was talking to a former colleague. He barely acknowledged his wife even though he hadn't seen her in nearly a week. He continued his phone conversation during the entire fifteen-minute drive to the restaurant, and even as they waited for their table. Finally, as they were being seated, he ended the call.

The dinner didn't turn out to be special—or romantic. Instead, the couple got into a heated argument over the travel arrangements to the wedding. Jason informed Michelle he planned to ride to Winston-Salem with the guys. They planned to play golf while the women attended the bridal luncheon. Since the women didn't have to be in Winston-Salem as early as the men, the guys had agreed to pile into a car in Raleigh early Friday morning and start the weekend together. The women would head out later. It made no sense, Jason told her, for Michelle to ride with him, as she would wind up waiting around for hours for the luncheon to begin.

Michelle didn't see it that way at all. She told Jason she had planned for them to have a romantic weekend — together — to make up for him being away on their anniversary. But Jason was adamant he was going to be playing golf with the guys. He had been looking forward to it for weeks. His friend Josh Dalton told him his wife Julie had left a voicemail inviting Michelle to ride to Winston-Salem with her. Michelle denied receiving any such message. That pushed Jason over the edge. He accused his wife of lying and being selfish.

His anger didn't subside during their ride home from dinner. "I'm going out!" he barked, as Michelle got out of the car.

She entered the house in tears. Michelle recounted for her mother how Jason had ignored her the first part of the evening and then argued with her the remainder of the night. She told her mom she was going to get in her car to try to find Jason. Linda tried to persuade her not to, but before long, she was gone.

Michelle and Jason soon were back inside, their argument now a full-blown screaming match with doors slamming throughout the house. "Fine!" Jason ultimately relented. "I'll take you." But he insisted they leave early enough for him to make his tee time. Michelle would have to keep herself busy between then and the bridal luncheon.

Jason arranged to meet the rest of the guys at a gas station in Greensboro early Friday morning. Michelle would take the Explorer from there to Shelly's parents' home in Tobaccoville, just outside Winston-Salem. The friction between them hadn't subsided as they began their journey from Raleigh. When they finally arrived at the designated meeting point, Jason looked Michelle dead in the eye as he got out of the car.

Through clenched teeth, he said, "I'm done. I'm out." His anger wasn't lost on his friends. Still seething, he told them as they drove off he was "done" with Michelle.

.....

When she opened the front door to her parents' home at 8:00 a.m., Shelly was shocked to see her best friend standing on the doorstep. She had no idea why Michelle had come so early without the other women from Raleigh. She was visibly shaken. She sat down with Shelly in the living room and shared her heartache.

This was her anniversary week, Michelle told her friend. Jason had conveniently arranged to be out of town on business for nearly the entire time. When he finally returned home, he virtually ignored her, she explained. What was supposed to be a romantic, belated anniversary dinner turned into an explosive, hours-long argument. They had argued during the entire car ride that morning, too. What really riled her, Michelle said, was in all the time her husband was away, he didn't even think to buy her a real present. Just a card postmarked from Orlando with some Starbucks gift cards inside.

Michelle seemed completely withdrawn, despondent, and depressed throughout the remainder of the day. She stayed to herself while Shelly got ready, during the bridal luncheon, and at the rehearsal dinner. While Jason carried on with the guys during dinner, Michelle was all alone at the far end of the room. Shelly sought out her friend and suggested they step outside so they could talk. She was very concerned.

Michelle would have none of it. This was Shelly's special weekend, she told her friend, and no matter what was troubling her, she wouldn't dream of spoiling the wedding festivities. Michelle tried to be in good spirits the following day at the wedding. She truly was happy for Shelly and wanted that to show through no matter how badly her own marriage seemed to be crumbling. She wasn't going to ruin this momentous occasion for her best friend.

Jason, of course, was having a blast—the life of the party as always. For him, the wedding was nothing short of a college reunion and a chance to relive his glory days. He tried his best to outdrink his college buddies and, unzipping his fly, reprised what he liked to refer to as his "dick tricks." If his wife was miserable, that was her problem, not his. She wasn't going to rain on his parade.

.....

Over the next few days, Linda couldn't help but notice the deterioration in her daughter's marriage. It seemed pretty obvious to her why there was no spark, no romance. At breakfast one morning, Jason looked at his wife and, in his mother-in-law's presence, told Michelle he liked how her boobs were looking so big.

Linda knew Jason was dissatisfied with the amount of sex in his marriage and later tried to use what he said as a teaching moment, telling him, "That type of comment doesn't make a woman feel like she wants to have a romantic interlude in bed. You should want to make love to your wife, not just have sex with her. Don't be so rude." She also cautioned her son-in-law that, above all else, he never should think about having an affair. "That will destroy the marriage," she warned.

Linda promised Jason she would talk with Michelle and discuss the importance of a physical relationship to complement an emotional one. And she did. But Michelle painted a very bleak picture. "Mom, you just don't understand," she said. "The way he talks to me is disgusting. It's not romantic. He just wants to fuck me."

The smiling, peppy, extroverted daughter Linda had always known seemed to be vanishing before her very eyes. She was constantly sad and withdrawn.

One night while Jason was upstairs, Linda sat with Michelle on the couch in the den, Michelle resting her head on her mother's lap. Linda stroked her daughter's hair just like she did when Michelle was a little girl. Though Michelle had a pulse and was breathing, Linda Fisher's beautiful child seemed totally devoid of life.

# 3

Mr. Garrison's furious barking announced Shelly Schaad's arrival moments before she knocked on the Youngs' front door. Michelle warmly greeted the new bride. They had arranged a week earlier, when Michelle picked up Shelly and Ryan from the airport, to get together for a girls' night the next time Jason was out of town. Michelle wanted to hear all about Shelly's Italian honeymoon and also share her own news. She had emailed her best friend during her honeymoon to let her know the baby she was carrying was going to be a boy.

As Shelly walked into the kitchen to deposit the bags of Italian food she brought for dinner, she immediately noticed how cold the house was.

"The heat pump's broken," Michelle reported, as she spread their sumptuous meal out on the kitchen counter. "We're waiting on the insurance to come through to be able to fix it."

Shelly decided to keep her coat on to stay warm.

Cassidy was upstairs playing in the bonus room right next to the home office where Jason was busily printing directions for his business trip to Virginia. The women went upstairs to get Cassidy for dinner. Just before they got to the top step, Jason peeked out to greet Shelly. While she and Michelle chatted, he ducked into the master bedroom to grab some clothes for

Shelly to return to her husband. Jason had to borrow them when he had too much to drink at Ryan's bachelor party, and had urinated on his own clothes.

Shelly took the clothes and asked Jason to join them for dinner. He politely declined, telling his wife's friend he needed to get on the road, explaining he planned to stop at the Cracker Barrel in Greensboro for dinner before driving an additional three hours to Galax, Virginia. That would leave him exactly two hours, he said, to drive to his 10:00 a.m. sales meeting the next morning in the Virginia mountains.

Shelly, Michelle, and Cassidy went downstairs for a girls-only dinner. When they finished, Shelly supervised the toddler using the toilet without any assistance. Though she had only recently begun potty training, Cassidy was proudly sporting big-girl underwear and was mostly accident-free. After she washed her hands—again all by herself—the three marched back upstairs for bath time. They were still in Cassidy's bathroom when Jason came out of the master bedroom at about 7:15 p.m., clutching his black suitcase and laptop bag, ready to depart. Unlike Shelly, he wasn't wearing a coat.

After saying goodbye to Cassidy, Shelly, and Michelle, Jason loaded up his Explorer, dropped the MapQuest directions on the front passenger seat, and drove to a local gas station to fill up. While there, he began an hour-long conversation with his mom, Pat Young, whom he was hoping to visit in Brevard—his hometown in the North Carolina mountains—following his business trip. Jason told her he might spend the night. He would need to wake up early Saturday morning, he explained, to get back to Raleigh in time for the N.C. State football game that afternoon.

. . . . .

Shelly and Michelle lifted Cassidy out of the bath, dried her off, put on a precautionary diaper, and dressed her in an undershirt and her cute, pink fleece pajamas. Cassidy insisted she put on her socks "myself." Michelle encouraged her daughter as she struggled with them and took over once she gave up. It was bedtime.

Cassidy pleaded with her mom for a little more time. She wanted to watch her favorite DVD, *Barbie Cinderella*. "Just for ten minutes," Michelle relented. As the movie played in the bonus room, Shelly filled Michelle in on her fairytale honeymoon. They put Cassidy to bed after ten minutes and nestled into the den to talk and watch *Grey's Anatomy*.

The contrast between their lives was stark: Shelly, a newlywed, madly in love and starting her new life as Ryan's wife; Michelle, just three years into her own marriage, a union that seemed to be disintegrating.

Michelle filled Shelly in on how she and Jason had been fighting about the upcoming holidays. Jason was refusing to allow her mom to be part of his family's Thanksgiving celebration in Brevard, Michelle explained, and was trying to limit Linda's time at their home over the Christmas holidays. She even shared details about their marathon counseling session with Meredith the prior Friday evening. To Shelly, Michelle appeared crestfallen and defeated. She told Ryan later that evening, "She's just in a deep, dark hole and I can't reach her."

One thing that seemed to lift Michelle out of her emotional abyss was her pregnancy and son on the way. That gave her hope. She beamed with pride as she showed Shelly the baby clothes she had picked out for Rylan and perked up as she talked about the nursery she was planning.

The phone rang. In the blink of an eye, Michelle was down again. Her father, Alan Fisher, had called to tell Michelle he wasn't going to make it to Raleigh that weekend after all. He had recently been diagnosed with prostate cancer. His poor health and the related treatments would prevent him from traveling, he said.

Michelle's relationship with her dad hadn't been easy since her parents divorced many years earlier, but she wanted him to be part of her children's lives. She was visibly upset—both about his declining health and his inability to come to Raleigh that weekend.

Just then, the pitter patter of little feet could be heard

coming down the staircase—Cassidy wasn't going down without a fight. Michelle excused herself and walked her toddler back up to her room. She tucked her in one final time, gave her a squeeze, and kissed her good night while finishing her conversation with her dad.

Michelle returned to the den and turned on *Grey's Anatomy,* which she had been recording on the DVR. The phone rang again, this time with Jason on the other end. Michelle told him she would call back later after Shelly had gone. It was already after 9:00 p.m. when the women were finally able to turn their attention to the doctors and drama on the TV.

Toward the end of the show, Shelly was overcome by an eerie sensation, almost as if they were being watched. She asked Michelle if she was ever scared living in such a secluded area. Her friend replied Jason had mentioned hearing some noises at night recently, and the trailer park behind their home was fully visible in the winter once the trees were bare, which did concern her. But then she remarked, almost casually, "If someone's going to break in to kill you, they're going to kill you," and little could be done to stop them.

Shelly was so spooked by the time she was ready to leave that she asked Michelle to walk her to her car. Michelle slipped on a coat and pair of slippers and stepped out into the driveway with her friend. They traded a warm hug by the car door and parted ways just before 10:30 p.m.

. . . . .

Less than ninety minutes after leaving the Cracker Barrel restaurant in Greensboro, Jason exited Interstate 77 and pulled into the parking lot of the Hampton Inn in the small town of Hillsville, Virginia, a crossroads community near Galax.

The wind was howling more than twenty miles an hour; it was bitter cold, barely above freezing. Though Jason hadn't booked ahead, he was able to get a room and took the elevator up to the fourth floor. He called Michelle just before 11:00 p.m. They spoke for less than five minutes—just long enough to let her know he had arrived safely and to say good night.

With his laptop out, Jason turned his attention to preparing for his sales meeting the next morning in Clintwood, Virginia, near the Kentucky border. This would be his first solo sales call for his new employer, ChartOne. Though he was a whiz at pharmaceutical sales, he hadn't yet perfected his pitch for the electronic medical records software ChartOne was selling. He reviewed some materials he planned to use at the sales meeting, made some calls, and looked at sports websites until nearly midnight.

.....

Jason arrived at Dickenson Community Hospital more than thirty minutes late the next morning. He told hospital personnel he had gotten lost on the tricky mountain roads. The meeting was brief. The hospital didn't seem interested in ChartOne's software. Jason got directions to Asheville—the largest city between Clintwood and Brevard—stopped for gas, and began the long journey to his childhood home.

En route, he made several phone calls, including one to Michelle's office at Progress Energy and another to her cell phone. Both calls rolled to voicemail. Jason decided not to leave her a message. He did, however, leave a message for Meredith about the eBay printouts he had neglected to pull off the printer. After not hearing from his sister-in-law for more than an hour, Jason called his mom and asked her to try to connect with Meredith, letting her know how important it was his wife not see those printouts. At 1:37 p.m., Jason placed a second call to Meredith. When that one also rolled to voicemail, he left her another message:

"Hey it's Jason, just calling you back. I wanted to get an update. And I also want to let you know I called my mom and I gave her that message. My phone has been a total suck up. Don't know if you heard the whole thing. So, I told her the deal. I think she's going to try to call you … I tried to call Michelle, but not super aggressively because I want to find out for sure if you've taken those papers or not. Anyway, I will talk to you again later. If you get a chance, call me. Bye."

Pat Young left Meredith a similar message just three minutes later. It was the first time she had ever called Meredith's cell phone.

After making a quick stop at the Transylvania County Hospital and leaving his business card, Jason pulled up to the familiar site of his boyhood home in Brevard. He slung his suit coat over his shoulder and began walking to the front door.

Something was wrong. His mother and stepfather Gerald were standing in the front yard, holding each other, shock and grief etched into their faces. Jason walked up to them and asked, "Is it Grandma?"

Gerald responded, "No, Jason. It's Michelle. Michelle is dead."

Jason instantly dropped to his knees and began to sob. His stepfather had to catch him to prevent him from falling face first into the ground.

Gerald and Pat helped him inside. Jason collapsed onto their recliner, still sobbing. By the time his younger sister Heather and her husband Joe got to the house, Jason was under a blanket, his eyes red and swollen, his face pale, and crumpled-up tissues strewn all around him. Heather began to cry at the sight. She put her arm around her big brother and told him how sorry she was. Michelle was up in heaven, Heather said, with their dad and Jason's sweet baby boy.

"You're going to make a good mother for Cassidy," Jason told her between sobs.

. . . . .

Joe was at the wheel of Jason's Explorer as the family headed east toward Raleigh, Gerald remaining behind to care for the family's pets. Jason was in the backseat with his mom, still wearing his dress clothes from his sales meeting that morning. He was slumped over with his head in his mother's lap. Pat tried her best to console him. At one point, he told her he would surely lose the house because there was no way to pay for it without Michelle's income.

Pat fielded several calls during the nearly 300-mile journey to Raleigh. After one of them, she told Jason the police had asked, "Are you headed back to Raleigh? Sure as hell better damn be!" He didn't understand why anyone would be so rude to his mother. Soon it was Meredith calling to let Jason know the police wanted to speak with him and he needed to come to her house because his home was now a crime scene.

It was nearly 11:00 p.m. when the group arrived in Fuquay-Varina, a bedroom community southwest of Raleigh where Meredith was living. When they were about five minutes from her home, Pat fielded a call from Ryan Schaad and Josh Dalton. They were calling to warn Jason investigators were asking a lot of questions and were already pointing at him as the most likely suspect. They told Pat Jason needed to get a lawyer before speaking with anyone. Joe pulled into a parking lot at Applebee's so they could discuss what to do.

Heather called a Raleigh attorney who was helping her with a personal injury case. Because it was after-hours, no one answered. Just a few minutes later, though, Ryan called back to let Jason know he had secured a high-profile criminal defense lawyer, Roger Smith, who would meet with him on Monday. Until then, Ryan warned, Jason shouldn't speak with the police.

Jason's family then headed for Meredith's home. When they arrived, Meredith and Linda—who had quickly arranged a flight from New York that afternoon—were standing outside by the front door. Ignoring Linda, Jason went straight to Meredith, hugged her, and sobbed. When she reiterated the police wanted to speak with him, her brother-in-law replied he wouldn't be talking with anyone until he met with his attorney.

"Where's Cassidy?" he asked.

"In the bedroom," Meredith answered.

Jason went straight to her bedroom, saw his daughter peacefully asleep in the bed, took off his shoes, and snuggled up next to her.

.....

The following Thursday, nearly 200 of Michelle's friends and family members gathered for her funeral. Many of them had attended her wedding just three years earlier. There was nothing but happiness and hope then. Now, they were filled with anguish, sadness, and a profound sense of loss of a life cut short, another never lived, and the smile and grace that had touched so many of them so often. It was excruciatingly painful for Michelle's family and friends to accept she would no longer be part of their lives.

Jason selected orange and yellow Gerbera daisies for the top of the casket. Those were the flowers Pat and his older sister Kim had scattered across the front yard the day Jason and Michelle brought Cassidy home from the hospital. Jason also had Gerbera daisies planted next to the mailbox when they moved into their Birchleaf Drive home. He knew how much his wife loved them.

As the funeral drew to a close, Jason and his family walked up to the open casket together. Jason dropped to his knees and began to gently rub Michelle's stomach, his way of saying goodbye to the son he would never get to know. His head slumped, and he cried softly. As he got up, he took a small piece of paper out of his wallet and placed it into his wife's cold, lifeless hand. It was something Michelle had slipped into his wallet to surprise him before they were married, the words his mom sang to him when he was a boy:

*I love you a bushel and a peck*
*A bushel and a peck and a hug around the neck*
*A hug around the neck and a barrel and a heap*
*A barrel and a heap and I'm talkin' in my sleep*
*About you, about you*
*'Cause I love you a bushel and a peck*
*You bet your purdy neck I do*
*A doodle oodle oh*
*A doodle oodle oh doo*

# 4

## MICHELLE MARIE FISHER

Sayville is a quaint hamlet located on the south shore of Suffolk County, Long Island, centered nearly precisely between the skyscrapers of Manhattan—some fifty miles to the west—and the luxurious, beachfront homes in The Hamptons—nearly fifty miles to the east. The Great South Bay beachfront, formed by the Atlantic Ocean, serves as the town's southern boundary. At barely more than five square miles, Sayville provides true small-town charm and comfort. The restaurants and small shops lining Main Street are a popular draw to a place which, in 1994, was anointed as the "friendliest town in America." When Michelle Fisher graduated from Sayville High the following year, about 16,000 people called the predominantly white town "home."

Alan Fisher made a good living as an auto dealer. Linda was a schoolteacher at Sayville Junior High, where she taught math and coached the cheerleading team. Alan and Linda had two daughters: Michelle, born in 1977, and Meredith, born in 1980. They lived a middle-class life in a modest home not far from the beach. Like most siblings, Michelle and Meredith could sometimes fight like cats and dogs. Michelle's weapon of choice was her incredibly strong fingernails. Meredith became quite adept using her teeth to even the odds against her big sister.

Michelle was very nurturing, even as a child. Linda would

sometimes find her in her room caring for her Cabbage Patch Kids dolls. She excelled in everything and was one of the most popular kids in school. Linda instilled in her elder daughter the importance of academics, and they came easily to her. She also got both girls into cheering at an early age and proudly coached them at Sayville Junior High.

But all was not hunky-dory at the Fisher home. By the time Michelle was fourteen, her parents lived in separate bedrooms and barely spoke to one another. They had decided to stay together for the sake of their girls, but the fractured relationship was difficult for Michelle and Meredith to ignore. Michelle coped with the acrimony and tension between her parents by pouring her energy into school and her friends.

At Sayville High, not only was she one of the most popular students in her class, Michelle was a member of the National Honor Society, became fluent in Russian and French, co-captained the cheerleading squad, and participated enthusiastically in talent shows and plays. In her senior year, the cheerleading team Michelle led won the Long Island Cheerleading Association's championship.

By the time Michelle graduated, she had a full semester of college credits racked up from completing AP courses. The pages of her high school yearbook were filled with photos of her in action. Her senior portrait perfectly captured her radiant smile and beautiful, long, lush, brown hair. A common refrain from those who knew her well was that her smile would "light up a room."

Always the planner, Michelle started contemplating her college selection not long after beginning high school. Using a school computer to help navigate her choices, she narrowed her list to four colleges. Linda took Michelle and Meredith on a road trip to visit each. When they arrived in Raleigh, North Carolina, Michelle and her mother instantly fell in love with N.C. State. With her stellar grades and resume, Michelle had no problem getting in, even though the university admitted very few out-of-state students.

Michelle flourished at N.C. State, earning straight As nearly every semester. It was of little wonder she made the Wolfpack cheering squad as a freshman—she and her pom poms were on the sidelines for football and basketball games during the 1995-96 season. When Michelle was chosen as a cheerleader for the opening ceremonies of the 1996 Summer Olympics in Atlanta, she was elated. Her mom couldn't have been prouder.

The Summer Olympics was both the pinnacle of the decade Michelle devoted to cheering as well as her last hurrah; she decided to focus her remaining time at N.C. State on her studies. That didn't mean she would stop cheering for the Wolfpack, however. As a student and huge fan, she attended nearly every home football and basketball game throughout her college years.

Without cheering filling so much of her schedule, Michelle decided to rush a sorority in the fall of her sophomore year. On the "rush bus," she met another girl named Michelle—Michelle Sauter. Not only did they share a name, both were from Long Island. They became fast friends and decided together to join Alpha Delta Pi.

The Michelles formed a clique with three other women in the sorority who affectionately referred to themselves as the "McBroads"—a sisterhood that would continue long after their respective graduations, even as they dispersed as far away as Massachusetts and Florida. As adults, the McBroads communicated frequently, attended one another's weddings, and got together at least annually for Wolfpack football games or to vacation in Myrtle Beach.

Just before Michelle's sophomore year, with money Linda obtained from her divorce with Alan, Linda purchased a condo just a few minutes away from the N.C. State campus. Michelle lived there with different combinations of her friends and sorority sisters—including Shelly Doub—until completing her master's in accounting in 2000 and taking the CPA exam, a four-parter she passed on her first try. She began her accounting career at Deloitte & Touche in downtown Raleigh.

To that point in life, Michelle had succeeded at virtually everything she tried. Quitting was not in her vocabulary. Once she committed to taking something on, she was "all in."

"She was beautiful. She was intelligent. She was determined,

She was completely Type A, so much so that we called her the 'camp director,'" Shelly would later say.

As she began to chart her career as an accountant, the only blemish in Michelle's life seemed to be her tattered relationship with her father. After Alan and Linda divorced in June of 1995—just as Michelle was graduating from high school—she and her father maintained some semblance of a relationship. But that changed quickly after he married June, his second wife, who Michelle would soon refer to as her "evil step-monster." For reasons that never became clear to Michelle, June detested her and forbade her to enter the New Jersey home she and Michelle's father shared. Faced with the choice between his new wife and his first-born, Alan chose the former. As a result, Michelle had very little contact with her dad thereafter. A new man, however, would soon enter her life.

.....

In February 2001, Michelle celebrated her 24th birthday with Shelly and some friends at the Pour House, a downtown Raleigh watering hole. Jason Young was at the bar, hanging out with some of his old college friends. While horsing around with the guys, he accidentally knocked over Michelle's glass of wine. He offered to buy her another glass and they began to talk. They discovered they were both recent N.C. State graduates and passionate Wolfpack fans.

Though there were no fireworks that night, there was certainly a spark. At the time, Jason was living with his mother and stepfather in Brevard while working as a salesman for Black & Decker. It wasn't long, though, before he was making frequent weekend trips to Raleigh to spend time with Michelle. Jason ultimately decided to move back to Raleigh and rented a townhome with his friend Ryan Schaad.

He got a job as a pharmaceutical sales representative with Pan American Labs.

If ever there were a couple that epitomized the idiom "opposites attract," it was Michelle and Jason—Michelle, the pretty, brunette city girl with a thick, New York accent; Jason, the handsome, blond mountain boy with a pronounced Southern drawl.

Ever the consummate planner, Michelle was attracted to Jason's wild and whimsical nature, his incessant practical jokes, and how he flew by the seat of his pants. His "bad boy" image and penchant for vulgarity somehow added to his appeal. Though he often acted more like a college frat boy than a man several years removed from school, Michelle enjoyed the playfulness and charisma that always made Jason the life of the party.

Pat Young very much enjoyed meeting Michelle, finding her to be just as beautiful as Jason had described, with a lovely smile and great personality. Michelle sat in Pat's kitchen and the two chatted about their common interest in cooking. She seemed completely at ease talking with her new boyfriend's mom about her childhood, cheerleading, and growing up. Pat felt an instant connection.

.....

Since she was a girl, Michelle had always envisioned a long courtship, orderly engagement, and majestic wedding replete with elaborate floral arrangements, an elegant, white bridal gown, and all her family and friends in attendance. That would of course be followed by a beautifully furnished and decorated house full of kids, a white picket fence, and life happily ever after.

But that's not the script that was written for Michelle Fisher. Fate—and unprotected sex—would intervene to derail this idealized vision of her future.

It was the summer of 2003 when Michelle learned she was pregnant. She and Jason already were living together, sharing one of the two bedrooms in a townhome Jason and Ryan had recently purchased on Arete Way in Raleigh.

Michelle wasn't sure how Jason would react to the news. Though they had been dating for two years, she knew marriage was a topic her boyfriend approached with trepidation and fear. Yet she was sure in her mind Jason was "the one" for her happily ever after and hoped the news of a child on the way might spur him to propose.

But when she told Jason about her unexpected pregnancy, his initial reaction was shock—and horror. He told Michelle he wasn't ready for marriage. Or to be a father. Over the course of the next week, though, slowly but surely she somehow persuaded him to change his mind. Jason gave Michelle a rubber band to put on her finger to symbolize his commitment until he went online and ordered an expensive diamond ring to take its place.

The baby on the way wasn't the only reason Jason felt pressured to get married sooner than planned. Michelle had recently left Deloitte & Touche after deciding she wasn't cut out to be a partner at a national accounting firm. She had taken a temporary job at N.C. State while looking for a more permanent position, but had lost her health insurance as a result. It was one thing to have no coverage while risking her own health. But now with a baby on the way, getting health insurance coverage had suddenly become imperative.

After discussing their options, she and Jason arrived at the obvious solution: they needed to get her onto his health insurance coverage—quickly. So on August 12, 2003, Jason Young and Michelle Fisher found themselves exchanging vows before a magistrate at the Wake County Public Safety Center in downtown Raleigh, with Linda and a complete stranger serving as their only guests. Although they didn't fully appreciate it at the time, both their engagement and their marriage had been constructed upon a foundation of unexpected circumstances, rather than genuine love and commitment.

Though the August ceremony may have been the official wedding in the eyes of the law, Michelle wouldn't have dreamt of giving up on the grand wedding she had always envisioned. She set the date for Friday, October 10, less than two months later. It was important to her for the ceremony to take place before she started showing.

A couple of weeks before the wedding, Michelle sent a ten-page email to the other members of the McBroads, all of whom were planning to attend. She described in meticulous detail the duties and responsibilities assigned to each: who would be picking up whom from the airport, where everyone would be staying, when and where they would go to get their hair and nails done, and the specific details of the wedding ceremony. None of the McBroads was surprised to receive such an email—they knew Michelle all too well.

For the wedding ceremony, Linda rented out the Long View Center in downtown Raleigh—an ornate, stucco building originally constructed in 1881 as a church. The floral arrangements were beautiful. Michelle looked elegant in her white bridal gown. Jason was equally dapper in his black tuxedo. Meredith was the maid of honor. Mr. Garrison, wearing a doggie tuxedo, served as the ring bearer. Thanks to Linda and Meredith's tireless efforts, they had pulled it off in record time, making Michelle extremely happy and hopeful. She and Jason delayed their honeymoon until the following summer, when they spent several enjoyable days in St. Maarten.

Not only was Michelle newly married and expecting a baby—she also had a new job. About a month before the big wedding ceremony, she landed a position as a financial specialist in the tax department of Progress Energy, a Fortune 500 company that served as one of the southeast's largest utilities. She absolutely loved the work, her fellow employees, and the many employee benefits. And her supervisors and co-workers adored her. She planned to take only a short maternity leave and to resume working as quickly as possible.

That plan led to "contract negotiations." With Meredith. Having recently graduated from college in New York, her baby sister was ready to leave her mother's nest, and the impending birth of her niece presented an excellent opportunity. They agreed Meredith would move to the Raleigh area when the baby was born and serve as Cassidy's nanny once her sister returned to work.

Cassidy's birth was not without its drama. She had turned into the breach position in the final weeks of Michelle's pregnancy. All efforts to reposition her before she entered the birth canal failed. Not one to take chances, Michelle insisted upon a C-section despite months of planning for a natural childbirth.

So it was that Cassidy Elizabeth Young sucked in her first breaths of life on March 29, 2004. When her daughter was handed to her on the operating room table, Michelle gazed into her eyes and, through tears of joy, exclaimed, "She's beautiful!" And upon hearing her mother's familiar voice, Cassidy instantly stopped crying and became calm. It was an "awesome moment," Jason later recounted.

Michelle reveled in everything about motherhood: breast feeding, changing diapers, buying cute, pink onesies, feeding her daughter by the "airplane" method, and falling asleep with her daughter at her side. She proudly pushed Cassidy around the neighborhood in her stroller, trying her best to smell the roses along the way.

The new mother would sing *Twinkle Little Star* to Cassidy using a toy karaoke machine, often inspiring her daughter to grab the microphone to complete the song. They would sit together at the kitchen table imitating each other's noises, Cassidy squealing with laughter each time Michelle duplicated her sound. They would rub noses together—"nosies"—and beg for kisses from one another. Unsolicited, Cassidy would sometimes look wistfully into her mother's eyes, saying, "I love you, Mommy."

.....

The only thing missing from Michelle's grand plan was a bigger house with a yard and a white picket fence. She and Jason had been house hunting for some time when they pulled into South Raleigh's Enchanted Oaks subdivision in April 2005. Michelle instantly fell in love with the charming neighborhood and Birchleaf Drive, Enchanted Oaks' main artery, which encircled the entire subdivision. The lots were large and wooded, and the houses spread out nicely for privacy. To Michelle, this was the perfect spot to settle down and grow a family.

The Birchleaf Drive house she and Jason were shown was a

fourteen-year-old, traditional, colonial brick home that sat on nearly two acres. It had a large kitchen, elegant light fixtures, and huge front and back yards. The community pool was just a short walk from the house. Michelle knew immediately. This was the home she needed to complete her grand plan.

She and Jason came up with the down payment, easily qualified for a mortgage and, just before Memorial Day 2005, became the proud owners of 5108 Birchleaf Drive. They moved in that July.

Having taken the step of purchasing their dream home, Michelle considered it prudent to have their wills prepared. That task fell to her former roommate and ADPi big sister, Fiona Ginter, now a lawyer. Michelle and Jason were able to agree on all provisions—except one: who would serve as Cassidy's guardian in the event they both perished simultaneously.

Michelle strongly believed Meredith would be the most logical guardian for their daughter. After all, her sister spent almost as much time with Cassidy during her first year of life as did Michelle—and probably even more than Jason. But Jason wanted his sister Heather to be guardian. Ultimately, he convinced his wife it was more sensible to name Heather because she was already married and worked during the daytime, unlike Meredith who was unmarried and worked at night. They agreed to revisit the issue in three years.

·····

Michelle had always been very close to her mother. Though she was blessed to have many close friends, the one person she could always turn to for advice and problem-solving—especially in her darkest days—was Linda. That was particularly true when she needed to vent about the problems she was having in her marriage.

Even though Michelle displayed tremendous self-confidence and poise as an adult, she frequently needed to hear her mom's soothing voice and wisdom. She called Linda on her cell phone as she drove home from work every day. They often spoke more than once a day.

Linda was there with Michelle to celebrate Cassidy's birth. She became a frequent visitor to the Youngs' Arete Way townhome and Birchleaf Drive home to spend time with her precious granddaughter.

Because she was a schoolteacher, Linda was able to spend considerable time in Raleigh during the summers, much to her daughter's delight. Michelle loved knowing Cassidy was spending the workday in her mother's care and company. And she loved coming home from work to her mom's warm and loving smile.

.....

By the spring of 2006, Michelle was pregnant again—this time, a planned event. She was beaming with pride and excitement and couldn't wait for Cassidy to be a big sister. She and Jason traveled to Brevard over the Memorial Day weekend to share the news with Jason's family.

During that trip, Michelle experienced one of the scariest moments of her life. Jason and Michelle left Cassidy with his mom and stepdad the morning they were planning to head back to Raleigh; they ventured off to get some coffee from Starbucks. Jason was driving his Mitsubishi SUV with Michelle in the passenger seat. Suddenly, without warning, Jason lost control of the car and it nearly went off the road to their right, causing Jason to steer sharply to the left.

Before either knew what was happening, they were descending more than 100 feet down an embankment, plunging into the French Broad River. Water rapidly started filling their car. Fortunately, Michelle and Jason were able to escape and climb up the side of the embankment as they watched the SUV sink into the river. Miraculously, they were both unscathed. Or so they thought.

When Michelle got back to Raleigh later that evening, something didn't seem right. She wasn't sure if the baby was still moving. She called Shelly—by then a nurse—to ask her advice. Shelly urged her to get an ultrasound as soon as possible. When Michelle went in for the ultrasound later that week, her worst fears were realized. There was no heartbeat. Just like that, she went from the high of being an expectant mother to the low of losing her baby. She was crushed.

Less than two months later, though, Michelle was hopeful again. Jason was out of town on a business trip when she learned she was pregnant again. She decided to have Cassidy surprise her father with the news. Michelle dressed her in a T-shirt with the words "I'm going to be a big sister" emblazoned across the front. When Jason got home, he looked at Cassidy's shirt, then his wife, and realized they were pregnant again. For at least that one moment, there was genuine happiness in the Young household.

The new pregnancy also had Michelle reconsidering her career. She loved working for Progress Energy, where she had recently been promoted to the position of Senior Financial Specialist. But she also loved being a mom and didn't want to miss out on Rylan's special moments as an infant and toddler as she had with Cassidy.

Though Rylan wasn't due until March 2007, by early October 2006, Michelle had prepared a five-page presentation for her supervisors she hoped would convince them to permit her to work part-time once her son was born. Michelle sought permission to work Tuesday through Thursday each week, ten hours a day—her mother would provide child care into the early evening. The proposal was well-organized and chock full of detail—no big surprise considering its author.

Shortly after receiving her proposal, Michelle's manager informed her that both he and his supervisor were agreeable to her plan. They were impressed with her dedication and passion for her job and confident she would be able to complete her work in a three-day, 30-hour workweek. Michelle was thrilled. She would be able to continue doing the job she loved with co-workers who had become like family, and also devote four days each week exclusively to her children.

Michelle was also excited about a family vacation her mother had been planning since her retirement from teaching that June. Linda was going to be on a mission trip in New Orleans beginning November 5 and planned to meet up with

Michelle, Jason, Cassidy, and Meredith at Disney World a week later. Her mother had even invited Jason's family to come, though they declined. The end of that trip was going to include a McBroads' weekend at an Orlando spa, as Michelle's sorority sisters were all celebrating their recent 30th birthdays.

But as fate would have it, that is a birthday Michelle Fisher Young would never get to celebrate.

# 5

## Jason Lynn Young

Brevard is a cozy, western North Carolina town, nestled in the picturesque Blue Ridge Mountains, approximately thirty miles south of Asheville.

Because it serves as the entryway to the Pisgah National Forest, tourists flood through Brevard on their way to the amazing rock climbing, hiking, kayaking, and whitewater river rafting Pisgah offers. Just as many tourists pass through Brevard to gaze at the breathtaking vista of cascading waterfalls adorning Pisgah's lush, green mountainside. Bluegrass music festivals fill the summer calendar, many performed at the famed Brevard Music Center. When Jason Young graduated from Brevard High in 1992, only about 5,000 people inhabited the town, the vast majority having been born and raised there.

Like Linda Fisher, Pat Young was a schoolteacher, teaching fifth grade at a small Transylvania County elementary school. She took an eight-year break from teaching to raise her three children: Kim, born in 1972; Jason, in 1974; and Heather, two years later. When Jason was five, his father Bob was stricken with cancer and died very quickly. The family struggled financially as Pat navigated life as a single mother.

Gerald McIntyre and Pat began their relationship when Jason was six, and ultimately married when he was in college. Gerald worked in a machine shop and as a power plant operator for a company affiliated with Winchester Corporation, one of the nation's largest manufacturers of rifles and shotguns. Through his connection to Winchester, he acquired a massive collection of guns and occasionally took Jason skeet and trap shooting.

Although Jason was close with his sisters Kim and Heather, he could also be a real pest, needling them at times for his own amusement, often making them the butt of his incessant jokes. He was constantly pulling pranks on friends and family members.

One Sunday afternoon, when Jason was twelve or thirteen, Pat's 80-year-old mother was visiting Brevard. Jason was walking slightly in front of her when, without any provocation, he pulled down his pants and mooned her. As Pat would later say, "Mother thought it was really funny. She kind of fell over on the ground as if she were so shocked that her grandson would show his behind to her."

"People were drawn to him," Heather recalled fondly, "because he was so much fun and you [could] never stay mad at him for very long because he'd have you laughing within minutes."

As a youngster, Jason loved the outdoors—hiking, camping, and playing basketball and soccer. He was an avid Boy Scout. He also enjoyed watching football games on TV with Gerald. Though his procrastination sometimes drove Pat bananas, Jason was a good student and was also very popular. His senior class voted him "best all around" and his teachers nominated him for the Brevard High "hall of fame."

Jason worked several summers at an all-girls Christian camp, Camp Illahee, where he was a counselor and kayaking and mountain climbing instructor. The girls adored him. One of them, Carol Anne from Atlanta, who was four years younger than Jason, developed a crush on him. He saw her once or twice a year after his days at Camp Illahee ended. Though Jason only considered her to be a friend, to him it was the type of friendship that came with "benefits." He never noticed that Carol Anne had developed genuine feelings for him.

. . . . .

An ardent Wolfpack fan, Jason never wavered from his intention to attend college at N.C. State. After completing his freshman year in 1993, he took the following year off to hike the 2,190-mile Appalachian Trail with a high school buddy. That trek from Maine to Georgia proved convincingly that though Jason could sometimes have a short attention span, he was also gritty and determined when he put his mind to something.

But when Jason returned to college in 1994, his studies often took a backseat to his attendance at Wolfpack football and basketball games—and to drinking and partying. He truly was the life of the party and easily formed a loyal cadre of friends, who loved his infectious personality, how Jason would do anything on a dare, and how he placed having fun above all else. Some of those friendships endured into his adulthood, most notably with Ryan Schaad and Josh Dalton.

After graduating in May 1998—nearly six years after beginning college—Jason, Ryan, and Josh pooled their resources to purchase lifetime rights to season tickets to Wolfpack football and basketball games.

Though it was important to Jason to attend the football and basketball games, the tailgating before them was far more significant to him. The parties would begin hours before the games and often involved dozens of students. Jason would frequently drink to the point of inebriation, as would many of his fellow tailgaters. They would then stumble into the stadium to find their seats. Sometimes, they never even made it to the game.

Jason was known among his college friends as a "horndog." He didn't seek lasting relationships with college girls. Rather, he viewed them as conquests and would flirt with them with the sole intention of ending the evening in bed together. His friends admired how successful he was in that arena. That was particularly true after Jason moved into the swanky, privately owned University Towers dormitory in his third year of college. He served as a resident assistant (RA) to subsidize his rent. As an RA, he was the one the students on his floor would come see when they were having issues or problems. And when pretty girls had a problem, Jason went to great lengths to solve them—as a means to the end of adding another notch onto his bedpost.

One of his fellow RAs at University Towers was a striking platinum blond named Genevieve Jacobs. They became friendly and started dating in early 1997 when both were a little more than a year away from graduating.

Following graduation, Jason landed a prized sales position at Nike in Charlotte. Genevieve remained at University Towers as an assistant general manager. Their relationship continued by telephone and with their trading weekends between Raleigh and Charlotte.

On October 3, 1999—Genevieve's 24th birthday—Jason proposed. He was making decent money at Nike and whipped out a three-stone, platinum engagement ring with a center-cut diamond in excess of a karat.

They planned to get married in May 2000.

Their engagement, however, didn't last long. Though Genevieve found Jason charming and affectionate, she began to notice his darker side, which would nearly always emerge when he was drinking. When he drank, she realized, he could get mad at her over nothing. Their relationship became increasingly volatile. When she discussed his drinking with Jason, he would promise to scale back, but repeatedly broke those promises. Genevieve ended their engagement in early 2000.

.....

When Jason first met Michelle in February 2001, he was struck by how pretty, smart, and sweet she was. Not long after their first meeting at the Pour House, Jason was in Raleigh visiting old college friends when he had another chance encounter with Michelle at a movie theatre—both were there with their own cluster of friends. They wound up sitting next to each other.

During intense scenes, Jason noticed Michelle would squeeze his arm. The next time he was in Raleigh, Michelle's roommate Shelly invited him to watch a movie with them in their apartment. From that point forward, it was clear they were in a relationship.

Even though Jason suffered from very few inhibitions, he was petrified by two things: singing and dancing. Michelle, however, was able to coax him onto the dance floor not long after they started dating. Despite being extremely self-conscious, Jason danced up a storm until his clothes were drenched in sweat. He realized he was able to shed that inhibition only because Michelle made him feel so comfortable. He told her he loved her.

Before long, Michelle was not only attending Wolfpack tailgates with Jason, she was organizing them. With Michelle in charge, tailgate cuisine no longer consisted of boxes of Bojangles chicken—home-cooked food was served instead. In the days leading up to the game, Michelle would send out an email to the tailgate group with specific assignments, organizing who would bring the food, condiments, plates, cups, and tables and chairs. Jason's friends affectionately referred to her as their "den mother." Even the drinking became a little more controlled under her adult supervision.

·····

A couple of weeks after learning of Michelle's pregnancy with Cassidy, Jason called his mother to tell her he and Michelle were getting married. Knowing her son all too well, Pat immediately asked, "Is she pregnant?"

He confessed she was. His mom then asked, "Do you love her?"

Jason said he did.

To his relief, Pat replied, "Then I think that's great." She knew how much Jason had always loved being around children. Now he was going to have a child of his own.

In his sister Heather's words, "It was like a big kid having a little kid."

Jason and Michelle visited New York soon after to discuss their wedding plans with her family. Linda, who found Jason to be very immature, told him point blank, "If you don't love her, don't marry her. She'll survive."

He didn't respond.

Jason ceded all wedding-planning responsibilities to Michelle and Linda. But he made very clear the three things he required: First, the wedding couldn't fall on a day of a Wolfpack football game. Second, they couldn't get married north of the Mason-Dixon line. Finally, he wanted to be able to invite as many friends as he could and have unlimited beer. Michelle and Linda made sure that all three of his wishes were granted.

.....

Though Jason may not have been "all in" on the wedding planning, he was very excited about Cassidy's impending arrival. He went to birthing classes with Michelle and was just as distraught as she was when they were unable to proceed with a natural childbirth. Yet he found the birthing process exhilarating and fascinating. He peeked over the curtain as the obstetrician performed the C-section—one tiny leg out, then another, then an arm, then the second, and within seconds, Cassidy's head. He held his breath until, finally, he heard his newborn girl begin to wail.

Jason was the first to hold Cassidy and the first to change her diaper. He was more than happy to get up with her in the middle of the night to feed her with breast milk Michelle had pumped. He loved giving her baths.

Though he could be lazy and procrastinate—especially when it came to household chores—Jason was always in the moment with his daughter. He loved playing with her and, true to his character, making her laugh.

As Michelle Sauter would later say, "He lit up her life—she would just laugh, and giggle, and play." When they were in that zone, it was as if no one else were in the room. Even those who didn't particularly care for Jason acknowledged he was a good dad.

Shortly after Cassidy's birth, Heather and Joe came to Raleigh to visit their niece and to babysit while Jason and

Michelle attended a wedding of one of the McBroads. While his sister was in town, Jason informed her he and Michelle had taken out life insurance policies on each other—for $2 million—which Michelle had been able to acquire at a very reasonable rate through her CPA Association.

Jason explained to Heather their father's premature death left them to grow up without many of the conveniences most of their friends enjoyed. He and Michelle planned to have more kids and wanted to make sure if something happened to either of them, their children would be able to enjoy a good lifestyle, go on great vacations, and attend the best colleges. Although Michelle thought the size of the policies was a little extreme, Jason convinced her, he told Heather, it was a wise investment for their children.

·····

To say Linda and Jason had the typical mother-in-law/son-in-law relationship would be an understatement. They were like oil and water. Linda didn't believe Jason was good enough for her daughter and found fault in virtually everything he did. She considered him juvenile, irresponsible, lazy, and crude. She didn't trust him to make good decisions for Michelle or Cassidy. Her intuition was he would inevitably hurt her daughter and hurt her badly.

For his part, Jason found Linda to be an overbearing, meddlesome, New Yorker who, like Marie Barone in the TV sitcom *Everybody Loves Raymond,* permeated every facet of his life. He couldn't stand how she and Michelle would commiserate by phone nearly every day about his shortcomings. Even worse, Linda literally moved into their townhome for an entire month during the summer of 2004, ostensibly to help out with her new granddaughter, but in reality—as far as Jason was concerned—to critique his every movement.

The thrill of moving into their Birchleaf Drive home wore off quickly, in Jason's eyes, when his mother-in-law came to Raleigh to spend another month with them, living in the guest bedroom just a few feet away from the master bedroom. Since Jason was working from home when he wasn't traveling, he spent far too many days feeling watched—and judged.

And Linda was doing just that. She was appalled that rather than focusing his energy on his toddler and household responsibilities, her son-in-law was gone nearly every evening playing in two softball leagues—and was signed up to play in two basketball leagues when softball season ended. Linda watched helplessly as Michelle tried in vain to persuade her husband to drop down to only one league each season so he could help out more with Cassidy and around the house.

Jason was well aware of Linda's disapproval of his priorities—and really didn't care. His goal was to be away from home as much as possible while his mother-in-law was in town. He viewed his relationship with Linda as a vicious cycle spiraling in the wrong direction. The more he complained to Michelle about her, the more his wife complained to Linda about him. And the more his mother-in-law heard about Jason's deficiencies, the more emboldened she became in spotting additional ones she would immediately report to her daughter.

Meredith would later describe their relationship this way: "My mom is a strong personality and they'd butt heads. I mean, initially, they kind of got along and quickly it became, when Michelle and him would get in a fight, Michelle would call my mom and cry and scream and yell and vent to my mom, so, as a mom, she's, you know, disappointed and aggravated and frustrated with the way that her son-in-law is treating her daughter."

On several occasions, Jason pleaded with Michelle not to call her mom every time she became upset with him, as her complaints were diminishing him further and further in Linda's eyes. But Michelle couldn't help herself—her mother had been the one person she could really lean on every time she struggled.

Oddly, the person whom Jason could most count on for consolation about his troublesome relationship with Linda was Michelle's father, Alan. His relationship with Alan was as good as his relationship with Linda was bad. His father-in-law served as an echo chamber for Jason's complaints about Linda's meddlesome nature and was more than happy to let Jason vent to him. Unlike Michelle, Jason was welcome at Alan and June's New Jersey home. It was almost as if Alan had more of a parent-child relationship with Jason than he did with his own daughter.

.....

Jason desperately wanted to have a son. Since he was the only boy born to his father Bob Young, it was up to him to preserve the family name. He also wanted Cassidy to have a brother that was close to her in age. He was thrilled to learn that Michelle was pregnant in the spring of 2006.

Following her miscarriage, they began trying again the moment his wife was cleared by her doctor—and conceived right away. Jason went with Michelle to most of her prenatal appointments. He wouldn't have missed for anything the appointment designed to learn the baby's sex. When his wife's obstetrician pointed out certain male features, Jason was overjoyed. He was now going to be the father of a girl and a boy. Even more important, the Young name would be extended down to another generation.

The only inconvenience of having a boy, Jason soon realized, was that traditional baby-boy clothing is that certain shade of blue, which happens to adorn the uniforms of the Wolfpack's arch-rival, the University of North Carolina Tar Heels. That made shopping for Rylan's first outfits a little challenging. Jason and Michelle made sure to complement those blue garments with others that were red—if their DNA didn't ensure a baby Wolfpacker, then perhaps his attire would do the trick.

.....

Jason played the role of Michelle's date for the weddings of each of the McBroads: her fellow Long Islander, Michelle (Sauter) Money in 2001; Susan Buchanan in 2003; and Lisa

Shroff in 2004. Throughout those years, the McBroads' weekend retreats and vacations were "girls only." Yet they ultimately realized their get-togethers would become more and more difficult to schedule unless husbands were invited.

The first "co-ed" McBroads' weekend took place in Myrtle Beach in May 2006, the weekend before Jason's and Michelle's fateful trip to Brevard that ended with their SUV plunging into the French Broad River. Another co-ed McBroads' gathering occurred that July. During that weekend, Jason struck up a friendship with Michelle Money, who he learned was having significant difficulties in her own marriage.

Jason and Michelle hosted some of the McBroads and their husbands at their Birchleaf Drive home in late September—the weekend of the N.C. State-Boston College football game. They were planning an epic tailgate to relive their college memories.

The Friday evening before the big matchup, a game of hide and seek broke out in their backyard. Jason and Money somehow ended up in the same hiding spot. While hiding, they quickly lost interest in the game and resumed their conversation about Money's marriage. She confided in him she believed her husband, Steve, had been cheating on her with Lisa Shroff—both of whom were staying with the Youngs that weekend. Jason told Money he had seen "some things" between the two that made him suspicious as well.

That Sunday afternoon, the day after the big game, while most of the women were out shopping and the guys were huddled around the TV watching football, Money and Jason snuck outside together. Minutes later, she was perched atop Jason's riding lawnmower with Jason on his skateboard racing down Birchleaf Drive, being pulled by a rope as if he were waterskiing on dry land. It was the most fun either had the entire weekend.

.....

Earlier that month, Ryan and Shelly hosted an impromptu gathering after an N.C. State football game. For some reason, Michelle didn't attend that particular game. Following the game, Jason called Michelle to let her know he would be staying at Ryan's house that evening for a "guys only" bachelor party. Which wasn't actually true. Several women were there, including Shelly and her cousin—who was spending the night with her boyfriend—as well as Shelly's co-worker, Allison Roach. Jason drank too much and soon was flirting with Roach in the living room. Suddenly, on a dare, he unzipped his fly and urinated, partially on himself, and partially on an expensive rug.

Ryan quickly sprang into action. He grabbed Jason, pulled him into the bathroom, and undressed him so he could throw him into the shower to get him clean and try to sober him up. But as Ryan was reaching for the spigot, Jason escaped and ran out into the living room—completely naked. He plopped down on the couch and joined the existing conversation—as if he were the featured guest on *The View*—smiling and posing for pictures. Exasperated, Ryan grabbed Jason again, shoved him back into the bathroom, and finally got him cleaned up and dressed.

Shelly made the sleeping arrangements that night to keep Jason as far away from Roach as possible. She had Ryan guarding Jason in the living room while Roach slept with her in the bedroom. The next morning, Jason left, dressed fully in Ryan's clothing. He had the entire drive home to come up with a good explanation for his unexpected attire.

.....

On Saturday, October 21, 2006, Jason was at the Raleigh-Durham Airport, patiently awaiting the arrival of his old Camp Illahee friend, Carol Anne Sowerby. She had flown in from Montana, where she lived with her husband, to attend a real estate training course in Raleigh. Michelle and Jason had offered her their guest bedroom the several nights she would be in town. Michelle was looking forward to finally meeting Sowerby when she returned from a business trip in New York.

Later that first evening, Sowerby fell asleep on the sofa in the Youngs' den. When she woke up, Jason was sitting near her, watching TV. He told her to make herself at home upstairs in the guest bedroom.

"Take a look in the mirror before you go back to sleep," he said, as she was halfway up the stairs. When Sowerby turned on the light in the guest bedroom, and looked in the mirror, she was startled to see a mustache drawn in black marker above her lips and an extra pair of black eyebrows above her eyes. Jason stood at the upstairs landing, laughing uncontrollably at the sight.

During dinner a few nights later, after Michelle had returned from New York, the three adults were engaged in casual conversation about weddings. Jason asked Sowerby if he could see her wedding ring. When she handed it to him, he immediately put it in his mouth, gulped, and said, "I've swallowed it. Now you can't go back to Montana!" She begged him to return it. Jason said she would just have to delay her trip home until the ring passed. Neither Michelle nor Sowerby was amused.

When Jason and Michelle were getting ready for bed that night, his wife confronted him. "How dare you do that Jason!" Jason then reached into his mouth and pulled the ring out from the inside of his cheek, where he had been hiding it all along. Grinning from ear to ear, he explained he was just playing a joke on his old friend and intended to return the ring the following morning.

Relieved, Michelle cracked a smile. "Typical Jason," she likely thought.

.....

Jason had been planning another big tailgate party for the Wolfpack game against Georgia Tech, which was scheduled for late afternoon on November 4. His college friend Brian Ambrose, who was now living near Charlotte, was planning to come into town with his wife and kids. Jason had invited them to stay at his Birchleaf Drive house.

His father-in-law, Alan Fisher, was planning to come in from New Jersey. Michelle had arranged for Meredith to care for Cassidy and had undertaken her usual pre-game organizing. Plans had been evolving throughout the week.

Instead, everyone who would have attended that tailgate spent the afternoon of November 4, 2006, mourning the loss of Michelle Fisher Young.

# 6

## INVESTIGATION

Within an hour of Meredith's arrival at 5108 Birchleaf Drive, Sheriff's deputies and detectives, and crime scene investigators from the Raleigh/Wake City-County Bureau of Identification (CCBI), were meticulously combing through every square inch of the house.

They found no sign of forced entry. Nothing on the entire first floor was disturbed or out of place. Only two small drops of blood were detected downstairs—both on the interior doorknob of the door leading from the kitchen to the garage. There was no blood on the back staircase leading from the kitchen area to the bonus room or on the front staircase leading from the front foyer to the upstairs bedrooms.

The second floor was an altogether different story. Cassidy's bloody footprints were all over the upstairs landing and her bathroom floor, including on a step-stool in front of her sink and on a green bathmat. Blood was smeared on the walls of her bathroom at toddler height, including behind where the open bathroom door would have come to rest.

Bloody footprints were visible on that corner of the floor. Logically, at some point following the murder, the toddler had been in the bathroom with the door closed. One of her bloody socks was on the bathroom floor along with a yellow hooded towel that also contained blood. A drop of blood was found on the side of her bathtub and another on a white towel. Yet there was no evidence of any blood within the bathtub, toilet, or sink.

There was little doubt Michelle had been attacked in her own bed—blood on the bed linens had dripped down onto the floor. Close by, just to the left of Jason's closet doorway near Michelle's side of the bed and about a foot above the floor, an oval-shaped gouge had been notched into the wall. The gouge mark appeared to be freshly made and included a fresh deposit of blood.

On the floor directly beneath the gouge mark, running along the baseboard and extending into the closet doorway, a large pool of partially coagulated blood had soaked through the carpet. Splotches and spattering of blood dotted the wall, baseboard, and door molding between the gouge mark and the floor.

Michelle's body was lying—facedown—diagonally across the floor with her head pressed up against Jason's open closet door, where a second thick pool of blood had formed under her severely battered face. Her legs were angled toward the middle of the bed. She was wearing black sweatpants and a white zip-up hooded sweatshirt with red and pink stripes rimming the bottom. A small patch of skin was visible below her sweatshirt, which was hiked up just above her left hip.

Michelle's left elbow and forearm were lying at the edge of the pool of blood directly beneath the oval gouge mark, the left sleeve of her sweatshirt soaked in blood. In her left hand—resting palm up by her waist against a decorative pillow—was a single strand of hair, caked in blood. A larger clump of hair was sandwiched between her body and the carpeting. Michelle's right arm was stretched beneath her body, with her right hand resting underneath, and just beyond, her left elbow, palm facing upward, fingers curled in.

Michelle's feet were bare, her right foot under the bed and her left foot resting against her right leg. A pink-and-white sock was found on the floor near her left leg. Decorative pillows of various shapes, sizes, and colors were strewn about on the floor to the left of her body and near the foot of the bed.

Cassidy's dark red, bloody footprints covered the carpeting

just inside of Jason's closet doorway. One of her baby dolls was lying outside the door opening with its head placed inches from Michelle's. The child had likely been standing just inside her father's closet when she placed the baby doll in that position.

After investigators moved Michelle's body and closed Jason's closet door, it became apparent the blood spatter pattern on the wall next to the closet continued onto the exterior surface of the door. It appeared she had been beaten while the door was closed. Her killer must have moved her body to open the door.

What perhaps were the most important clues were left on a rectangular, white, embroidered pillow found next to the footboard beside Michelle's side of the bed. Investigators discovered two distinct adult-sized, bloody shoeprints on the surface of the pillow.

They also discovered that two of the three drawers from Michelle's wooden jewelry box, which was on top of a dresser near the bedroom's entrance—beside a framed wedding photo of Jason and Michelle kissing—had been removed. The only other items noted to be missing were Michelle's engagement and wedding rings, which weren't on her ring finger. Nor were they found anywhere in the house.

In the master bathroom, crime-scene investigators used a chemical—phenolphthalein—which enhances traces of blood the naked eye is unable to detect. They fully expected one of the dual sinks, bathtub, or shower to reveal evidence of blood, if not the assailant's bloody fingerprints.

But to their surprise, they couldn't detect even a speck of blood anywhere in the bathroom. The only bloody fingerprints investigators found anywhere in the house belonged to Cassidy. Every drop of the blood found at the house—including on the downstairs kitchen doorknob—was confirmed to be Michelle's.

Investigators did find the eBay printouts Jason had asked Meredith to retrieve. Just as his voicemail had indicated, they were lying on the printer in the second-floor office. The only other clue investigators initially found significant was a garden hose in the middle of the concrete pathway by the back deck.

Water was trickling out the nozzle and a small patch of the pathway was wet. But not a single drop of blood was found on the hose, deck, or pathway. And despite their best efforts, investigators' search for a murder weapon—at 5108 Birchleaf Drive or anywhere in the neighborhood—came up empty.

.....

The autopsy left little doubt that Michelle had been beaten repeatedly—and forcefully. It also revealed the 29-year-old pregnant mother actively defended herself and struggled with her assailant, before finally succumbing to the brutality of the attack. Her right hand was covered in scrapes and bruises. Her left arm had bruising from the forearm down to the thumb and fingers. The Medical Examiner was certain these injuries resulted from Michelle trying to fight off the blows.

His report noted Michelle's head sustained more than twenty separate blunt-force injuries. Lacerations were found all over the back of her head—some as long as four inches, and a few deep enough to expose her skull. Others, also very deep, were noted on the left side of her head, the longest just shy of four inches. The Medical Examiner concluded that, based on the crescent shape of the lacerations, the attacker's weapon was a heavy, blunt object with a rounded surface.

The blows fractured Michelle's skull in multiple places and resulted in hemorrhaging of her brain. She suffered another blow to the front of her face, resulting in both her lips being cut and several teeth being knocked out. She was hit so hard across her left jaw that there was a clean break of her jaw bone through her skin.

The Medical Examiner also documented extensive hemorrhaging to the soft tissue on Michelle's neck, around her thyroid gland—leading him to conclude her killer had tried to strangle her. Fingernail marks visible on the left side of her neck, he believed, were made by Michelle's own fingers, as she desperately tried to free herself from her assailant's choke-hold.

Despite the enormity of the beating inflicted on Michelle,

the autopsy revealed no evidence of sexual assault. She was wearing panties beneath her sweatpants. Not a single scratch or bruise was detected anywhere below her neck.

Though the Medical Examiner was able to determine the cause of death—blunt-force injury to Michelle's head—he was unable to determine the *time* of death. Based on her body temperature and the degree to which her blood had coagulated, Michelle had clearly succumbed to her injuries several hours before her sister arrived around 1:15 p.m. that afternoon. But beyond that, it wasn't possible to determine when.

. . . . .

Ryan Schaad and Josh Dalton were correct—investigators had begun to focus on Jason as the primary suspect long before he arrived at Meredith's home the evening of November 3. Within seconds of his arrival, uniformed Sheriff's deputies seized his Ford Explorer and brought it to downtown Raleigh to conduct a thorough search. They expected it to be chock-full of clues linking Jason to the murder scene.

But it wasn't. Once again, investigators relied on phenolphthalein to assist them in detecting traces of blood. Yet after hours of scouring the vehicle, not a single drop was found. Not inside the Explorer. Not on its exterior surface. And not on or inside of Jason's luggage, its contents, or any of his family's luggage.

Investigators did find several pieces of paper inside the SUV—the MapQuest directions Jason had printed prior to leaving for Virginia, three different gas receipts, a check-out receipt from the Hampton Inn, and the weekend edition of the *USA Today* newspaper, which bore a sticker from the hotel. They also found a Rand McNally road atlas opened to a page that showed Virginia and North Carolina highways. A handwritten telephone number at the top of the page was determined to be Meredith's cell phone number.

. . . . .

Now that investigators knew the exact location of Jason's hotel, a group was dispatched to Hillsville, Virginia. They arrived the afternoon of November 4 and began interviewing the hotel manager and staff. To the extent Jason had an alibi, it was the hotel. Investigators therefore wanted to learn everything they could about his arrival on November 2, the time of his departure, and everything he did in between.

The hotel was 169 miles from the Youngs' Raleigh home. Detectives had already determined from cell phone records that Jason's phone pinged a cell phone tower in Wytheville, Virginia—27 miles northwest of Hillsville—at 7:40 a.m. on November 3.

Based on the distance between Hillsville and Raleigh, it would have taken Jason at least six hours to drive to Raleigh to commit the murder, return to the Hampton Inn long enough to retrieve the check-out receipt and newspaper, and then to drive on to Wytheville.

Investigators needed to confirm the last time he could be placed at the hotel and determine whether that timeline left even the slightest possibility Jason could have been Michelle's killer.

They also wanted to determine if any evidence from the murder scene—blood in particular—could be detected in his hotel room. But a search of Room 421, which had been assigned to Jason upon his arrival, turned up no such evidence, even aided by the use of phenolphthalein.

Though the room had been cleaned by maid service prior to the investigators' arrival, the chemical should have permitted them to detect trace amounts of blood had any been deposited the prior day.

Security video captured by surveillance cameras revealed that Jason first appeared at the hotel's front desk between 10:49 p.m. and 10:51 p.m. on November 2. The grainy, black-and-white video showed him wearing a light-colored, long-sleeved, pullover shirt with buttons from the mid-chest area to his neck. He arrived at his room at 10:56 p.m., which was the only time he used his plastic keycard to unlock the door.

At 11:59 p.m., security video revealed Jason at the front

desk a second time, wearing a different shirt—a dark-colored, long-sleeved, pullover shirt with a light-colored, thin stripe across the chest.

Less than a minute later, another security camera captured him headed toward the side exit at the western end of the hotel, adjacent to a stairwell. That was the last time Jason's presence at the hotel could be documented—right at midnight. That left him a little over seven and a half hours to have driven to Raleigh, committed the murder, returned to Hillsville, and driven as far as Wytheville. Very possible, the detectives reasoned.

Additional evidence discovered at the hotel made this scenario even more plausible. At about 5:00 a.m. on November 3, a hotel employee discovered that a small red landscaping rock had been placed in the door jamb at the western emergency exit to prevent the door from closing.

He kicked the rock out and the door latched closed. There was a sign next to the glass door beside the emergency exit door that let guests know they would need a keycard to reenter the hotel through that door between 11:00 p.m. and 6:00 a.m. If Jason had wanted to avoid using his keycard upon returning to the hotel following the murder—had he anticipated returning prior to 6:00 a.m.—keeping the emergency exit door propped open would certainly have allowed him to do so.

Another discovery by hotel employees that morning further intrigued investigators. The security camera in the western stairwell—just a few feet from that same emergency exit door—had been unplugged.

The last image that camera produced prior to the morning of November 3 was at 11:20 p.m. on November 2—about twenty minutes after Jason entered his room. The camera had apparently been unplugged from then until a hotel employee plugged it back in at 5:50 a.m. on November 3.

Less than an hour later, however, the same camera was tampered with a second time. From 5:50 a.m. until 6:34 a.m., it appeared to be functioning properly and produced a running stream of video footage of the western stairwell. But at 6:35 a.m., the camera suddenly began capturing footage of the ceiling.

When a hotel employee went to investigate the problem, it appeared to him as if someone had shoved the camera upward toward the ceiling. The employee repositioned the camera to face the stairwell, and it worked perfectly well thereafter.

If Jason had returned to the hotel at about 6:35 a.m., he could have walked through the glass door without using a keycard, pushed the camera toward the ceiling, and taken the stairs to his fourth-floor room without being detected. And if he had made sure not to let the door to his room lock when he left the prior evening, he could have reentered the room without needing his keycard to unlock the door. While at the hotel, investigators confirmed it was possible to make the door to Room 421 appear to be closed without causing it to lock.

The hotel had no record of Jason checking out, but it wasn't uncommon for guests to leave without taking the time to check out at the front desk. Check-out receipts were slipped under guests' doors between 3:00-5:00 a.m. A *USA Today* newspaper was hung on the outside handle of each guest's door in the same time frame.

If Jason had returned to the hotel at around 6:35 a.m.—after driving back from Raleigh—both would have been there waiting for him. He would then have had more than thirty minutes to shower, shave, gather his belongings, and drive the 27 miles to Wytheville by 7:40 a.m.

.....

There was a significant problem with this theory, however. Math. And fuel. Chronologically, the first gas receipt found in Jason's Explorer was from a Handy Hugo near downtown Raleigh at 7:32 p.m. on November 2. The second was from a Get-It Mart in Duffield, Virginia at 12:06 p.m. on November 3. Investigators didn't find any evidence of fuel purchases between those two points in time.

Yet it simply wasn't possible for one 22.5-gallon tank of gas—the size of the Explorer's gas tank—to have lasted Jason the 701 miles he would have traveled between 7:32 p.m. on

November 2 and 12:06 p.m. on November 3 if the investigators' theory were correct.

In that time, Jason would have made three 169-mile trips between Raleigh and Hillsville, a 144-mile trip from Hillsville to Clintwood, and a final 50-mile trip from Clintwood to Duffield. Jason's Explorer likely would have run out of fuel before making it back to the hotel the second time. If investigators were going to prove their theory, they had to find a gas station at which Jason had refueled between Raleigh and Hillsville, likely between 4:00-6:00 a.m. on November 3.

So on Monday, November 6, several Sheriff's investigators were dispatched to canvass gas stations along the main highways between Raleigh and Hillsville. Armed with photos of Jason and his Ford Explorer, they spoke with every gas station manager and cashier they could find who was on duty between 4:00-6:00 a.m. on November 3. They were hoping someone would recall a 30ish-year-old white male in a white Explorer who used cash that morning to buy gas. Miraculously, they hit pay dirt within hours.

Gracie Dahms Bailey was a cashier at the Four Brothers BP station on Highway 52 in King, North Carolina, just north of Winston-Salem, and about fifty minutes south of the Hampton Inn. She was on duty during the early morning hours of November 3. When Sheriff's investigators asked whether she remembered a man filling up a white SUV early that morning—and paying with cash—she answered without any hesitation or equivocation. "Yes, I do," she replied.

The convenience-store worker told investigators a man had pulled his white SUV up to the pump farthest away from the store and repeatedly tried to get the pump to work. When he couldn't, the man came into the store—frustrated and angry—and cursed at her for refusing to cut the pump on.

Bailey explained to him, at that time of day, she needed customers to provide identification, or cash or a credit card, before she was permitted to turn on the pumps. The man threw a $20 bill at her and went back outside while she activated the gas pump. He filled his SUV with only $15 worth of gas and quickly drove off, Bailey said, without returning for his change.

Investigators showed her a photograph of Jason. "That's the man!" Bailey exclaimed. She told them she remembered him vividly because no customer had ever cursed at her like that. His language made such an impression she couldn't forget the early-morning incident.

As they looked through the store's receipts to confirm her account, the investigators discovered one cash purchase of gas at 5:27 a.m. for $15 and a second at 5:36 a.m. for $20. One of those, they believed, was Jason's.

That timing fit neatly within their working timeline, which had Jason tampering with the Hampton Inn's western stairwell security camera about an hour later. More importantly, if Jason had been purchasing gas in King, North Carolina at about 5:30 a.m. on November 3, the only logical explanation for his being there was that he was on his way back to the hotel after killing his wife.

·····

Revelations from the Hampton Inn and Four Brothers BP station weren't the only puzzle pieces that began falling into place during the investigation's first few days. Jason's cell phone records provided a bonanza of additional information—much of it incriminating. It wasn't terribly surprising that the most frequently called and texted telephone number listed in those records belonged to a woman named Michelle. Yet that particular phone number wasn't the one assigned to Michelle Young. Rather, it belonged to Michelle Young's sorority sister and fellow McBroad, Michelle *Money*.

Jason's phone records revealed that in the thirty days leading up to the murder, he and Money had exchanged more than 400 text messages and phone calls. They also established Money was the last person Jason had spoken with on November 2 while at the Hampton Inn, approximately fifteen minutes before he appeared at the front desk the second time.

The two had exchanged more than *fifty* text messages and calls that very day. And Jason was back on the phone with her beginning at 7:49 a.m. on November 3 when he was near Wytheville.

Curiously, just after Jason began that call, he placed Money on hold and called his home phone. He left a message on the answering machine stating he was aware of his wife's 9:00 a.m. doctor's appointment and was just calling to let her know he was going to head onto Brevard after his sales meeting to spend the evening at his mother's home.

After finishing that message, Jason spoke with Money for another eighteen minutes. He was also on the phone with her that afternoon as he was headed toward Brevard, at the very time Linda was frantically trying to contact him to inform him of Michelle's death. Both her messages rolled to voicemail, which Jason apparently never checked.

.....

On November 16, Wake County Sheriff's investigators and detectives descended upon Ocoee, Florida—about twelve miles from Orlando—to interview Money. She immediately confessed to having an extramarital affair with Jason.

The "business meeting" Jason told his wife he was flying to Orlando to attend on Saturday, October 7—three days before their third wedding anniversary—was actually a tryst he had arranged with Money. Her husband Steve was out of town that weekend, which allowed Jason to slip in undetected. He stayed at Money's home the entire weekend. She told investigators that they had sex twice while he was there. Money drove Jason to the airport that Monday morning for him to catch his flight to Denver—for an actual business meeting.

With search warrant in hand, investigators trolled through Money's computer. Sure enough, there was an email stream between the two to complement their text message stream. One email exchange in particular stood out. In that exchange, dated October 28, 2006—six days before the murder—Jason said:

*i feel lucky just to know you, much less love you, but i do.*
*i don't know how all this happened, but i know how it will end*

*up…two broken hearts…but, i don't care. i know there is pain in my future, but you are so worth it, even if it's only for a "blink" in time.*

Money responded:

*Missing you so much!!! I won't even get into my husband's lack of romance, affection, attention, etc…*

*I wish things were different for all of us. Miss you tons!*

By the time they read this email, detectives had already unearthed the $2 million insurance policy on Michelle's life—on which Jason was listed as sole beneficiary. If the prospect of recovering on that policy didn't qualify as sufficient incentive for Jason to want his wife out of the picture, his professed love for Money certainly did. To the extent a jury needed to hang its hat on a motive, detectives had now established not one, but two.

·····

While one set of Sheriff's investigators canvassed gas stations between Hillsville and Raleigh, another was dispatched to canvass the Enchanted Oaks neighborhood. They were particularly interested in learning whether anyone happened to see anything unusual at 5108 Birchleaf Drive during the early morning hours of November 3.

Terry Tiller delivered the *New York Times* to 5200 Birchleaf Drive, a little farther down the road from the Youngs' house, which she typically passed by between 3:00-4:00 a.m. She told investigators that the Youngs' house jumped out at her the morning of November 3 because all of the interior and exterior lights were on—she assumed there must have been a late-night party. Normally Tiller wouldn't have even seen the house because it was set so far back from the road, she told investigators. She also noticed a light-colored, medium-sized SUV parked in front of, and parallel to, 5108 Birchleaf as well as a silver-blue van parked directly across the street. She didn't see anyone in, or near, either vehicle, however.

Cindy Beaver lived about ten houses farther down Birchleaf Drive from the Youngs. She was a postal worker who had a 6:00 a.m. shift at a post office near the N.C. State campus. She told investigators on November 7 that at about 5:20 a.m. on November 3, she was in her Volkswagen Beetle heading down Birchleaf Drive toward the subdivision's entrance. She had her bright headlights on to spot any deer that might cross the road. As she rounded a bend in the road, she saw a vehicle at the edge of the Youngs' driveway, facing the street. She recalled it being light-colored and similar in size to what a "soccer mom" might drive.

As best Beaver could remember, the vehicle was edging toward the street, with its headlights on, when the beam of her bright lights crossed its windshield. She couldn't make out if the passenger was a man or woman, but could see that person's head jerk away. She recalled being mortified she had scared this person, who she could only describe as having thick hair. She was able to get a better glimpse of the driver, someone she recalled being a white male whose hands were gripping the steering wheel.

Another neighbor investigators spoke with was Fay Hinsley, a spry, elderly woman who lived alone on the street behind the Youngs. She had a regular hair appointment every Friday morning, and was on her way there at approximately 6:15 a.m. on November 3, when she noticed a medium-sized, grayish SUV parked at the very end of the Youngs' driveway, facing and nearly into the street. At first she was startled because she thought the vehicle was going to race out at her, but then noticed the driver's seat was empty.

Of the three accounts, only Tiller's was consistent with the timeline established by the 6:35 a.m. tampering with the Hampton Inn's security camera. Detectives determined that it would have taken Jason at least two hours and 25 minutes to drive from Raleigh to Hillsville in the early morning hours — not including his stop to refuel. Based on Tiller's account, Jason could have been on the road back to Hillsville prior to 4:00 a.m. Her account fit neatly within their working timeline.

But neither Beaver's nor Hinsley's were at all consistent with that timeline. In fact, those accounts were quite similar to one another in that they placed a vehicle at the edge of the Youngs' driveway, facing toward the street, though at different times. And if Beaver's account were correct, it was most unlikely that the white male she saw was Jason Young, as there was irrefutable evidence his phone pinged a cell tower in Wytheville, Virginia — some 200 miles away — at 7:40 a.m.

.....

On Monday morning, November 6, Jason was in downtown Raleigh for his first meeting with his lawyer. The law firm of Tharrington Smith was widely regarded as one of North Carolina's leading criminal defense firms. Brothers Wade and Roger Smith — both former football players for the University of North Carolina Tar Heels — had been involved in numerous high-profile murder cases during the nearly four decades they had practiced law together.

Wade Smith was one of the defense attorneys for Jeffrey McDonald, the surgeon and Green Beret who in 1979 was convicted of killing his pregnant wife and two children while stationed at Fort Bragg, North Carolina. He had also represented one of the Duke University lacrosse players who had been falsely accused of sexually assaulting an African-American exotic dancer.

Though Ryan Schaad had informed Jason his appointment would be with Roger Smith, the Roger Smith who extended his hand to greet his new client that morning was considerably younger than what Jason had been expecting. Roger Smith, Jr., Roger's son and Wade's nephew, had been practicing criminal law at Tharrington Smith since graduating from law school in 1999. Having learned from the best — as much through osmosis from his father and uncle as from his studies in law school — he had already established himself as an excellent lawyer in his own right.

Based on Smith's advice, Jason refused to have any contact with the Sheriff's Office or its detectives, despite their repeated requests. Smith informed the Sheriff's Office Jason would be exercising all rights granted to him under the Constitution, most particularly, his right to remain silent. In fact, based on his lawyer's advice, Jason refused to discuss the case, his whereabouts on November 3, or his relationship with his wife, even with his friends and family.

On November 8, Smith accompanied Jason to the CCBI office in downtown Raleigh to respond to a "non-testimonial order" the Sheriff's Office had obtained to photograph Jason, gather head and pubic hair, take fingerprints and footprints, and collect samples of saliva and blood for DNA analysis. The CCBI was also authorized to obtain his body measurements and to fully inspect Jason's body for any cuts, scrapes, bruises, or abrasions.

The Constitutional right against self-incrimination didn't protect Jason from having to submit to such an examination. It was a fairly routine procedure following a homicide and didn't necessarily indicate that Jason was being treated as a suspect, let alone the primary suspect.

By this time, investigators were fully aware Michelle had actively defended herself against her killer. Logic suggested her assailant's body would bear some indication of the struggle. Investigators were hoping they could turn Jason's body into a critical piece of evidence against him.

But their hope quickly dissipated. They carefully inspected and photographed Jason's arms, hands, and fingers. Not a single scratch or bruise was visible.

The skin on his face was silky smooth and clear. Investigators had Jason strip and photographed every square inch of his body. Above his ankles, there wasn't a single blemish anywhere to be found.

The only aberration was on Jason's left foot. There was some black bruising underneath the nail on his left big toe, at the base of the toenail. There also was some minor blistering along the left side of the same foot, near the pinky toe. But beyond those two findings, investigators found nothing whatsoever to indicate that Jason had been involved in a savage attack against a woman who had clearly defended herself.

.....

As the calendar turned from November to December, and

then into 2007, much of the investigative work moved from the crime scene, neighborhood, and hotel to the crime laboratory at the State Bureau of Investigation. It would take some time for SBI serologists, chemists, biologists, and forensic computer examiners to analyze all of the blood, fingerprints, DNA, hair, carpet fibers, shoe impressions, digital, and other evidence investigators had collected.

Though the lead detectives continued to be wedded to their theory and timeline that placed Jason at the murder scene, they hadn't yet come up with a murder weapon, a reliable eyewitness, or any forensic evidence connecting Jason to the crime. They also were still at a loss as to how to explain Cassidy's remarkably clean appearance when she was discovered in Jason's and Michelle's bed.

Michelle's mother, sister, friends, and co-workers—and the public at large—were eager for answers and closure. But Wake County Sheriff Donnie Harrison cautioned everyone to be patient. His staff had accomplished a lot during the first few months of the investigation. Ultimately, he believed, they would make an arrest and, if necessary, prove their case.

If Jason Young did commit this despicable act, in due course, they would bring him to justice.

# 7

## CUSTODY AND WRONGFUL DEATH

$B$y November 2006, Cassidy Elizabeth Young had become as central to the lives of Meredith and Linda Fisher as she had been to Michelle Young's. Meredith, after all, had moved to North Carolina the day her niece was born to be her nanny. The two had an incredibly strong bond—it was rare for them to be apart for more than a few days.

If Michelle needed someone to care for Cassidy, her sister was always her first choice. And as it turned out, Cassidy spent her first two nights following her mother's death with her Aunt Emmy.

For her part, Linda had devoted large chunks of her summers to be with her only grandchild. She too had a special relationship with Cassidy. When she stayed at 5108 Birchleaf Drive, Cassidy spent far more time with her grandmother than she did with her own father—even when Jason was working from home. Having recently retired from teaching, Linda had been making plans to move to North Carolina permanently. She couldn't wait until Cassidy was part of her daily life.

But now that Michelle was dead, neither Meredith nor Linda had begun to process how her absence would affect their time—and relationships—with Cassidy. Before they could give that question any considerable thought, Cassidy was gone.

Immediately after Michelle's funeral, Jason had Heather

and Joe whisk Cassidy away to the mountains to insulate his daughter from the swirl of media attention surrounding the murder. Not only were Meredith and Linda not involved in that decision, they hadn't the slightest hint Cassidy was being relocated until she was long gone. They weren't even given the opportunity to say goodbye.

When investigators released Jason's Ford Explorer a few days later, he joined Heather and Joe in Etowah, about a twenty-minute drive from his mother's home in Brevard. At the time, Heather and Joe had no children. Though Heather had been with her niece only a handful of times, she began caring for her as if she were her own child. Cassidy and Jason lived there until December 2007, when Heather needed to turn Jason's room into a nursery, as she and Joe were expecting their first child. Jason and Cassidy then moved in with Pat and Gerald.

It didn't take Meredith and Linda long to realize Jason was now Cassidy's gatekeeper. If they wanted to speak to Cassidy by phone, that would occur only upon her father's express approval. If they wanted to visit her in person, Jason would get to dictate if, when, where, for how long, and under what conditions that visit would occur. For instance, Linda tried to make arrangements to see Cassidy in Brevard during the 2006 Thanksgiving and Christmas holidays. To her shock and dismay, she was rebuffed.

Pat and Jason apparently were wedded to the notion that Meredith and Linda were planning to kidnap Cassidy and take her back to New York. Pat told her son the funeral director pulled her aside during Michelle's pre-funeral visitation to inform her she had overheard Linda telling Meredith, "We ought to just take Cassidy and go." Yet as it turned out, it was Jason, not Linda, who had quietly orchestrated her relocation.

Meredith ultimately prevailed upon Jason to allow her to exchange Christmas gifts with Cassidy just before New Year's Day 2007.

Jason arranged for a "neutral site" visit at his friend Brian Ambrose's home near Charlotte, about half way between Raleigh and Brevard. The visit was short—and tense—and entirely under Jason's watchful eye.

Linda was first permitted to see her granddaughter at her third birthday party at Pat's home in late March 2007. She had asked if she and Meredith could have a separate party for Cassidy, but that request was denied. As a consolation, Pat indicated Meredith and Linda could have some "alone time" with Cassidy at her home both before and after her party. But neither actually occurred.

In the spring and summer of 2007, Pat did accommodate a handful of visits at the Holiday Inn Express in Brevard. Meredith and Linda would make the five-hour trek from Fuquay-Varina, spend the night at the hotel, and patiently await Cassidy's arrival the following morning.

The visits were usually over in two hours or less. According to Meredith, these visits were "extremely supervised" by Pat and one of her friends. Jason never attended.

"There was always someone a few feet away," she explained. When she tried to take Cassidy to the bathroom during one of the visits, Pat's friend stood guard just inside the bathroom door, presumably to ensure that Meredith didn't try to snatch Cassidy and run.

That fall, Pat arranged a visit at her home when Jason was away. About two hours into the visit, while Cassidy was napping, Pat sat Meredith and Linda down in her living room. She left momentarily and returned holding a piece of paper. Visibly annoyed, she dropped a photocopy of an article from New York's *Newsday* on the coffee table in front of them. The article indicated Pat and Jason hadn't been permitting Linda and Meredith to visit with Cassidy.

Clearly perturbed, Pat asked, "Why are you saying this when you're having visits? We'd like you to correct this and let the media know that yes, you are seeing Cassidy, you are having visits." Linda promised to let the media know they were indeed having visits. But Pat also pressed another issue— that Linda had been bad-mouthing Jason about his affair with Michelle Money.

Through squinted eyes, Pat glared at Linda, saying, "You don't know that he had an affair."

Now annoyed herself, Linda shot back, raising her voice, "Sure I do! She told the investigators she did." That statement and Linda's tone only riled Pat more. Turning to face Meredith, she said, quite sternly, "We need you to stand up for Jason and support him publicly."

But Meredith was having none of this, telling Pat, "We'd be happy to support Jason publicly—once he starts cooperating with the police."

"He needs to get up with his lawyer and go talk with the detectives," Linda chimed in.

That was about all Pat could bear. "If you won't retract that statement, if you won't support Jason publicly," she warned, "I'm afraid that we can't arrange for any more visits with Cassidy."

It was an ugly confrontation. Meredith and Linda felt like they had been ambushed. After two hours of joy being with Cassidy, the entire day had been ruined. They departed in an angry state, fearful even more restrictions would now be placed on their time and contact with Cassidy. Their stomachs churned during their long drive back to Fuquay-Varina.

Pat apparently meant what she said. From that point forward, all of Meredith and Linda's attempts to contact Cassidy by phone were rebuffed. All gifts and cards were returned—unopened—including their Christmas gifts that December. Neither Pat nor Jason would accept their calls or respond to their emails. They were completely cut off from Cassidy.

Months went by without any indication this pattern would change. With Cassidy's fourth birthday approaching in March 2008, Meredith and Linda formulated a plan. They knew where Cassidy attended daycare and decided to take a chance. Without breathing a word to anyone, they drove to Brevard on Cassidy's birthday and pulled up to the daycare center.

Instead of announcing their presence in the office, they headed directly to Cassidy's classroom, bearing balloons and birthday gifts, as well as the Christmas gifts that had been returned unopened. They even baked and decorated cupcakes for the whole class.

To their incredibly good fortune, the daycare's director was absent. Not quite knowing what to do, Cassidy's teacher allowed Linda and Meredith into the classroom where, for the very first time since Michelle was buried, they were able to spend quality time with Cassidy, without Pat or Jason—or Pat's friend—hovering over them as if they were convicted child molesters.

They repeated this gambit just before Mother's Day. Once again, they were able to gain entry into Cassidy's classroom. To their surprise and delight, that day was "spa day" for all of the moms. They spent the afternoon having Cassidy pamper them, apply makeup, and paint their fingernails. For that moment, at least, it was like old times.

But their joy was short-lived. Soon after that May 2008 drop-in at the daycare center, Jason had a note placed into Cassidy's file directing that Meredith and Linda were no longer authorized to visit his daughter. Once again, they were being shut out of Cassidy's life, this time, without any obvious path forward. It was time—indeed, long past time—to fight back.

.....

By 2007, Mike Schilawski was widely recognized as one of Raleigh's best—and smartest—family-law attorneys. Prior to passing the bar exam in 1982, he served as Editor in Chief of the prestigious *Law Review* at Campbell Law School, some eleven years after obtaining his bachelor's degree from the University of North Carolina at Chapel Hill. He also held a master's degree in education from N.C. State. Schilawski had been practicing family law for about twenty years when Meredith and Linda first came to see him in the spring of 2007.

At that point, they simply wanted to better understand their legal rights as Cassidy's maternal aunt and grandmother. What they learned confirmed their worst fears. Neither had legal standing to force Jason to allow them to visit with Cassidy. If Jason wanted to exclude them from his daughter's life altogether, as her biological father, he had every right to do so. No court would intervene even to allow them to have phone contact with Cassidy. Whatever informal arrangements they could work out with Jason would be more than they could ever hope to achieve through legal action.

But there might come a time, Schilawski advised them, when that could change. A blood relative—such as an aunt or grandmother—could obtain standing to challenge a biological parent for custody or visitation if the parent had acted inconsistently with his Constitutionally protected rights as a parent.

Schilawski told them that if Jason had brutally murdered Michelle while his daughter was just a few feet away—as Meredith and Linda knew investigators had all but concluded—that criminal act would support their argument that he had forfeited his Constitutionally protected rights to be Cassidy's father. If Jason were charged with Michelle's murder, he said, he could then pursue action on their behalf in family court.

By August 2008, however, investigators still hadn't wrapped up their investigation. It wasn't clear how much longer it would be until they charged Jason with Michelle's murder—or if they ever would. Meredith and Linda had been completely excluded from Cassidy's life for three months. They hadn't been able to speak with her by telephone for nearly a year. Their frustration was mounting, as was their hostility toward Pat and Jason.

"We know we don't have standing to file a lawsuit," Linda lamented. But she implored Schilawski to do something— anything—to induce Jason to allow them to visit with Cassidy.

Schilawski agreed to write Jason a letter, which would insist he agree on a visitation schedule. The letter was delivered by registered mail to Pat's address in Brevard in mid-August. Schilawski informed Jason he had been retained by Meredith and Linda "to assist them in securing visitation opportunities and telephone contact with Cassidy."

He noted that Meredith and Linda had been completely cut off from Cassidy since well before May. His letter invited Jason "to enter into negotiations to voluntarily provide access" to Cassidy. Schilawski warned Jason—in what was essentially an empty threat—that if he were "unwilling to attempt to negotiate a visitation schedule with Meredith and Linda, I would advise them to proceed with other remedies that may be available."

Though Meredith and Linda had no idea whether Schilawski's letter would alter the status quo, they were relieved something was finally being done to force the issue and cautiously optimistic it might result in renewed contact with Cassidy.

Two weeks later, Schilawski received a call from Alice Stubbs, Roger Smith, Jr.'s law partner at Tharrington Smith. She indicated she was responding to his letter and would be representing Jason on all matters related to Cassidy. "This is good news," Schilawski thought. With Stubbs involved, at least there was a possibility of a dialogue.

Alice Stubbs was only thirty when Governor Jim Hunt appointed her to the Wake County District Court bench in 1997, barely five years after she graduated from the University of North Carolina School of Law. She had a stellar resume, having attended the prestigious Phillips Academy prep school in Massachusetts and Davidson College near Charlotte—widely regarded as one of the best private universities in North Carolina—before heading off to law school.

By 2002, Stubbs was one of four Wake County judges hearing family court cases. Four years later, she joined Tharrington Smith and became an integral part of its family-law practice. Though she had only been a family-law practitioner a short while as of 2007, her time on the family-court bench—not to mention her bulldog tenacity and ferocious, take-no-prisoners style—made her a force to be reckoned with.

When Schilawski had sent Jason his letter, he wasn't certain he would even receive a response. After all, Jason had rebuffed every effort detectives had made to speak with him for nearly two years. It was reasonable to assume Jason would take the same approach to his letter.

But now that Stubbs was involved, Schilawski was more optimistic a favorable outcome might actually be possible.

He considered it unlikely she would advise her client to continue insulating Cassidy from all contact with the aunt and grandmother who had been such a central part of her life prior to Michelle's death. Stubbs knew all too well from her time on the bench that this type of "restrictive gatekeeping" generally backfired on family-court litigants.

In early September, Stubbs invited Schilawski to propose a visitation schedule for his clients. With their lawyer's assistance, Meredith and Linda crafted a monthly schedule from September 2008 to August 2009, with visits to take place in Brevard, Fuquay-Varina, and even New York. Unsupervised long weekends were proposed for September 2008 and during the Christmas holidays. Their proposal also would have restored telephone contact with Cassidy on a regular basis. Schilawski was hopeful this proposal would begin a dialogue with Stubbs that would lead to a formal, written agreement.

At the same time, as a showing of good faith, Stubbs arranged for an *unsupervised* weekend visit in Brevard that October—the longest visit Meredith and Linda had with Cassidy in the two years since Michelle's murder. It was amazingly wonderful. But the weekend flew by and, just like that, they were right back to where they had been since the confrontation in Pat's living room in 2007. All further discussion over their proposed visitation schedule came to a screeching halt.

Stubbs informed Schilawski the October visit had gone so well, Jason and Pat believed a formal agreement simply wasn't necessary. She explained Jason was perfectly willing to allow further visits in Brevard. He just wasn't willing to commit to anything in writing or to be boxed into specific dates and locations that far in advance.

Yet with the sting of the "keep-away" game Jason and Pat had been playing for nearly two years still all too fresh in their minds, Meredith and Linda had little appetite—or reason—to return to visitation being dictated by Jason and Pat's unfettered control. They told Schilawski that Stubbs's suggestion was unacceptable. At their urging, he insisted to Stubbs that she and Jason make a counter-proposal, so they could keep the discussion going.

Days and weeks passed. Schilawski's entreaty was met with dead silence. No counter-proposal of any kind was extended. Once again, Meredith and Linda were back to square one.

.....

Paul Michaels had been a successful Raleigh personal injury attorney for nearly thirty years. He worked exclusively on a contingency-fee basis—paid only if he succeeded in recovering money for his clients, typically taking one-third of their recoveries. Meanwhile, his younger brother Jack spent most of his career as an insurance defense lawyer, defending against personal injury claims brought by lawyers like his brother. In 2000, Jack decided to join forces with Paul, forming the law firm Michaels & Michaels, P.A.

In August 2008, Paul received a voicemail from Howard Cummings, Wake County's first Assistant District Attorney. Though they were casually acquainted from attending the same YMCA, their professional paths didn't ordinarily cross— Cummings tried cases in criminal courtrooms, not the civil courtrooms with which Michaels was most familiar. He had no idea why the Assistant DA might be calling.

When Michaels returned the call, Cummings explained that he had been working with detectives involved in the Michelle Young murder investigation. He had gotten to know Linda and Meredith Fisher very well, he said. They had become increasingly frustrated with the lack of progress in the investigation and wanted to know if they could do anything to push things along.

In addition, Cummings told Michaels that Linda and Meredith were apoplectic that Jason stood to receive $4 million as the sole beneficiary on Michelle's life insurance policy when—they all believed—he was the one who killed her. Though the Prudential policy was for only $2 million, it was going to pay double indemnity because her death was caused by "accident," rather than illness or disease.

Cummings confessed to Michaels that the criminal investigation was at somewhat of a standstill. And that was precisely why he was calling. He knew there were tools available in the civil discovery process he and Sheriff's investigators couldn't use. He wanted to know if Michaels and his brother could pursue a wrongful death case against Jason which—through the civil discovery process—might lead to additional evidence.

"You can ask him questions under oath in your case," the prosecutor explained. "We can't do that and he absolutely refuses to talk with us. Either he answers your questions under oath about what happened to Michelle, or he'll forfeit the $4 million." He promised the personal injury lawyer access to detectives and their files so long as he agreed to share with the DA's Office whatever additional information the civil case uncovered. Michaels told Cummings he would discuss the matter with his brother Jack and get back with him.

Time was of the essence. The statute of limitations on the wrongful death case was two years—they had less than three months to decide whether to take the case and file suit. Though neither Paul nor Jack Michaels had ever before filed a wrongful death suit based on the victim's murder, they were certainly aware of other lawyers who had obtained civil judgments against murderers.

Cases of that type were rarely contested and typically resulted in judgments of well over $1 million. But the judgments were almost always worthless, as the defendants found liable for wrongful death—typically in prison by then—ordinarily lacked the resources to pay even the first penny. A wrongful death judgment against Jason Young would be equally worthless, they believed.

Nonetheless, the appeal of a potential civil case against Jason was the possibility they could obtain a judgment declaring him to be Michelle's killer under the "slayer statute." Were that to happen, not only would Jason be precluded from recovering the $4 million in insurance proceeds under North Carolina law, those proceeds could then be redirected to Michelle's lineal descendant—Cassidy.

Michaels got back to Cummings to let him know he and his brother were happy to meet with Linda and Meredith, though they couldn't yet commit to pursuing a case. When that meeting occurred, however, the Michaels brothers were surprised to learn that Linda and Meredith weren't as eager to file suit against Jason as the Assistant DA had advertised. Linda, in particular, was concerned doing so might further doom their efforts to reestablish meaningful visitation with Cassidy.

The lawyers had other concerns as well—substantial concerns. For starters, they were civil attorneys, not prosecutors. They had never before proven a murder case, and weren't sure they could—after all, the Sheriff's Office had been investigating the case for nearly two years and hadn't even obtained an indictment, let alone a conviction. And as they researched the slayer statute, they couldn't find a single instance in which it had been applied *before* a murder conviction—every prior case they found applied the statute only *after* a conviction.

Compounding their concern was the risk the insurance company, Prudential, might take the position the policy would be voided altogether if Jason had murdered Michelle. For instance, had Jason secured the policy because he intended to kill Michelle, Prudential could argue the policy was obtained fraudulently and would therefore be void. Thus, there was grave doubt Prudential would pay a single penny without a separate court battle.

Jack Michaels spoke with two of his former insurance defense lawyer colleagues, both of whom predicted Prudential would fight vigorously rather than pay. Even more alarming, the Michaels brothers learned Cummings had actually approached another prominent personal injury attorney before calling them, who declined to take the case due to all these risks.

The attorneys' reluctance to get involved began to subside only after they were given access to the criminal investigation files. For two long days, they reviewed investigators' interview notes, the autopsy report, SBI reports, and crime-scene photos.

They were also put in touch with the lead detective, Sergeant Richard Spivey, who helped them connect the dots and put the puzzle pieces in place. The brothers became convinced not only that Jason had in fact killed Michelle, but that there was sufficient evidence available for them to prove he had. Though they still had reservations and concerns, they decided to take the case.

On October 29, 2008—five days before the statute of limitations expired—Paul and Jack Michaels filed a wrongful death complaint with Linda, as the executrix of Michelle's estate, named as the plaintiff. The lawsuit named Jason Lynn Young as the sole defendant.

The complaint alleged, "In the early morning hours of November 3, 2006, Jason Young brutally murdered Michelle Young at their residence."

Linda sought "compensation for the horror, pain and suffering of Michelle Young caused by Defendant's fatal assault" as well as "the present monetary value to Cassidy of her mother's reasonably expected net income" and "society, companionship, comfort, guidance, kindly offices and advice."

She also sought punitive damages to punish Jason for killing Michelle. Finally, she asked the court to declare that Jason was Michelle's "slayer" under the slayer statute and therefore barred from collecting any life insurance proceeds.

The following afternoon, a private process server appeared at Pat Young's doorstep in Brevard. When she opened the door, she was handed the summons and complaint suing her son for the wrongful death of his wife. Jason had thirty days to respond, or the relief requested in the complaint could be granted.

Linda and Meredith assumed someone from Tharrington Smith would file some kind of a response. Yet there was no response at all. As was permitted by the civil rules when a defendant fails to respond to a complaint, on December 2, Jack Michaels had the Clerk of Court enter a "default" against Jason.

The following day, he filed a motion for a default judgment under the slayer statute and personally walked a copy over to Tharrington Smith. He asked the receptionist to ensure the motion's delivery to Roger Smith, Jr. The hearing was set to take place just two days later.

The afternoon of December 5, 2008, would ultimately represent a critical turning point in Linda and Meredith's quest for justice. At 3:30 p.m., Judge Donald Stephens called the case of *Linda Lee Fisher v. Jason Lynn Young* on for hearing. Sitting at the plaintiff's counsel table was Linda Fisher, flanked on either side by Paul and Jack Michaels.

Meredith sat behind them in the first row of the gallery. In stark contrast, the chairs behind the defense counsel table were empty. No Roger Smith, Jr. No Jason. No one at all. Judge Stephens asked whether anyone in the courtroom was there on behalf of Jason Lynn Young. No one responded.

Jack Michaels then asked for permission to approach the bench and handed Judge Stephens three sworn affidavits: one from him, one from his brother Paul, and one from Sergeant Spivey. The lawyers' affidavits recounted the extensive efforts they had made reviewing the criminal investigation files and asserted their belief that those materials established Jason had killed Michelle.

Sergeant Spivey's affidavit went even further, stating, "Based on my experience in law enforcement ... and my knowledge of the evidence gathered in the investigation of the death of Michelle Young, in my opinion, the allegation in the Complaint that 'in the early morning hours of November 3, 2006, Jason Young brutally murdered Michelle Young at their residence' is true."

Peering over the top of his wire-rimmed reading glasses, Judge Stephens asked, "Do you have a proposed judgment?"

"I do, Your Honor," Michaels responded as he walked toward the bench to hand the judge the unsigned judgment he had drafted.

Judge Stephens perused the judgment, scribbled his name on the signature line, and handed it to the Clerk to enter into the file. The judgment decreed "that the Defendant, Jason Lynn Young, willfully and unlawfully killed Plaintiff's decedent, Michelle Marie Fisher Young, within the definition of 'slayer' under General Statute § 31A-3(3)d" and he was therefore barred from recovering any life insurance proceeds on her life.

Rather, those proceeds would be owed to the person

who was next in line to receive them had Jason predeceased Michelle—namely, Cassidy Elizabeth Young.

Linda and Meredith were elated. Finally, more than two years after Michelle's murder, justice, at least at some level, had been attained. They could now publicly refer to Jason as Michelle's killer. And their leverage over Jason and Pat in their effort to establish a formal visitation schedule with Cassidy had now changed considerably.

.....

With the civil judgment in hand that decreed Jason had murdered Michelle, Mike Schilawski could now assert Jason had forfeited his Constitutionally protected rights as Cassidy's father. The blood relatives with greatest past relationships with her—Meredith and Linda—finally had standing to file suit in family court.

On December 17—just twelve days following the wrongful death hearing and judgment—Schilawski filed a custody lawsuit, naming both Meredith and Linda as plaintiffs and Jason as the sole defendant. Two days later, Pat Young was greeted at her front door by yet another process server, who, this time, handed her a custody complaint.

Much like the wrongful death suit, the custody complaint contended, "In the early morning hours of November 3, 2006, the Defendant brutally murdered Michelle Marie Fisher Young ('Michelle') at their residence. Michelle was pregnant with Defendant's son at the time of her murder. Upon information and belief, Cassidy was in the residence at the time the Defendant murdered her mother."

The complaint further asserted, "Extreme tension exists between the Plaintiffs and the Defendant and between the Plaintiffs and Defendant's family. Defendant and his family are unable and/or unwilling to encourage Cassidy's relationship with the Plaintiffs." It contended Jason had "consistently denied telephone and personal contact between Plaintiffs and Cassidy."

Schilawski included even more incendiary language in

the complaint, detailing a pattern of conduct that had been "degrading to Michelle, erratic, and inappropriate," including Jason's extramarital affairs, drinking alcohol in excess — including the occasion at Ryan and Shelly's home in which he sat on their couch stark naked while engaged in conversation — and his frequent display of "penis tricks" at social gatherings.

The complaint alleged Jason had "not behaved as a grieving spouse would since Michelle's murder," noting he was still in touch with at least one woman with whom he had a sexual affair, and was posting pictures of Cassidy online in an effort to solicit dates. It also alleged Jason hadn't cooperated with law enforcement officers investigating Michelle's murder.

The custody complaint quoted from the wrongful death judgment that declared Jason had "willfully and unlawfully killed Michelle." It alleged Jason was "not a fit and proper person to have the care, custody and control of Cassidy. By his conduct as set out herein, the Defendant has acted inconsistently with his Constitutionally-protected status as the biological parent to Cassidy."

Meredith and Linda asked the court to award them "the exclusive care, custody and control of the minor child, Cassidy Elizabeth Young" and also "appoint a qualified physician or psychologist to conduct a psychological evaluation of the Defendant to assist the Court in making a determination regarding custody and visitation." Their request for temporary custody, as well as their motion for a psychological evaluation of Jason, were set for a one-hour hearing on February 4, 2009.

At the time he filed the complaint, Schilawski anticipated Stubbs would contend the proper venue for the custody case was Transylvania County, where Cassidy had resided since moving in with Pat and Gerald in December 2007, rather than Wake County, where she hadn't lived for over two years.

He therefore wasn't at all surprised when, instead of responding directly to the complaint, Stubbs filed a motion to dismiss it for improper venue. Recognizing this likelihood even before Stubbs filed her motion, Schilawski had been in touch with an attorney in Brevard who agreed to represent Meredith and Linda if venue were actually transferred.

Since the family court needed to resolve Stubbs's venue motion before hearing the custody issues, Schilawski and Stubbs agreed that the February 4 hearing would be devoted solely to her venue motion. Everything else would have to await the outcome of that hearing.

But that didn't stop Meredith's and Linda's lawyer from continuing to press for a visitation schedule and restoration of telephone contact with Cassidy. He proposed a schedule to last them until his request for temporary custody could be heard.

In late January 2009—with the scheduled hearing just a week away—Stubbs informed Schilawski she had a proposal to discuss. The two lawyers met at Tharrington Smith a couple of days later.

Jason's attorney let Schilawski know she had a lengthy discussion with her client about the custody case. She then outlined the type of arrangement to which Jason could agree and asked Schilawski to draft a consent order fleshing out that arrangement.

When he got back to his office, Schilawski called his clients to schedule a meeting. "I think you're going to like this proposal," he told them, without providing any details.

The following day, Meredith and Linda found themselves sitting at a conference room table at Schilawski's law office, anxiously awaiting his arrival. They assumed he was going to tell them Stubbs had convinced Jason to accept their proposed visitation schedule. That would have allowed them monthly, unsupervised weekend visits, just like the one they had in Brevard in October 2008. They were also hopeful their telephone contact with Cassidy would finally be restored.

After what seemed like an eternity, Schilawski finally entered the room, holding three copies of a document. He placed one in front of Meredith, another in front of Linda, and the final copy at his seat. The eight-page document was entitled "Child Custody Consent Order."

He explained that this proposal was not at all what he was expecting when Stubbs asked to meet.

Rather than providing a visitation schedule, the proposed

order would actually transition Cassidy's *custody*—to Meredith. Under the proposed order, Jason's daughter would spend three- to five-day blocks with Meredith each month from February to May; a full week in June; and two weeks in July. As of August 1, Meredith would have permanent custody of Cassidy in Wake County, where she would attend kindergarten.

From that point forward, Jason would have visitation only every other weekend during the school year and four weeks over the summer. Ironically, the order called for custodial exchanges to take place at the Cracker Barrel restaurant in Statesville, about half way between Fuquay-Varina and Brevard. It also provided for telephone contact for both Meredith and Linda while Cassidy was in Jason's care.

Meredith and Linda were stunned. The only reason they had Schilawski file the lawsuit was to obtain *visitation* rights with Cassidy and to ensure they had access to her by telephone. Though the complaint included a claim for custody, their actual goal was merely to ensure their legal right to be part of Cassidy's life. They never expected to be awarded custody. And they certainly didn't expect Jason to voluntarily surrender custody.

"Why is he all of a sudden agreeing to this?" a bewildered Linda quizzed her lawyer. Though Stubbs never revealed Jason's motivation directly, the answer to this question seemed obvious.

"He doesn't want to have to answer any questions about what happened to Michelle," Schilawski responded. The consent order ensured he wouldn't have to. He wouldn't need to respond to the complaint's allegation he had brutally murdered her. He wouldn't be examined under oath at a deposition. No psychological evaluation would be performed.

In exchange for those provisions—through which he protected himself against possible repercussions in a criminal courtroom—Jason signed the consent order, legally transferring custody of his nearly five-year-old daughter to Meredith. Without much fanfare, the family-court judge affixed her signature and entered the order on February 6.

Meredith and Linda were overjoyed. Their relationship with Cassidy would finally be restored. For the second time in two months, justice had prevailed.

.....

To the great relief of Paul and Jack Michaels, Prudential Insurance Company didn't put up any fight at all. Instead, the insurer paid the full $4.25 million owed under Michelle's life insurance policy. Seventy-five percent of that amount was placed in trust for Cassidy's benefit until her eighteenth birthday; the other 25% was paid to the Michaels brothers as legal fees.

But there was still the matter of establishing damages for Michelle's wrongful death. A hearing for that purpose was set for March 16, 2009, before Judge Osmond Smith. Once again, neither Jason nor anyone representing him appeared. On this occasion, Jack and Paul Michaels presented live testimony from several witnesses, including Linda, Meredith, Sergeant Spivey, and two of Michelle's Progress Energy co-workers. They also played a video showing Michelle interacting with Cassidy at her kitchen table. "I love you, Mommy," a smiling Cassidy beamed at the end of the video.

Meredith's testimony was heart-wrenching. She told Judge Smith Cassidy had recently asked her, "'How did my mommy used to hold me?'" Fighting back tears, Meredith testified that she "grabbed her real tight and told her that her mom loved her so much and that she would squeeze her and hug her like this every chance she could."

Through her own tears, Linda told the judge she felt as if "my heart's been ripped out of me," and the void in Cassidy's life would never be filled.

Sergeant Spivey testified Michelle's murder involved "the most severe physical beating I've ever seen someone encounter." He described it as "pretty extreme, a pretty vicious attack that she underwent."

The detective told Judge Smith the evidence the Sheriff's Office had amassed pointed directly at Jason, and established

Michelle's murder was "premeditated."

When the evidence closed, Jack Michaels asked the judge, in calculating damages, to "send some sort of message to the community that what happened here to Michelle Young is not the way to end a marriage."

Judge Smith found that Linda, as executrix of Michelle's estate, was entitled to $3.9 million in compensatory damages for Michelle's pain and suffering and funeral expenses, as well as the value of Cassidy's loss of Michelle's income, care, comfort, society, and companionship. He awarded an additional $11.7 million in punitive damages, finding Jason's conduct "was a premeditated, brutal intentional tort" and that he "willfully and maliciously" caused Michelle's death.

Though no one expected any part of this $15.6 million to be collected, the magnitude of the award did send a powerful message and served as yet another measure of justice for Michelle Fisher Young.

# 8

## CIRCUMSTANTIAL EVIDENCE

A criminal case can be proven by direct or circumstantial evidence, or some combination of the two. In a murder case, unfortunately, the eyewitness in the best position to provide direct evidence of the crime—the victim—is of course unable to do so. That is why circumstantial evidence tends to be so critical in proving murder.

There is a common misconception that circumstantial evidence is, by its very nature, less compelling than direct evidence. Yet the opposite is often true. In a simple car crash case, three different eyewitnesses might each have a different perception—or recollection—of what actually happened. The human mind, after all, has many imperfections and frailties.

A qualified accident reconstructionist, however, after measuring the skid marks of both vehicles, and evaluating the extent and location of damage to each, can typically conclude with amazing precision exactly how the accident occurred. Thus, when circumstantial evidence is grounded on hard science such as physics, chemistry, or biology, it can be extremely powerful.

In a similar vein, in the criminal arena, a sexual assault can be proven by establishing the presence of the defendant's DNA on the victim's body. Because DNA is so incredibly unique, a match between the defendant's sample and a swab taken from the victim often constitutes irrefutable proof that the defendant was the perpetrator—even absent eyewitness testimony from the victim.

But circumstantial evidence doesn't need to be grounded on hard science to be convincing. Sometimes, common sense alone is sufficient to make circumstantial evidence powerful.

If one wakes up in the morning to find snow covering the ground, they know it snowed overnight. Yet the evidence one is relying on to reach that conclusion is entirely circumstantial and not at all based on science. It is based solely on life experience.

Sometimes circumstantial evidence establishes beyond doubt *what* happened, but not *who* was responsible. Upon discovering Michelle Young's lifeless body lying beside her side of the bed in the master bedroom, investigators quickly concluded she had been murdered and a weapon of some kind had been involved. But without a murder weapon lying by her side—bearing the assailant's fingerprints or DNA—those revelations did nothing to establish who had killed her.

Circumstantial evidence is most powerful when clustered or layered. Human hair had been found in Michelle's left hand and on the floor beneath her body. Had SBI crime lab personnel been able to match that hair to Jason, that additional layer likely would have been sufficient to solve the crime.

Because the crime lab concluded the hair matched Michelle's, however, its discovery did nothing to identify her assailant. Similarly, had Michelle's blood been found on any of the clothing in the luggage in Jason's Explorer, that additional layer also would have been enough to establish his guilt. But none of her blood was found on any of his clothing.

Even more ideal layering of circumstantial evidence would have been a bloody fingerprint, which would have clearly placed that finger—and the body to which it belonged—at the murder scene. But not a single bloody fingerprint, other than Cassidy's, was ever found.

On the other hand, the bloody shoe impressions found on the embroidered pillow held the promise of solving the crime. Like a bloody fingerprint, those impressions had to have been made at the time of the murder and were quite obviously made by someone other than Michelle or Cassidy. Though shoe impressions are not nearly as unique as fingerprints or DNA, if they turned out to match the size and type of shoes Jason owned, that would have constituted powerful circumstantial evidence pointing directly at him.

Yet the SBI crime lab had been hard at work analyzing the shoe impressions for many months without being able to reach firm conclusions.

Another way of looking at circumstantial evidence is through the lens of coincidence. Using the shoe impressions as an example, if they did turn out to match the size and type of shoes Jason owned, how astronomical would the odds have been that those facts would have been mere coincidences, rather than circumstances pointing to Jason's involvement in the murder?

The Hampton Inn presented several such examples. Was it a coincidence the shirt a surveillance camera captured Jason wearing during his second appearance at the front desk wasn't found in his luggage or his Explorer? Or did the absence of that shirt suggest he had been wearing it at the time of the murder and discarded it because it contained Michelle's blood? Was it a coincidence the hotel's western stairwell security camera had been disabled some twenty minutes after Jason's arrival, and was then pointed at the ceiling at 6:35 a.m. the next morning? Was it plausible someone else besides Jason tampered with that camera—twice—within hours of his wife's murder?

Similarly, was it a coincidence a rock was found propping open the emergency exit door adjacent to the western stairwell? And that Jason's keycard hadn't been used a single time after he first entered his room shortly before 11:00 p.m.—even though he clearly left his room just before midnight? Could each of these pieces of evidence merely have been coincidences or, at some point, did their cumulative weight make that likelihood entirely implausible?

Motive is nearly always proven by circumstantial evidence. Several pieces of evidence clustered around Jason's motive. The $2 million life insurance policy with a double-indemnity provision. Jason's affair with Michelle Money—evidenced by several dozen calls and texts with her on November 2 and 3 as well as his profession of love for her. His deteriorating relationship with Michelle. And his extreme displeasure with the thought of his mother-in-law descending upon his home for the holidays—and then perhaps permanently following the birth of Rylan.

Was each of these pieces of evidence a mere coincidence, disconnected entirely from whether Jason was the one who bludgeoned Michelle to death? Or did all of them—piled together—establish precisely why he was the most logical person to have done so?

Was it also a coincidence that Jason successfully pulled the MapQuest directions off the printer before leaving home on November 2, but, for some reason, left the eBay printouts lying on the very same printer? Or that in the space of less than ninety minutes during the afternoon of November 3, he made three calls designed to get Meredith to go to 5108 Birchleaf Drive (two to her and one to his mother), specifically trying to get her upstairs where both Cassidy and Michelle's body were found? Did those three calls, in such rapid succession, create the inference he was desperate for Michelle's dead body to be found? And equally desperate to ensure Cassidy was safe? Were those calls circumstantial evidence of a guilty mind? Were the eBay printouts circumstantial evidence of premeditation?

In the same vein, was it merely a coincidence that Jason made calls to the home phone that morning, and to Michelle's work phone and cell phone that afternoon? Or were those calls intended to make it appear he had no idea she had been killed? How many coincidences were necessary to reach the tipping point? At what point would common sense dictate there was simply no way each and every one of those pieces of evidence was merely a coincidence?

Against all of this incriminating circumstantial evidence, there were also two significant pieces of *exculpatory* circumstantial evidence: Rylan and Cassidy. If Jason had been the assailant, he didn't just extinguish Michelle's life—he also extinguished Rylan's.

From their interviews, detectives had learned how eagerly Jason had been anticipating his son's arrival. Even had he desperately wanted Michelle out of the picture, how could he have done this to Rylan—and himself? Likewise, there was little doubt Jason cared deeply for Cassidy and loved being her dad. Surely he would have known that her mother's brutal murder would scar Cassidy emotionally and result in life-long psychological issues.

Could he nevertheless rationalize that murdering Michelle would somehow leave his daughter better off?

Cassidy also presented a forensic enigma. Irrefutable evidence existed that she had walked through and played in Michelle's blood—she had smeared blood all over her bathroom walls and walked through it in both her socks and her bare feet. She had left bloody footprints in Jason's closet. Yet she somehow wound up on his side of the bed squeaky clean—as were the comforter and linens on that side of the bed. And though she had no diaper on, the two-and-a-half year-old child hadn't urinated or defecated on herself in the more than nine hours she had been alone in the house, had Jason departed prior to 4:00 a.m., as the detectives' working theory and timeline presumed.

Thus, rather than pointing to Jason's guilt, or helping to solve the crime, the circumstantial evidence surrounding Cassidy made no sense at all.

There was also another living occupant at 5108 Birchleaf Drive—Mr. Garrison—and the circumstantial evidence surrounding him was equally confounding. Meredith had found the dog inside the house when she arrived. At one point during her 911 call, she actually addressed him by name. He too had presumably been left alone in a very bloody house for more than nine hours. Yet not a single bloody paw print was detected. How could that be? Investigators hadn't the slightest idea.

This much was clear: if Jason Young were charged with his wife's murder, the case against him would be based entirely on the assembly and interpretation of circumstantial evidence. Some of that evidence was strong, particularly when considered cumulatively. Some of it, however, tended to point away from Jason. And some of it prosecutors would never be able to explain.

# 9

## ARREST

During his fifteen years in law enforcement, Sergeant Richard Spivey had investigated many violent crimes, including murder. The burly, no-nonsense officer joined the Wake County Sheriff's Office in April 2004, following nine years as a detective with the Durham City Police Department.

In late April 2007, Sheriff Donnie Harrison assigned Sergeant Spivey as the "case agent," or lead detective, in charge of the Michelle Young murder investigation. Sheriff Harrison hoped a new set of eyes, and the sharp mind and steely determination for which the detective was known, might lead to new developments that would finally solve the case.

Sergeant Spivey began his assignment by taking a fresh look at the mountain of evidence Sheriff's investigators had amassed. As he was sorting through digital images of Cassidy's bedroom, something struck his eye—something that didn't seem to belong in a toddler's bedroom. He zoomed in on a plastic bottle on the top shelf of the hutch above her dresser.

As the label came into focus, he was able to make out the words "Tylenol Extra Strength Adult Rapid Blast." The bottle contained a red liquid. He also spotted a medicine dropper lying on the same shelf that appeared to have some red liquid remaining in the chamber.

As he zoomed in on the shelf below, the detective noticed a white bottle with a purple wrapper bearing the name "Pancof

PD." Since he was unfamiliar with that medication, the detective conducted some research. He learned that Pancof PD is a strong cough medicine—for *adults*.

One of the ingredients is dihydrocodeine, which causes dizziness and sleepiness. The package insert indicated that it should be used with extreme caution with children.

He also discovered Pancof PD was manufactured by Jason's former employer, Pan American Labs. Sergeant Spivey spoke with human resources personnel at the company and confirmed Jason had been supplied over 1,000 samples of Pancof PD during his three years of employment and had been thoroughly trained on all of its side effects.

The Sheriff's Office had preserved these items since November 2006, including the medicine dropper. Sergeant Spivey had them sent off to the SBI crime lab for analysis. The SBI found a match of Cassidy's DNA on the medicine dropper. It also confirmed that dihydrocodeine was present within the red liquid in the chamber.

Suddenly, the toddler's shockingly clean appearance the afternoon of the murder wasn't quite so enigmatic. The notion she had been cleaned up before 4:00 a.m. and placed under the covers on Jason's side of the bed—and remained asleep in precisely that spot for more than nine hours—didn't seem so implausible. Cassidy had apparently been drugged. And who was more knowledgeable about the effect these medications would have on a young child than Jason Young?

. . . . .

Shortly after being assigned to the murder investigation, Sergeant Spivey arranged a meeting with Gracie Dahms Bailey. Having read her account of the gas purchase that supposedly placed Jason in King, North Carolina around 5:30 a.m. on November 3, he wasn't quite convinced her identification would stand up in court. He wanted to know—without her being prompted by a photograph of Jason—how she would describe the person who had cursed and thrown a $20 bill at her.

When they met, Bailey recalled that, despite the frigid weather, the man who cursed at her that morning wasn't wearing a coat. He was wearing a long-sleeved shirt and blue jeans.

She told the detective that he was white, had blondish hair, and was somewhere between his mid-20s and early-30s. In every respect, that identification matched the Jason Young Sergeant Spivey had seen from surveillance camera footage at the Hampton Inn at 11:59 p.m. the prior evening. He was now more comfortable Bailey's identification would stand up in court.

.....

SBI forensic computer examiners discovered several important items on Jason's home and laptop computers. For starters, it turned out the eBay printouts Jason sent Meredith to retrieve on November 3 were created at 7:08 p.m. the prior evening, just minutes before he departed for his business trip. That timing made it seem much more likely the printouts were merely a prop in Jason's plan rather than a genuine effort to find a belated anniversary gift for Michelle—especially because the auctions displayed in the printouts closed before he even sat down for dinner at the Greensboro Cracker Barrel.

The second helpful piece of information was an email Jason sent to Michelle on July 12, 2006:

*I just got home and the goddamn power is out. I called [P]rogress [Energy] and a crew is already out. Cass pissed herself all over the floor, it's hot as hell inside and I can't entertain her enough w/o tv to finish the goddamn yard. I am taking beer and her to pool. I am in a mood that makes our trip to myrtle seem mild, pray the beer kicks in. I could kill u for not letting me finish the yard this morning.*

Another email exchange on October 24—ten days before the murder—made it clear Jason was suffocating from Linda's constant presence at 5108 Birchleaf Drive. He complained about the nearly two weeks she was at the house prior to and following Ryan and Shelly's wedding.

Michelle responded:

*I agree 4 days or so would be more ideal and when she moves here, that will be the deal. We talked about how she'll only be at our house 3 nights a week and one of those nights will be a designated "date night" for you and I to go to dinner, take a walk, play some tennis, whatever—just make sure that we get some quality time together.*

Jason was mortified at the thought of his mother-in-law spending three nights a week at their home.

*i don't get this ... when she MOVES here, she shouldn't BE here at all. THAT is what HER house is for. If she wants to come have dinner for a few hours ... fine, but she is not going to LIVE here.*

Jason also addressed the upcoming Christmas holiday:

*i do not want your mom here a week before Christmas and i don't want her here through new years eve. if she wants to come AT Christmas and stay for two or three nights, then fine. i am not spending my entire holiday season with my mother in law at my house. i'm not wavering on this and i don't think i'm being extreme.*

If Michelle didn't comply with his wishes, Jason threatened:

*i will simply choose to spend my Christmas elsewhere. Enough is enough and i've told you this until i'm blue in the face.*

The emails between Jason and his wife were certainly illuminating. But the email that really caught detectives' attention was one he wrote to his former fiancée, Genevieve Jacobs, on September 12, 2006, about seven weeks before the murder. By that time, she was married, living in Austin, Texas, and went by her married name, Cargol.

In the email he sent from his work-issued laptop computer at 5:32 a.m. that morning, Jason told Cargol she had been "haunting" his dreams and he was "just full of nostalgia and old memories, but your visits make me feel whole and complete again."

He explained:

*I outwardly moved on from you, but I'm not sure my heart and my soul did. I now have a family, career and a totally different life. I have a daughter who I never realized a person could love something so much. I am happy, but I don't feel complete. Will I ever? In my heart, I sometimes imagine that our paths will cross again ... as old people, in a different life, in heaven, or however you want to think of it ... that's what I do to suffice myself when you're strongly embedded in my thoughts. You're the psychologist specialist ... am I going crazy?*

*Does any part of your mind have these thoughts or are they completely buried?*

*... I know the possible negative outcomes from this correspondence and don't want to put either one of us in jeopardy. I just need to open my heart for a minute to tell you how I feel b/c the possibility of leaving this world w/o expressing your love and passion would be a travesty ...*

*The biggest mistake I ever made was asking you to marry me when I did. I wish we could have dated and grown in maturity a few more years together, but it simply wasn't meant to be. Timing is almost as important as love and feelings, it just doesn't withstand eternity ... which unfortunately for me, is what I have to live with now. I can remember moments with you like they just happened; I remember breaking apart after our failed engagement and then being drawn back again. I remember you hugging me and snuggling on me out in Clayton and saying, "this feels like home" (not the house, the hugging part). Those are memories that I will take to my grave ... and I have so many. You made me feel love ... true, passionate, timeless love, I will always love you even though I know we will never be together. I still somehow think we will one day find each other, and that might be totally one sided, it might be a fantasy I've created for myself to get by. I don't know if our love was as profound for you, I actually hope it wasn't ...*

*I have rambled far too much already. I've got so much I want to say, but it would just come out as an incoherent mess, so I will leave it at this; I love you Genevieve Ann Jacobs Cargol, I know that is inappropriate for a married man to be saying to a married woman, but I do. I always have and I always will. It doesn't mean I will act on it or speak of it again, but it is what it is. I know you probably realize this now and it doesn't need to be said, but I will always be here forever for you. Please don't feel like you need to respond, b/c that is not what I am looking for ... I just needed to get that off of my chest. Now take your big fat hiney and get OUT of my dreams! I'm getting too old and tired for that nonsense and it's been YEARS since I've seen you. If you do insist upon these visits while I'm trying to sleep, at least gain 60 or 70 lbs and start losing your teeth so I will wake up, call it a nightmare and go back to sleep. ;-) You know I could never end something heartfelt and important on a serious note. always JY*

"Wow!" thought Sergeant Spivey. In the four months preceding Michelle's murder, her husband had literally told her he could kill her, had heated screaming matches with her that involved doors slamming, had professed his enduring love for his now-married former fiancée, and was in the midst of a torrid affair with another married woman to whom he had also professed his love. Even without any forensic evidence connecting Jason to the murder scene, the detective had more than enough, he believed, to build a case against Jason.

The final bombshell the SBI discovered while rummaging through the Youngs' home computer were searches Jason had apparently conducted on yahoo.com, ask.com, and webmd.com in the months preceding the murder.

His search topics included: "anatomy of a knockout," "head trauma knockout," "divorce," and "right posterior parietal occipital region," medical terminology for the back of the head. Considering the manner in which Michelle had been bludgeoned to death, these searches seemed to reveal further evidence of premeditation and deliberation.

. . . . .

Sergeant Spivey was well aware the bloody shoe impressions found on the embroidered pillow in the master bedroom held the potential to crack the case wide open.

By late 2007, the SBI had determined one of the impressions matched a size 10 Franklin brand Air Fit athletic shoe—a fairly common shoe sold at stores like Dollar General for about $10.

Investigators weren't sure what to make of that revelation because they knew from the CCBI's measurements that Jason wore size 12 shoes, not size 10.

With the help of a footwear specialist from the FBI, detectives were able to determine that the other impression was made by a Hush Puppies-brand shoe. The FBI, in turn, enlisted the assistance of a Hush Puppies product specialist in Michigan to determine which models of Hush Puppies shoes matched the outsole design of the shoe impression found on the pillow.

After conducting some research, the product specialist determined that two separate models of Hush Puppies shoes matched: the Belleville and the Sealy. But both models had been discontinued and were no longer carried in stores.

When this information got back to Sergeant Spivey, he recalled that investigators had found a DSW Shoe Warehouse rewards card during a search of 5108 Birchleaf Drive. Pursuant to a court order, DSW had provided a printout showing purchases that had been made with the rewards card. That printout revealed that on July 4, 2005, Jason had purchased four pairs of shoes. Lo and behold, one of them was a pair of brown, Hush Puppies Orbital plain-toe, slip-on, men's casual leather shoe, size 12.

Sergeant Spivey could feel his heart beginning to beat faster. He logged onto his computer and pulled up still images from the surveillance video footage investigators had obtained of Jason paying his bill at the Greensboro Cracker Barrel. As he looked down toward the bottom of the image—at Jason's feet—his heart nearly leaped out of his chest. There, as clear as day, were brown, plain-toe, slip-on, casual leather shoes.

He then pulled up the still image of Jason walking down the hallway toward the western exit of the Hampton Inn just before midnight. "There they are again!" he thought to himself, as he zoomed in on Jason's footwear.

Finally, he pulled up photos of the shoes Jason was wearing when CCBI agents photographed him a few days after the murder. Though those particular shoes had been purchased earlier that morning, it sure was interesting, the detective mused, that what Jason had selected to wear to the CCBI office were brown, plain-toe, slip-on, casual leather shoes.

The critical question that remained unanswered, however, was whether the Hush Puppies Orbital shoes had the same outsole design as the Belleville and the Sealy. Sergeant Spivey asked the SBI to consult again with the Hush Puppies product specialist. Upon completing his research, the product specialist was able to provide a definitive answer: yes, the Orbital did have the same outsole design as the Belleville and the Sealy.

The shoes Jason purchased sixteen months before the murder, therefore, matched one of the bloody shoe impressions left at the murder scene. "Houston, we have liftoff!" the detective thought to himself, grinning with satisfaction.

Of course, that revelation naturally raised an additional, obvious question: where were Jason's Orbital shoes now? To try to answer that question, in February 2008, Sergeant Spivey obtained a search warrant to see if the shoes might be at Pat Young's home in Brevard, Heather McCraken's home in Etowah, or in a storage unit in Etowah that held items removed from 5108 Birchleaf Drive. The warrant also permitted investigators to examine Jason's vehicle and the shoes on his feet.

With Sergeant Spivey leading the way, investigators and SBI agents searched Heather's house and the storage unit in Etowah. No Hush Puppies shoes were found at either location. The group then ventured on to Brevard and met with Pat Young. They showed her the warrant and were granted permission to search her home. But after turning her house upside down, they didn't find any Hush Puppies.

Sergeant Spivey asked Pat where her son was. She informed him Jason was working in medical sales in Greenville, South Carolina, some fifty miles away.

"Our search warrant allows us to examine him in person," the detective told her. "He's going to need to meet us here or somewhere else."

Pat told Sergeant Spivey she would call Jason and try to arrange a place to meet at a midpoint between Brevard and Greenville. After speaking with her son, she told the detective they would meet at a public park near the South Carolina border.

The entire group, including Jason's mother, piled into Sheriff's vehicles and headed in that direction. They arrived at the park and waited.

It had been more than a year since any law enforcement officers had personal contact with Jason. Sergeant Spivey relished the opportunity to look into his eyes to see for himself whether he looked the part of a cold-blooded killer.

Jason finally arrived in his Ford Explorer. He was wearing business attire, looking more the part of a professional salesman than a cold-blooded killer.

Sergeant Spivey handed him the search warrant and explained what they were looking for. Upon the officer's request, Jason hiked up the bottom of his slacks and showed him his dark, lace-up shoes. He then permitted the detective to search his vehicle. No Hush Puppies Orbital shoes were found.

"I really appreciate how courteous and respectful you've been to my mom," Jason said, his gratitude seemingly sincere despite the difficult circumstances.

"Thanks," Sergeant Spivey replied. "Jason, we sure would like to speak with you about all this."

But Jason didn't respond. Instead, he took the search warrant, folded it in half, tossed it onto the dashboard of his Explorer, and said goodbye. His attorney had advised him not to speak with anyone about the murder—especially not the police. And he was following that advice to the letter.

.....

As part of his investigation, Sergeant Spivey spent some time getting to know Michelle Young's father, Alan Fisher. Alan informed him that Jason, Pat, and Cassidy had flown up to New Jersey the week before Cassidy's third birthday in March 2007. They stayed with Alan, and his wife June, for four days.

Alan told him he and June had turned half of their dining room table into a shrine to Michelle—pictures, a photo album, and newspaper clippings, all focused on the amazing life she led. Birthday presents for Cassidy were set out near that end of the table. June had placed them there deliberately, Alan explained, so Jason would have to confront the "Michelle shrine."

On their first day in New Jersey, Pat walked over to the table, on her own, and slowly took it all in. She became very emotional.

When Alan walked into the room, Pat instinctively reached

out and hugged him, her eyes welling up with tears. "But Jason made it a point not to go near that table," Michelle's dad told the detective.

When Cassidy began opening her gifts, Jason "stayed far away from that end of the table," he continued. "It's like he couldn't face it. Now why would someone that had nothing to do with this avoid that? If that were my wife and I had nothing to do with it, I would have been over there looking at everything."

"Jason and I spent some time one-on-one with just Cassidy," Alan said. Jason "had every opportunity" to tell him he had nothing to do with his daughter's murder. Michelle's father told the detective that he would have done exactly that had their roles been reversed. "I would have said, 'Look, off the record I just need you to know, I shouldn't be talking about it, but you need to know that I had nothing to do with this and I could never do this and I feel horrible and you know I have advice from my attorneys and I can't talk. You need to know that I wasn't involved.'"

But during the four days they were together, Alan lamented, Jason never pulled him aside to say anything like that. And that made him and his wife that much more suspicious of Jason.

"He can be a very smart boy," Alan continued, now showing a hint of anger. "There's a side of him that, some sides of him that I found after the murder that I never knew existed … He has the personality that—we're convinced he's a chameleon. He is what you want him to be and he's got multiple personalities and he leads you to believe that that's the person he is. The minute he's out of your presence, he's a chameleon to someone else."

Michelle's father told Sergeant Spivey he knew it was tempting to believe Jason wasn't smart enough to have pulled off the murder without leaving any forensic evidence behind. "That's what he wanted you to believe," Alan said. "He's very smart to get away with this … He is very capable of doing this and thinking that he can get away with it."

Sadly, Alan Fisher would never learn the outcome of the investigation. He succumbed to prostate cancer on July 31,

2008. The quest for justice for his daughter would have to carry on without him.

.....

By December 2009, prosecutors in the DA's Office decided they had enough evidence to submit to the grand jury. Sergeant Spivey, their first witness, highlighted the key evidence. Before prosecutors could even call their next witness, the foreperson signaled he and his fellow grand jurors had heard enough. He scribbled his signature on the indictment, charging Jason with first-degree murder.

Sheriff Harrison assigned Sergeant Spivey to lead the contingent of officers heading to Brevard to make the arrest. At about 1:30 p.m. on December 14, a caravan of Wake County Sheriff's Office vehicles pulled up to the curb near an auto repair shop in Brevard.

The group had been tipped off that Jason was there having some work done on his Explorer. Sure enough, they spotted him leaving the shop with his mother, approaching her car. As he was about to enter the driver's side of the car, Sheriff's deputies swarmed the vehicle, telling Jason to put his hands up high and remain still. Jason complied, offering no resistance at all.

The Jason Young officers encountered that cold December afternoon couldn't have looked more different from the professionally dressed salesman Sergeant Spivey met with in February 2008. His blond hair was greasy and had grown down to his shoulders. He was wearing a khaki and black baseball cap, blue Nike T-shirt, jeans, and a thick, gold rope necklace.

As handcuffs were placed on Jason, Sergeant Spivey informed him he had been charged by the grand jury with the first-degree murder of his wife, Michelle Young. He then read Jason his Miranda rights and directed him to the backseat of another white Ford Explorer—owned by the Sheriff's Office. The five-hour journey back to Raleigh was eerily reminiscent of Jason's backseat ride across North Carolina in his own Explorer the evening of the murder.

This time, though, the Explorer's destination was the Wake County Public Safety Center in downtown Raleigh, where the magistrates and county jail were located. The irony was lost on no one that this was the very location where—six years earlier—Jason had cemented his relationship with Michelle "till death do us part." Poetic justice if ever there were any, the officers must have thought as they readied Jason for his perp walk.

Sergeant Spivey ushered Jason into the building, where Sheriff Donnie Harrison had been patiently waiting for hours. The Sheriff broke out in a huge smile as the detective, striding alongside the handcuffed Jason Young, came into full view.

As Jason stood before the magistrate and was formally informed of the charges against him, a slew of uniformed deputies and Sheriff's officials looked on, satisfied they had gotten their man. Jason was then booked, issued an orange-and-white striped jumpsuit and slippers, and assigned to the jail cell he would call "home" for the next eighteen months while awaiting trial.

That evening, an exuberant Sheriff Harrison met with reporters in his office. Grabbing the photo of Michelle he had kept on his desk the last three years, he explained it was there to remind him why he and his staff had been working so hard and for so long.

"Her mother gave it to me, and it was a reminder every day that we had a case to solve, and we've been working diligently to solve it," he said. "It makes me feel good today to look down at the picture and say we've gotten one part of that puzzle."

# Part II
# Trial

# 10

## OPENING STATEMENTS

Donald W. Stephens had served as a Wake County Superior Court judge for 27 years, the last ten as "senior resident." His no-nonsense style and acerbic comments from the bench were well-known to the practicing bar.

He wasn't averse to sarcasm or even a tongue lashing if, in his judgment, a lawyer had misstated the law or embellished the facts. He especially frowned on hyper-technical legal arguments that ignored logic and common sense.

Judge Stephens was famous for the "look" he would transmit from his perch on the bench when something had been said or done that displeased him. He would glare icily over the top of his wire-rimmed reading glasses with his piercing, grey-blue eyes, making the lawyers below him want to crawl under the counsel table and hide. He expected—demanded— that attorneys coming before him be prepared, and parties and witnesses respect his authority.

The judge had been involved in the Jason Young case since its inception, signing several search warrants in the immediate aftermath of the murder, conducting status conferences and preliminary proceedings with prosecutors and defense counsel, and also presiding over the hearing that resulted in the civil judgment that declared Jason to be Michelle's slayer.

Both Jason's defense team and the prosecution team were composed of a pair of attorneys. Because he had run out of money by the time of his arrest, Jason was no longer able to afford the services of Roger Smith, Jr. To his good fortune, however, Bryan Collins, Wake County's Public Defender, had been appointed to represent him.

Collins also hailed from the North Carolina mountains, though his hometown of North Wilkesboro was a good 135 miles northeast of Brevard.

Like Alice Stubbs, Collins had received his undergraduate education from Davidson College and obtained his law degree from the UNC School of Law.

After graduating from law school in 1985, Collins began his career, coincidentally enough, at Tharrington Smith. While there, he learned criminal law from Wade and Roger Smith and civil law from a young personal injury attorney named John Edwards—the same John Edwards who would later become a United States Senator and candidate for both Vice President and President before falling from public grace as the result of his own torrid affair.

After a few years at Tharrington Smith, Collins struck out on his own as a criminal-defense lawyer. Because Wake County didn't yet have a Public Defender, it relied on private practitioners, like Collins, to volunteer to represent indigent defendants at a modest hourly rate paid by the court system. Collins accepted many such indigent cases—in addition to cases in which he was privately paid—and appeared regularly before Judge Stephens and his brethren in Wake County courtrooms.

Collins was a gifted courtroom lawyer. His tall frame and imposing presence complemented his baritone voice and deep Southern twang, which bore an uncanny resemblance to actor Andy Griffith's. Indeed, his folksy courtroom demeanor was cut from the same cloth as the *Matlock* character Griffith portrayed in the late 1980s. He was smart, thorough, and quick on his feet.

Collins had developed such a good reputation representing indigent criminal defendants that, when the Wake County Public Defender's Office was established in 2005, he was the natural choice to fill it. He had served in that role for nearly six years when Jason's case came on for trial in May 2011.

Collins was joined at the defense counsel table by Mike Klinkosum, an excellent defense attorney in his own right. Ironically, "Klink"—as he was better known among his colleagues in the bar—first became interested in becoming a lawyer marveling at Andy Griffith's portrayal of a folksy and sharp-witted criminal lawyer during episode after episode of *Matlock*. And just like Collins, he was reared in the mountains of Wilkes County. The similar roots and upbringing between the defense lawyers and their mountain-boy client allowed them to develop a quick and easy rapport with Jason.

After beginning his career as an Assistant Public Defender in Chicago, Klink returned to Wilkes County, where he had a private, criminal-defense practice for five years, followed by another four as an assistant capital defender—working exclusively on cases in which prosecutors were seeking the death penalty. He joined Collins as an Assistant Public Defender in March 2007. In early 2010, he helped exonerate a man named Greg Taylor, who had spent 17 years in prison for a murder he didn't commit.

Though he had recently gone back into private practice in Raleigh, Klinkosum agreed to continue representing Jason at the court-appointed rate.

District Attorney Colon Willoughby had assigned Howard Cummings as lead prosecutor shortly after Michelle Young's murder. When the case came on for trial, however, Cummings was exhausted and needed a break. He had just completed a highly complex eight-week murder trial—in which he had obtained a murder conviction against a man named Brad Cooper, who had also been charged with killing his wife.

As a result, Assistant DA Becky Holt—who had worked with Cummings on Jason's case from the beginning—was elevated to lead prosecutor.

Holt and Collins had a lot in common. She too grew up in North Carolina, though in Jacksonville, near the beach. She was a sophomore at Davidson College when Collins was a senior and a first-year student at UNC Law when he was a "3L."

Like Collins, Holt spent her first few years of law practice learning from experienced lawyers at a private law firm in Raleigh. She had built her own reputation over twenty years as a prosecutor, both in Wake County, and for a short stint from 2008 to 2009 with the United States Attorney's office in Raleigh. Because she had been assigned to Jason's case since 2006, made several trips to the murder scene and Hampton Inn, and participated in interviews of key witnesses, Holt had mastered the factual details long before Collins had been appointed as Jason's counsel.

The same, however, could not be said for David Saacks, the Assistant DA who sat beside Holt at the prosecution counsel table. Saacks had joined the Wake County DA's Office less than a year before Jason's trial began, after spending eighteen years as a prosecutor in neighboring Durham County. He had been on the prosecution team that had obtained a conviction against Durham novelist Michael Peterson in the "staircase murder" of his wife Kathleen—a case that garnered national and even some international media attention.

Because he had only recently replaced Cummings on the Young case, Saacks was a solid step behind the other lawyers, finding himself drinking from a water cannon as the trial neared.

On June 7, 2011, after a week of jury selection, seven women and five men were empaneled as the group who would eventually deliberate on Jason's guilt or innocence and render a verdict. Jason—to whom the prosecutors would frequently refer as the "defendant"—sat at the far end of the defense counsel table. He had exchanged his orange-and-white striped jumpsuit for a sharp-looking suit. His hair was neatly cropped—much shorter than the day of his arrest.

The courtroom gallery was packed with spectators filled with anticipation. Pat Young and Jason's sisters, Kim and Heather, sat in a pew directly behind Collins and Klinkosum. Sergeant Spivey, the lead detective, sat right behind the prosecution counsel table, in front of the gallery. Linda and Meredith sat behind him, in the gallery's first row. Jack Michaels, the lawyer who helped the pair with the wrongful death case, was one row farther back.

Judge Stephens gave jurors several instructions and admonitions and then asked the State to proceed with its opening statement. Holt stood up, walked over to a lectern centered before the jury, and readied her notes. She looked up, and with a stern expression, began her remarks.

"Michelle ... Marie ... Fisher ... Young ... was just 29 years old when she was strangled and brutally beaten to death by her husband, Jason Young, in their bedroom on Birchleaf Drive in the early morning hours of November 3 of 2006. At the time of her murder, Michelle Young was five months pregnant with a little boy that she had already named Rylan. Just down the hall from where she lay was her two-year-old child, her two-year-old daughter Cassidy."

"After the defendant beat her to death," Holt continued, "he fled the home and left Cassidy behind. And it was Cassidy Young that found her mother. Cassidy Young placed a doll baby by her mother's head to comfort her as she lay in a pool of blood in her bedroom. It was Cassidy Young who walked through her mother's blood into the closet and into the bathroom just down the hall."

Holt traced Meredith's steps into the house, through the garage, into the kitchen, then upstairs, and into the bedroom where she found her sister's lifeless body. She described Meredith's frantic 911 call and the sudden appearance of Cassidy from under the covers.

Jason had planned to kill his wife, the prosecutor asserted, because he "didn't want to be married." Instead, he wanted "to live as if he were single again, to go to parties, to go to the football games and the tailgates, to get drunk, to spend time with his friends."

"Things began to get more tense," Holt contended, after Michelle became pregnant with Rylan and when she tried to make plans for Linda to move down from New York to help take care of their children. "But that was a problem for Jason Young, because Linda Fisher, Michelle's mother, wasn't going to put up with his antics. She told him, 'Don't mess up your marriage like I messed up mine. Don't do the things that I did.'"

The Assistant DA told the jury that Linda and Michelle had talked about turning the third floor of the Birchleaf Drive house into a little apartment for Linda. But Jason, she said, "wouldn't have any of that. Absolutely not." In the fall of 2006, "pressure began building and building." There were disagreements about the upcoming holidays, she explained. "Jason wanted to spend Thanksgiving with his family in Brevard, and there was some back and forth about Linda Fisher, Michelle's mother, and her being invited to go to Brevard. And he said, 'Absolutely not. She is not going to Brevard.'"

Holt described the four-hour counseling session with Meredith the Friday before Michelle's murder, noting that all that talking had not resolved the couple's problems. "So what you'll learn is that at the end of October and the first of November, that the defendant had a plan. This plan was to murder his wife and get on with his life on his terms." When Alan Fisher canceled his plans to come to Raleigh on Friday, November 2, she contended, "Jason Young saw his opportunity."

Jason had left his house between 7:00 and 7:30 p.m. the evening of November 2, she told jurors, "purportedly to go out of town." Holt traced his steps to the Greensboro Cracker Barrel and Hillsville Hampton Inn, where he checked in just before 11:00 p.m. "What you'll also learn is that an hour later, just before midnight, that the defendant is caught on camera at the Hampton Inn wearing completely different clothes and carrying two bottles of water. What you'll learn during the course of this case is that the defendant left that hotel and that he went to murder his wife."

"But there were a few things that didn't go according to plan," the prosecutor told jurors. "He didn't expect that when he got to that residence that there would be a fight. He didn't expect that there would be blood." Jason had planned a surprise attack on Michelle, Holt argued, expecting to "strangle her to death. But that's not how it happened. He struck her and struck her and there was blood all over the place. He left evidence that he didn't expect to leave."

She recounted Jason's stop for gas in King, North Carolina on his way back to the hotel. And how the woman inside the convenience store "requires either an ID or a driver's license or a credit card or cash payment. He becomes irate, he throws a $20 bill at her, and curses at her. He made an impression. She didn't forget him."

Holt described the lengths to which Jason went to sneak out of the hotel without anyone noticing. How he propped the back door open with a rock and unplugged the security camera in the stairwell. How, after hotel staff had plugged the camera back in, "it had been pushed up so it no longer was facing the door to capture the image of anyone that came through."

"The defendant had a plan. His plan was to murder his wife. His plan was to get away with it," Holt concluded. "Listen to the evidence in this case that's presented over the next couple of weeks. Find the defendant guilty of first-degree murder. Don't let him get away with it."

Klinkosum delivered the opening statement for the defense. He placed his notes on the lectern, walked a bit to his right, and then held up his right hand, palm facing the jury. "Right now, none of you can say you've seen my hand," he began. "Now I know all of you are sitting there going, 'What is he talking about? He's holding his hand up right in front of us.'"

"The reason I say none of you can say you've seen my hand is because none of you can say you've seen my hand," he continued, turning the back side of his hand to face the jury, "until you've seen the other side of it. Ladies and gentlemen, Jason Lynn Young did not murder his wife. He did not murder their unborn son, and this case has not been solved."

Klinkosum focused first on the two distinct sets of shoeprints in the master bedroom, "one belonging to a shoe that they believe was a size 12 and that they tried to match to shoes Mr. Young once owned, but also a size 10 Franklin athletic shoe, a size of shoe two sizes smaller than what Mr. Young wears."

He told the jury that Jason's sister, Kim, had hired an investigator named Dr. Maurice Godwin to examine the crime scene after investigators had released it. Between Kim and

Dr. Godwin, he stated, they located one of Michelle's teeth investigators had missed as well as a hair found on a picture frame. He foreshadowed that a witness from the SBI would testify that the hair had been ripped out of someone's head, but that its DNA profile matched neither Jason's nor Michelle's.

That wasn't all the investigators had missed, Klink added. Dr. Godwin also found two cigarette butts in the house, one in the garage and another in the doorway leading into the kitchen, both of which were sent to the SBI for testing. Pausing for emphasis, Jason's lawyer told jurors that "the DNA came back to two separate male individuals who have not been identified."

There was even more evidence that didn't fit the prosecution's theory, he continued, noting the jewelry box with two missing drawers was swabbed for DNA and, "just recently, the prosecution sent those DNA swabs to LabCorp, a genetic testing company ... and what they found was that it was a mixture of DNA, containing at least two individuals whose DNA doesn't match Michelle and it doesn't match Jason."

Klinkosum then grabbed an enlarged North Carolina roadmap to show the jury that Hillsville, Virginia is nearly a three-hour drive from the Youngs' home in Raleigh.

Pointing to the map, he continued, "They're going to try to convince you that he drove almost three hours to Hillsville, Virginia, stayed up there for about an hour ... and then drove almost three hours back to his house, beat his wife to death in the most brutal and bloody way possible, that his little girl Cassidy walked around in this blood so much so that whoever did this must have picked her up or walked her to her bathroom across the hall, set her down and she made little footprint impressions in her mother's blood in her bathroom."

"They're going to try and convince you that he made this three-hour trip back," Klink stated, "did all that, cleaned himself up, cleaned her up, got her back to bed somehow and then got in his Ford Explorer and went back to Hillsville, Virginia, without getting one drop of blood in his Ford Explorer ... without getting any blood anywhere in his hotel room, and without transferring any fibers from the carpet of the hotel room back into his house."

Klinkosum then shifted gears to acknowledge Jason's shortcomings, suggesting the prosecution would try to convict his client because he wasn't a great husband. Confronting that likelihood, he told jurors that the defense team agreed Jason wasn't a good husband—not at all. "He could be obnoxious. He could be juvenile. He would get drunk at parties and embarrass his wife." At times, Klink conceded, Jason acted "like an immature jerk. That's the only way to describe some of the things he did. It's the only way to describe it but that does not make him a killer."

But there was also another side to Jason, his attorney explained. "He was a great father." That came across in the interviews conducted by Sheriff's investigators—even from those who considered Jason to be a jerk. Why was that important? Klinkosum asked. Because the prosecution wanted to convince the jury "that he killed his wife in the most brutal way possible while his child was in that house, let her walk around in the blood, and then cleaned her up and left her in the house for her to be found almost ten hours later."

He then transitioned to the evening of November 2, 2006, and Jason's internet searches to find his wife a Coach purse for their third anniversary. He told the jury Jason had taken grief because he hadn't done much for their anniversary other than give Michelle a card. Both Linda and Meredith had given his client a hard time about his lack of thought, Klink explained. "And so, because this was the leather anniversary, he thought it would be a neat thing if he got her a leather Coach purse. He prints off these eBay papers just to get examples and leaves them there. He forgets about it because he's busy packing."

Jason left about 7:30 p.m. that night, he continued, and drove to Hillsville, Virginia. At about midnight, "he went out to his car to get some more paperwork, smoke a cigar—because Michelle didn't like him smoking cigars in the house—and so he snuck a cigar while he was in Hillsville, and then he went back to his room and went to sleep. Got up the next morning and made the trek to Clintwood, Virginia."

After his sales meeting, Klinkosum told jurors, Jason headed toward his family's home in Brevard, refueled, and, at some point, remembered he left the eBay printouts on the printer. He called Meredith, whom he knew had a key to the house, and asked her to retrieve the printouts before Michelle saw them.

Jason's attorney then told jurors how Meredith found Michelle's body and how Cassidy popped out from under the covers. "You've heard, ladies and gentlemen, that she walked around in the blood, that she had blood on her feet, and that there was blood in her bathroom from her footprints but, oddly enough, when Meredith found her she was clean, she didn't have any blood on her feet, there was no blood on the side of Jason's bed where, according to Meredith, she popped out from."

He described how Jason learned of Michelle's death later that afternoon, when he arrived at his mother's home in Brevard. Painting the picture, Klinkosum told the jury that his mom "put her arms around him, she said, 'We love you,' and he looked at her and said, 'What's up?' and she told him that his wife was dead. And the man dropped to his knees and started sobbing, and one of the first things he said was, 'My little boy is gone. My little boy is gone.'"

While Jason and his family were on their way back to Raleigh, Klink explained, they received a call from Ryan Schaad alerting Jason that "law enforcement is already investigating this, they've been investigating it for several hours." Even more alarming, Ryan told him, "'They think you did it. They're looking at you as a suspect. You need to get a lawyer—you need to get a lawyer before you talk with them.' And that's exactly what Jason did. And his lawyer told him, 'Do not talk to the police.'"

And in the days and weeks that followed, not only did Jason have to endure Michelle's funeral—where he was throwing up in the bathroom—"he also endured a lot more," Klinkosum added. The police were constantly making him and his lawyers aware they wanted to speak with him. The press "descended on him." There were media trucks parked outside his house.

He had to get a new cell phone because he was getting so many calls.

"It got so bad that people started blogging about this case—they started writing blogs about him. They started driving by 5108 Birchleaf and taking pictures. And also his family's home in Brevard. People were posting pictures of both houses on the internet. And at that point," Klink stated, "he just shut down. He knew people were after him—the mob wanted him and he shut down and he didn't talk to anybody."

The prosecution would make a "big deal about him not talking to the police and that he didn't cooperate," Klinkosum predicted. "Well, it's true, he didn't talk to them—he followed his lawyer's advice to the letter and he didn't talk to them." But Jason, he noted, did cooperate with "non-testimonial identification orders for him to give hair samples, saliva samples, blood samples."

"They brought him down to the City-County Bureau of Investigation and took pictures of him. And at one point during that process, they had him strip naked—naked, no underwear, nothing—make him stand up straight and they took pictures of his naked body from all angles. And not once, not once did he ask his lawyers to stop this, to try and do something to stop any of this. Not once."

The defense lawyer tried to take the sting out of one of the punches he knew the State would land. He told the jury his client was having an affair with Michelle Money, his wife's friend. And that on his way to Virginia the night before the murder, he was on the phone with Money constantly.

"You're going to hear that she was having problems with her marriage, he was having problems with his marriage, and they kind of were sounding boards for each other about what was going on and they had a sexual relationship. That doesn't make him a killer, ladies and gentlemen," he insisted.

Klinkosum suggested it was okay for jurors to dislike Jason because of his affair. And because his wife was pregnant during the affair. "It's okay to not like him, maybe even despise him for the things you're going to hear when he was acting like an immature jerk. But that while he may not have loved his wife like a lot of us think of love, he did love her in a way. She was the mother of his little girl. She was the mother of little Cassidy and they were trying to make it right."

He told jurors they would also hear about a different side of Jason, about the emails he and Michelle would send each other joking about their communication issues, "where she would say things to him about, 'I wish we could talk like this when we're face-to-face,' and he would say, 'I know, and I really want to work things out 'cause I do love you, JY.' That's how he ended his emails."

"Ladies and gentlemen, at the end of this case," Klink concluded, "when you look at everything, when you look at this case in the objective light of day and realize there's no physical evidence linking him to this, you're going to understand, ladies and gentlemen, that this man did not murder his wife and his unborn child, and you're going to be compelled to find him not guilty. Thank you."

The themes on which each side would rely throughout the trial were now established. The prosecution would focus on Jason's relationships—with Michelle, Linda, and Money—and his desire to live a life unshackled from responsibility and adulthood.

The defense, while candidly conceding Jason's flaws as a husband, would focus on the forensic evidence—the absence of evidence connecting him to the crime scene as well as the presence of evidence that pointed in other directions.

The battle lines now drawn, it was time for the State to attempt to convince the jury that Jason Young was the monster who had savagely bludgeoned his wife to death.

# 11

## EVIDENCE BEGINS

By long-standing custom, trial attorneys in North Carolina examine witnesses while seated at counsel table, rather than standing at a podium or roaming the courtroom like Perry Mason—or Ben Matlock.

Thus, when Becky Holt called Meredith Fisher as the State's first witness, she remained planted in her seat next to David Saacks, her notes carefully spread out before her. She plodded slowly and deliberately through the myriad of topics she planned to cover with Michelle's younger sister.

Meredith testified about growing up in Sayville, New York, her parents' divorce, Michelle going off to college at N.C. State and obtaining her master's degree in accounting, and the progression of her career from Deloitte & Touche to Progress Energy. She described her own relationship with Michelle growing up, fighting like "sisters do, but we always got along, we always, you know, teamed up when it counted." They became closer as adults, she noted.

She told the jury about her sister's involvement in the ADPi sorority and the McBroads' clique, including how the group stayed close following college and would attend each other's weddings and vacation together. She described how Michelle was a planner and would, "in every area of her life, in work, at home, really tried to think things through."

Meredith testified she relocated from New York to Raleigh

the day Cassidy was born. She agreed to be Cassidy's nanny for a year while working nights at the Lucky 32 restaurant, hoping to enroll in a master's program in social work. She lived with Jason and Michelle in their Arete Way townhome the first three months, she told jurors, before moving to an apartment. Her mother briefly relieved her of nanny duties in July 2004.

After Linda retired from teaching in June 2006, Meredith testified, she wanted to purchase a beach house on the Outer Banks. Michelle was planning to reduce her work schedule to Tuesday through Thursday once Rylan was born. The plan was for their mother to care for Cassidy and Rylan on days Michelle was working. Linda would then return to the beach or stay with Meredith on days her elder daughter was off.

Holt led her witness through the tensions building up between her sister and brother-in-law during 2006. Meredith testified that "they just would continue to fight and not be able to resolve problems. Michelle would ask me if I would mind kind of playing the role of counselor after they had been to marriage counseling that hadn't worked."

Because Meredith was planning to specialize in marriage counseling, Michelle thought it would be good practice for her sister to help her work through her problems with her husband—even though Meredith believed those problems were significant enough to require a professional, she agreed.

She told jurors, "Michelle's main issues were Jason being more responsible, helping out around the house, understanding her more. And his main concern was their lack of sex life, and that Michelle would immediately, after an argument, either call my mom or me. That made him mad, too."

Jason confided in her, she told the jury, saying, "'Sometimes I just want to throw in the flag and forget it and divorce her.'" But he would ultimately conclude that "it would be even worse being divorced from her."

For her part, Michelle "really wanted to make it work," Meredith added. "She didn't want Cassidy to grow up with divorced parents. She wanted to at least give it a good effort."

Holt eventually turned to the events of November 3, 2006. Meredith testified she was awakened by her cell phone ringing at 12:14 p.m. that afternoon. In his voicemail, Jason asked her to go to his house to retrieve some papers he had inadvertently left on the printer, so they wouldn't spoil his surprise about the Coach purse he had been planning to buy for Michelle.

When she got to her sister's home, Meredith recounted, she noticed several unusual things outside the house and then red streaks on the walls and footprints on the floor. She then turned and saw her sister's lifeless body beside the bed. Fighting back tears, she testified Cassidy popped out from under the covers and stared at her. "She said, 'Mommy has boo-boos everywhere. She needs a washcloth,' and she kept asking for band-aids to help mommy and her boo-boos."

Through a steady stream of tears, Meredith described her call with the 911 dispatcher and her fruitless efforts to aid her sister. When the Assistant DA played the 911 recording for the jury, the courtroom fell dead silent, while Meredith sobbed softly.

Holt then shifted to Meredith's interactions with Jason at her home later that evening. She testified that not long after Jason and his family arrived, and after he had gone to lie down with Cassidy in her bedroom, the police came to her front door. They wanted to speak with Jason. She went back to her room, where her brother-in-law was lying in her bed with her niece, and informed him the police wanted to speak with him. But Jason responded that he was staying right where he was, Meredith told the jury.

When officers later insisted they had to speak with Jason, she went back to her room a second time and asked to speak with him on the back deck.

While they were on the deck, she said to Jason, "'I don't believe that this is real.' I told him, you know, 'You can stay here as long as you like. I'm here for you. If you need me to watch Cass or anything, you know, we're here.' He ultimately gave me a hug then and shook and made the sounds as if he were crying, but when he pulled away, his eyes were not bloodshot and no tears fell. It seemed to me it was a fake cry."

A little later, officers repeated to Meredith—a third time—they needed to speak with Jason, who again refused. This time, she said to him, "'They just want you to listen to what they have to say. Just listen. You don't have to go out. Just to listen.'"

But Jason responded "that he wasn't willing to have any contact with the police until he had his attorney." He told her he would discuss the matter with his lawyer the following Monday "and answer any questions that they had once his attorney was present."

He later told Meredith, however, his attorney told him not to discuss the matter with anyone, "'not even you.'" And it wasn't long thereafter when she concluded, "He killed my sister."

Holt shifted gears again to discuss with Meredith the difficulties she and her mother had visiting with Cassidy in the months and years that followed. When their family-law attorney informed them Jason was agreeing to give up custody of his daughter, Meredith testified, "I was shocked. That's not what I was going for. I wanted visitation. I wanted to be able to see her and have some schedule enforced so that the plug couldn't be pulled at will."

Before turning the witness over to Collins, Holt played the voicemails Jason had left on Meredith's cell phone the morning of November 2 and early afternoon of November 3. At the prosecutor's prompting, Meredith told the jury that before those calls, her brother-in-law hadn't called her on her cell phone a single time since she ended her service as Cassidy's nanny in the summer of 2005. And Pat Young—who also called Meredith's cell phone the afternoon of November 3—had never called her before.

Bryan Collins handled Meredith's cross-examination. He treated her gingerly, not wanting to give the jury the impression he was pouncing on the victim's grieving sister. He got Meredith to agree that Michelle could sometimes "scream and holler" at Jason and she "gave just as good as she got" when they fought. She agreed Michelle was "no shrinking violet." Meredith also confirmed she had informed investigators the day of the murder that she found Cassidy "shockingly clean" in view of all the blood on the second floor.

The Public Defender then shifted his focus to the morning

of the murder. Meredith admitted she was drinking at the Carolina Ale House until after 2:00 a.m. on November 3—perhaps as many as five drinks.

She conceded her alcohol consumption left her a little concerned about driving home and she therefore sat in the parking lot for a while before driving off. She even considered stopping by her sister's house, she testified, as she wasn't sure she could successfully drive all the way back home to Fuquay-Varina.

She ended up at a Sheetz gas station near her home, where she ordered a pretzel. The security cameras revealed she was there from 3:37 to 3:59 a.m. Even when she finally got home, she didn't go straight to sleep. Rather, between 4:00 and 4:30 a.m., Meredith testified, she placed calls to her bank and cell phone carrier to pay bills.

Though Collins didn't make clear to the jury why he was asking these questions, he was subtly suggesting that Meredith's own whereabouts at the time of her sister's murder were unclear. She didn't arrive at the gas station until 3:37 a.m. The Carolina Ale House closed at 2:00 a.m.

Had she stopped at her sister's house—as she acknowledged she was considering? If so, what had she done while she was there? And with all the alcohol she drank, was there the slightest possibility that she had behaved irrationally, perhaps even violently? Jason's lawyer didn't ask those questions. He wanted jurors to make—or leap to—their own conclusions.

Toward the end of his cross-examination, Collins had Meredith recount how she had taken Cassidy to Target the afternoon of the murder to get her some food and buy her new clothes to wear.

Meredith changed her niece into the new clothes in the Target bathroom, she testified, and brought her pink fleece pajamas and undershirt home to put in the wash. Thus, if Cassidy's clothes had any blood or DNA on them, Meredith had made it disappear in the wash. Which Collins was perfectly happy to have the jury consider along with the other curious circumstances surrounding Michelle's younger sister.

The first day of evidence also included testimony from the

Medical Examiner, Dr. Thomas Clark. In response to David Saacks' questions, Dr. Clark testified a tremendous amount of force had to have been used to cause the deep lacerations to Michelle's head. He estimated it would have taken at least thirty blows to inflict that much damage.

Michelle's jawbone had sustained a very clean, sharp break—the fractured bone had pierced through the skin on her cheek. Most of the wounds, Dr. Clark stated, couldn't have been made by a hand or fist—though the blow that knocked out her teeth and cut through her lips could have been.

For the rest of her wounds, he testified, some kind of weapon had to have been used—likely a heavy, blunt object. The Medical Examiner's opinion was that Michelle's death had been caused by blunt-force trauma to the head.

As jurors sat on the edges of their seats, the Medical Examiner displayed one gruesome autopsy photo after another on a large TV monitor, pointing out his findings. Linda and Meredith quietly stepped outside the courtroom, finding the grisly carnage displayed in the photos too much to bear.

Dr. Clark testified there was extensive hemorrhaging in the soft tissue of Michelle's neck, in the muscles nearby and around the thyroid gland. That meant her killer had either hit her with a blunt object in that area or wrapped his hands around her neck tightly enough to burst the blood vessels. Michelle also had bruises and swelling on her hands, signs that she had tried to deflect her attacker's blows.

The Medical Examiner told the jury he also removed a gestational sac that contained a male fetus, approximately twenty weeks in gestation.

During cross-examination, Mike Klinkosum had Dr. Clark confirm the fingernail marks on Michelle's neck were most likely made by her own fingers—not her assailant's—as she attempted to pry his (or her) hands from her neck.

Oddly, neither Saacks nor Klinkosum asked the Medical Examiner for an approximate time of Michelle's death. Considering the extremely tight timeline on which the prosecution team was relying, jurors were surely left to wonder why no one asked such an obvious question.

.....

The second day of testimony featured Michelle's best friend, Shelly Schaad. Shelly described her relationship with Michelle, starting from when she was her little sister in the ADPi sorority to the pair becoming best friends, roommates, frequent lunch companions, and running partners.

When Holt asked her to describe Michelle's relationship with Jason, Shelly responded, "Um, volatile. Good days, bad days, but it seemed to be a lot more bad, then worse. A lot of arguments, I guess is how I would sum it up." She also testified, "Jason made it very well known that, you know, he was upset about the lack of sex in the relationship."

Shelly described the events surrounding her October 2006 wedding—how Michelle was very upset the entire weekend, though tried her best to put on a brave face so as not to spoil her best friend's festivities. That was in stark contrast to a lunch she had with her during the summer.

Shelly recalled Michelle as "just bursting at the seams, very happy, and she said, 'I'm pregnant.'" Michelle was on a similar high on October 26, when she picked up Shelly and Ryan from the airport following their honeymoon in Italy. "She was very happy, you know," Shelly said. "She was pregnant and ... on cloud nine a little bit that night."

Holt then focused on the evening of November 2, when Shelly came over with Italian food to catch up with Michelle and watch *Grey's Anatomy*. The prosecution witness recalled telling Jason there was plenty of food for him, but he responded he planned to stop at a Cracker Barrel for dinner. "I just remember him saying, 'I'm driving three hours to Virginia'— for some reason Galax stands out in my mind—and then he was getting up and driving two hours the next morning to a 10:30 meeting."

Shelly also recalled Jason stopping by while Cassidy was in the bathtub—luggage in hand—before he left the house. They discussed whether he would return in time for the N.C. State game that Saturday. Jason told her his plans were somewhat up in the air, she testified, and hinged on whether Alan Fisher would be able to come down from New Jersey, given his recent prostate cancer diagnosis.

The Assistant DA asked her witness whether she saw "any interaction between the defendant and Michelle at that time."

"Yeah. I mean, I think they gave each other a little, like a hug," Shelly recalled. "Not like a big bear hug. They said 'goodbye' and he left." She testified that Alan Fisher called not long thereafter and informed his daughter he wouldn't be coming to Raleigh that weekend after all.

Shelly found her best friend to be "very sad and very down and for a good reason—her father was just diagnosed with cancer, and we talked a lot about that and then she kind of went into detail a little bit about an argument her and Jason had had. To my knowledge, it was the day before, and Michelle mentioned that, you know, Meredith had mediated a fight for them and it was about Linda and the holidays."

She found Michelle's depression very upsetting. "She was just sad, um, and almost to a point where I just couldn't reach her," Shelly told jurors. "She was just in a dark hole and, you know, she just kind of turned off."

Shelly also testified about a strange interaction she had with Jason hours after Michelle's funeral. She had gone to his hotel room to give Cassidy a Barbie doll—unaware that Heather and Joe had already taken her to the mountains. While they spoke, Jason asked her something she found both odd and troubling. "'If something happens,'" he said, "'do you think the living will will stand?'"

During cross-examination, Klinkosum had Shelly confirm she had told investigators that, although Jason wasn't a great husband, he was a great father. He also got her to acknowledge that though Michelle arrived for her wedding festivities complaining about her difficulties with Jason, that situation improved significantly over the course of the weekend.

Agreeing with Klink, Shelly testified, "By the end of my wedding, you know, Jason was hanging all over her. He's like, 'My wife's crazy, but I love her.' That's what he said." Finally, Shelly told the jury, when Jason left the Birchleaf Drive home on November 2, she didn't notice any tension between him and Michelle and saw them embrace as he was leaving—even giving his wife a "peck on the cheek."

.....

Next to take the stand was a succession of witnesses who worked at the Hampton Inn in Hillsville, Virginia in November 2006.

Keith Hicks, a young man who worked the third shift, testified that sometime between 4:00 and 5:00 a.m. on November 3, he noticed an emergency exit door leading to the side parking lot was propped open with a small landscaping rock. He also noticed the security camera facing that door was unplugged. Hicks considered those circumstances "weird."

He had worked at the hotel for more than three years and had never seen anything like that before. He kicked the rock out from the doorjamb to make sure it closed and had the maintenance man, Elmer Goad, grab a stepladder to plug the camera back in.

Then, while scanning the various security camera feeds in the office later that morning, Hicks noticed the same camera was now pointed toward the ceiling. "Someone had come in— I'm assuming it's whoever unplugged the camera ... and they took their hand and they shoved it up into the ceiling," Hicks testified, adding this discovery gave him an "uneasy feeling."

During cross-examination, Collins had the prosecution witness confirm he would have personally placed Jason's check-out receipt under the door to Room 421 sometime between 3:30 and 4:00 a.m.

Since the checkout receipt was found in Jason's Explorer when it was seized later that evening, that had to mean, Collins and Klinkosum would later argue, Jason was in his hotel room that morning.

Saacks next called Elmer Goad, an older gentleman, who by then had been the maintenance man at the hotel for nine years. He testified he reconnected the security camera—the video feed connection rather than the power—which Hicks had described as being unplugged.

He then confirmed on the monitor in the office that the camera was pointed at the bottom part of the stairwell, as intended. But within an hour of fixing the camera, the monitor displaying its feed was showing something fuzzy, rather than the stairs.

When Goad went to investigate the problem, it appeared to him "somebody reached up and smacked it and flicked [it] up." In his entire nine years at the hotel, that was the only time Goad could recall such an event occurring.

Saacks also asked the witness about records the hotel kept of when rooms had been accessed with their keycards. Goad confirmed that Jason's room had been unlocked with a keycard only a single time during his stay, prior to 11:00 p.m. on November 2.

Jennifer Marshall, the hotel's general manager, testified next. Saacks had her review documentation confirming Jason didn't have a reservation that night. Rather, Marshall testified, he was a walk-in.

.....

The next morning began with one of the prosecution's most important witnesses, Gracie Dahms Bailey—recently divorced and now going by "Dahms."

Holt was well aware Dahms's testimony held the potential to win the case for the State, virtually single-handedly. That was because if Jason had been at the Four Brothers BP station in King, North Carolina at 5:30 a.m. on November 3, there was only one explanation for him being there—that he had killed his wife in Raleigh and needed more gas to make it back to the Hampton Inn to preserve his alibi.

If jurors believed Dahms's account of Jason cursing and throwing a $20 bill at her, it was pretty much "game over" for his defense.

But Dahms wasn't a strong witness—and Holt knew it. She had little formal education and even less poise—precisely why she was working third shift at a gas station in the middle of nowhere that cold November morning.

She had a very thick, country accent and spoke in monosyllabic language with very little inflection, poor grammar, and somewhat of a speech impediment. The Assistant DA had her work cut out for her. Mike Klinkosum, on the other hand, was licking his proverbial chops, ready to pounce when his turn came.

Holt asked Dahms whether she recalled anything unusual happening at the gas station during the early morning hours of November 3.

Her answer well-rehearsed, the convenience-store worker testified, "A white SUV come through. It went to the far pump of the gas station where I couldn't see what the license plate was or anything—tried to get me to cut the pumps on. I wouldn't cut the pumps on and he come in. When he come in, he asked me what happened and I told him. I said, 'Either you got a credit card or ID. I can't cut the pump on without either one of them.' And he threw a twenty at me and told me that he was going to get twenty and he only got fifteen. And as soon as he got fifteen, he drooved off, around the McDonald's to the other exit and out the road."

This incident, Dahms told jurors, occurred between 5:00 and 5:30 a.m. She was alerted to the far pump when the man pressed the nearby button three to four times, which repeatedly set off a buzzer inside the store.

One of her "regulars" was there, she testified, and he stepped outside to tell the man at the pump he had to come inside and pay. When the man finally came inside the store, Dahms said, he was angry. He got right in her face, close enough for her to touch him.

"He asked me what was up," she continued, "and I told him, I said, 'Either you got to have a license or credit card or cash before I was able to cut the pumps on,' and he started cussing at me and stuff. And I told him, I says, 'Well, that's my job.' And he threw a twenty at me."

Holt asked the prosecution witness if there were security cameras at the gas station back in November 2006. Though there were, Dahms answered, they weren't functioning at the time. The prosecutor asked her if some police officers stopped by the gas station a few days later asking about a white SUV. Dahms replied they had, and showed her a picture of a white SUV, which she told them appeared to be the same one she saw on November 3.

"Did they ask you to look at a photo and see if you recognized a person?" Holt asked.

"Yes, ma'am," the witness responded.

"Ms. Dahms, as you sit here today, do you recognize the person that came into the Four Brothers convenience store at about 5:00 or 5:30 and cussed at you and had the discussion that you've described here today? Do you recognize that person?"

Dahms replied that she did, and pointed her finger at the defense counsel table, in Jason's direction. "Let the record show the witness has identified the defendant," Judge Stephens announced.

To cement Dahms's identification, the prosecutor handed her the photo of Jason investigators had shown her on November 6, 2006. Dahms confirmed she told the investigators the person in the photo was the one who cursed and threw a $20 bill at her. With that, Holt turned Dahms over to Klinkosum for cross-examination—and held her breath.

Right out of the gate, Klink began poking holes in the approach Sheriff's investigators relied on to get Dahms to identify Jason.

"Ms. Dahms, before they showed you that photo," he asked, "they did not ask you to describe the person you saw, correct?"

Dahms acknowledged she didn't recall investigators asking her to provide any description.

Klinkosum followed up by establishing that, in three additional meetings Dahms had with investigators and prosecutors—in April 2009, October 2009, and May 2011—she also wasn't asked to provide any description. He then directed her—and the jury's—attention to a pretrial hearing at which she had testified on May 20, just before jury selection began.

"And one of the things you were asked was, 'Was he bald-headed or did he have hair,' correct?"

"Correct," the witness responded.

"And your answer was, 'I think he had a little bit. I can't remember right off the bat.' That was your answer, correct, about the hair?"

"Right," Dahms agreed.

The defense lawyer then got her to admit that, at the pretrial hearing, she couldn't recall anything about the man's hair color. Finally, he reminded Dahms she was also asked at the hearing whether she remembered anything about the man's height or weight.

"And you said, 'He was just a little bit taller than me,' correct?"

"Correct," she responded.

"About how tall are you, Ms. Dahms?"

"I'm about five foot."

"So this person was a little bit taller than you," Klinkosum asked again, for emphasis.

"Yes," she replied, as Klink glanced at the jury box with a wry smile, hoping jurors understood how badly he had just undermined her testimony that Jason—a lanky six foot one— was the customer she saw that morning.

During her redirect examination, Holt did her level best to bolster Dahms's identification.

"Why did you remember your dealings with the defendant on that day?" she asked.

"I don't forget anybody that cusses me," Dahms responded. "I've been through my ex cussing me and stuff like that, so I don't forget nothing like that."

Holt ended by asking her whether she was "sure that the defendant sitting here today is the same man that came into your store early morning hours of November the 3 and cussed you out because you wouldn't turn on the gas pump?"

"Yes, ma'am," Dahms answered, nodding her head, trying to project confidence.

Having completed her testimony, the State's star witness stood up and walked down from the witness stand, a mere 53 minutes after swearing to tell the truth. Whether she had in fact done so, however, would surely be the subject of intense discussion and debate when the jury finally was set free to deliberate on its verdict.

# 12

## OTHER WOMEN

Michelle Money would have preferred to have been any other place on Earth. Yet on June 14, 2011, she found herself on the witness stand in a Wake County courtroom, Jason Young staring at her from one side of the room, and Linda and Meredith Fisher from the other. Not to mention the dozens of spectators or the TV camera that would capture every word of her testimony and stream it live across the internet. She had been dreading this day for years.

As she took her seat, Money's evenly-parted, light-brown hair fell naturally upon her shoulders, framing her long, oval-shaped face. She wore just a hint of eye shadow and dangling earrings. While discussing her background, she flashed a broad smile as she recalled first being attracted to N.C. State by North Carolina's warm weather. She quickly settled into the rhythm of Becky Holt's questioning, projecting considerable poise and composure.

Money testified she and Michelle Fisher "hit it off" from the moment they met on the rush bus, as they realized they shared the same name and were both from Long Island. Their sorority sisters at ADPi affectionately referred to Money as "Little Michelle" and Michelle as "Big Michelle" or "Fish." The McBroads' clique would occasionally substitute "McBroad" as their own surnames, she testified—Michelle Fisher was therefore "Fish McBroad."

She described Michelle as "very loving and very caring," "very organized," and "meticulous."

Money first met Jason when he attended her wedding in 2001 as Michelle's date. Yet she didn't get to really know him until 2006, when spouses and children were first invited to attend McBroads' beach trips.

They both attended a Myrtle Beach outing during May 2006, and then again around the July 4 holiday. During the latter, Money testified, she confided in Alexis Anderson and Jason she was having troubles in her marriage to her husband Steve and suspected he might be having an affair.

Some of the McBroads next got together in Raleigh for the N.C. State-Boston College football game in late September, Money said, noting they all stayed at the Youngs' Birchleaf Drive home.

While playing hide and seek that Friday night in the backyard, she found herself in the same hiding spot as Jason. They started chatting about her marriage, she testified. Jason "seemed to be fairly concerned and very supportive."

The next day, Money told the jury, Jason told her he had observed "several interactions" between Steve Money and one of the McBroads that "confirmed my worries of an inappropriate relationship."

By the time she was back home in Florida, she found herself talking to Jason every day. "It basically grew very quickly," Money explained. "We just started talking all day about anything—football, potty training, mortgages—anything that you would talk to a friend about." As their conversations continued, Money confessed, "Jason and I expressed interest to be more than friends."

They discussed the possibility of him coming to Florida for a visit, as Jason had already reserved the weekend of October 7-8 for a guys' outing in Wilmington, North Carolina. He could just tell Michelle a business trip to Florida had suddenly come up instead, Money testified. They vacillated for several days about whether his coming to Florida was a good idea, but ultimately decided they really wanted to see each other.

"He flew in on a Saturday," Money recalled, "and I believe

that, as late as Thursday night, I was saying, 'Maybe you shouldn't come. This is wrong.'"

The prosecution witness testified she and Jason spent the entire weekend together while her husband was at a NASCAR race in Alabama. "We basically just hung out at the house," she told the jury, "and we had an intimate relationship for the two days that he was there." Holt didn't ask her for more graphic details. Considering the subject, Money didn't volunteer any.

Not long after that weekend, she and Jason discussed the possibility of getting together again the first weekend in November when her husband was next scheduled to be away.

The primary reason that didn't happen, Money explained, was because Jason "had a business meeting that he said he couldn't get out of." She also knew he and Michelle would be staying at her house after their trip to Disney World in mid-November, when all of the McBroads were planning to gather in Orlando for a spa weekend to celebrate their thirtieth birthdays.

Ironically, when Jason called Money on his way to the Hampton Inn the evening of November 2, she was watching *Grey's Anatomy*. She recalled their conversation being interrupted by two calls Jason received on his end—one from Michelle and a second from Meredith.

After Jason arrived at the hotel, he and Money spoke again, the call ending with Jason telling her he was about to go to sleep. She called him once more, she told jurors, just to say "good night." Although Jason didn't pick up then, he called back a couple of minutes later, told her that he was sorry he missed her call, and said "good night."

Money next spoke with Jason the following morning, she said, while he was on his way to his sales meeting at the hospital. During that call, they discussed the Coach purse printouts Jason had left on his home printer—he told Money he didn't want his wife to see them.

Later that afternoon, during another conversation following Jason's sales meeting, he told her he had asked Meredith to retrieve the printouts. Money recalled that Jason "sounded a little bit distracted" during that conversation "and I don't know if frustrated is the right word, but he didn't get the account. The hospital wasn't looking for what he was proposing to them."

When she learned of Michelle's death later that evening, Money testified, she immediately booked a flight and traveled to Raleigh early the next morning. She and other members of the McBroads gathered at Meredith's house. She recalled hugging Jason on the front porch, though not much about their conversation.

Later that month, when the McBroads were in Orlando for their spa weekend, Money told jurors, Wake County Sheriff's officers showed up unexpectedly and took the fingerprints of each woman. Detectives confronted her about the more than 400 phone calls and text messages she had exchanged with Jason in the weeks leading up to Michelle's murder.

She told them everything they wanted to know about the affair, she testified.

As Holt neared the end of her direct examination, she asked Money about a meeting she had with Jason in Myrtle Beach in June 2007—over six months after his wife's death. The two sat on the beach talking for hours, Money testified. Jason confided in her that "some days were harder than others." They discussed how some people had taken to the internet "saying things that were just absurd and not true."

Holt asked her witness why she had met with Jason.

"I really felt that he was the only one that suffered the way I suffered," Money explained, "in the sense of just that trauma of the media showing up at my home and invading my life and, I don't know, I kind of felt like I needed closure, actually needed to like see him and talk to him and know it was okay."

After that meeting, she and Jason continued to have contact by phone, occasionally talking about Michelle.

Money finally cut off all contact with Jason in January 2008, she told jurors, after an SBI agent dropped by her Florida home and told her she was an "idiot." The agent told her, "I needed to never speak to him again," she recalled, "and I was going to get myself in trouble if I did. And I sent Jason a text message saying I needed to put my life first and I can't do this. And he wrote back that he understood."

During his cross-examination, Mike Klinkosum had Money focus on the media frenzy to which she and her family had been subjected in the months following Michelle's murder. She testified how "the national TV shows started to put my name up there, 'the other woman,' and all this kind of stuff and it was just horrible, I mean, it just broke me, broke me down to feel, I don't know, so violated."

Klink drilled down deeper on her interaction with the SBI agent who told her she was an idiot for speaking with Jason. She recounted being told that "he would take me down as an accessory if I continued to have contact with Jason." The defense lawyer also had Money confirm that, in all of her communications with Jason the day before and day of Michelle's murder, "it was just regular Jason," not someone who appeared to be plotting a murder—or who had just committed one.

All in all, Money's testimony turned out to be less than advertised, as Holt ultimately left several arrows in her quiver. She never showed Money—or the jury—the email Jason sent her six days before the murder, gushing:

*i feel lucky just to know you, much less love you, but i do.*

And that whatever "pain in my future" their affair might cause, "you are so worth it, even if it's only for a 'blink' in time."

The Assistant DA didn't review with Money the phone records that demonstrated the increasing frequency and duration of her communications with Jason in the days leading up to the murder. Even Money's description of their sexual activity was so brief and innocuous, it barely would have qualified for a PG-13 rating.

. . . . .

It was evident from the moment Carol Anne Sowerby took the witness stand she was a tortured soul. She was choking back tears before Holt asked her first question, painful discomfort etched into her face. She knew she was moments away from revealing a dark, shameful secret she had been suppressing for nearly five years.

Sowerby discussed meeting Jason as a six-year-old camper when he was her kayaking instructor. She stumbled through Holt's background questions, unable to recall precisely when she transferred from the University of Georgia to the University of Montana or when she graduated. She testified she had seen Jason four to five times between moving to Montana and Michelle's death.

The prosecutor quickly pivoted to Sowerby's visit to Raleigh in October 2006—less than two weeks before the murder—and asked if she had met Michelle prior to that visit. Oddly, that question evoked a puddle of emotions, with Sowerby having difficulty getting the words out. Finally, through her streaming tears, she was able to say, "I was excited to meet Michelle and Cassidy."

The prosecution witness told the jury Michelle was on a business trip when she arrived in Raleigh. She described how, on her first night at the Youngs' Birchleaf Drive home, she had fallen asleep on the couch. When Jason woke her, he was laughing and told Sowerby to go look in the mirror. She told the jury, "There was like marker drawn on my face."

Holt then asked her what had happened the following night. Sowerby immediately hung her head, in obvious shame, and began sobbing, raw emotion bubbling to the surface. The courtroom fell silent as she struggled, for what seemed like an eternity, to respond.

Finally, she raised her head just long enough to reveal, with a contorted, painful expression, she and Jason had sex on the living room couch while Cassidy was asleep upstairs. Her body began to quaver, her head sank low again, and she continued to sob.

Holt soldiered on, asking Sowerby if she and Jason discussed keeping their indiscretion a secret from her husband.

"I remember telling him that we couldn't tell him because I didn't want to hurt him," she responded, revealing she hadn't told her husband until just before the trial.

The Assistant DA then shifted to the topic of a dinner at

the Youngs' home a couple of nights later, after Michelle had returned. Sowerby testified that while they were seated at the table, Jason asked to see her wedding ring.

He then took the ring, put it in his mouth, and either pretended to swallow it or actually did—she wasn't sure which. When she asked for the ring back, Jason said she couldn't get it back until it passed. Though he gave it back the next morning, he wouldn't give her a straight answer as to whether he had actually swallowed the ring and retrieved it from his stool.

Treading very gingerly, Klinkosum had Sowerby acknowledge Jason had told her Michelle was an "unbelievable mother."

"It seemed that Cassidy meant everything to him," she told jurors, "and he talked about how excited he was about being a dad … because it was such an amazing experience."

Three questions into Holt's redirect examination, Sowerby broke down again, this time sobbing uncontrollably. As an act of mercy, the prosecutor abruptly ended her questioning.

.....

The State then called Genevieve Jacobs Cargol to the stand.

Before Cargol even had a chance to state her name, Collins jumped to his feet, seeking permission to approach the bench. In their sidebar, the Public Defender explained to Judge Stephens that the defense intended to object to much of her testimony as being unfairly prejudicial to Jason.

To prevent that prejudice, he insisted, the judge would first need to hear her proffered testimony outside the presence of the jury. Reluctantly, the judge excused the jury so that the State could preview her testimony.

With the jury out of earshot, Holt began her questioning.

Cargol testified she became engaged to Jason in October 1999. Later that year, she and Jason traveled to Grapevine, Texas to attend a wedding. Prior to the trip, the couple had reached an agreement that Jason wouldn't drink very much because his behavior had been "out of control when he was drinking," she testified. But at lunch the day before the wedding, a friend challenged him to go "beer to beer," and he drank heavily.

Cargol sensed that her fiancé was unhappy with her for judging the amount he was drinking, recalling, "He had a scowl on his face."

When they got back to the hotel, Jason immediately passed out on one of the two beds in their room. After he awoke, she began questioning him about why he had broken their agreement about drinking.

Jason became irate, telling her, "If I'm going to be such a horrible husband, give me back my ring." Cargol couldn't oblige Jason's request, she testified, because her engagement ring was too small and wouldn't come off her finger.

Jason started grabbing her hand, attempting to pull off the ring. His fiancée tried in vain to get away from him.

"I didn't get very far," she testified. "He grabbed me by the arms and the shoulder and began throwing me around the room … I was thrown from one bed to the other, kind of slipping in between and trying to get back to the beds because I felt I'd be safer that way. And he was jumping on top of me, repeatedly pinning my arms as far as they would go behind me."

She recalled crying, yelling, screaming, "and begging him to get off of me." Jason eventually pulled the ring hard enough to remove it, cutting her finger in the process. They continued to struggle, with Cargol climbing on Jason's back and putting him in a choke hold until he finally relented.

For a moment, she stayed in the room, sobbing in disbelief about what she had just been through. She then ran out of the room to find refuge in a friend's room. Cargol testified she had bruises on her body from the fight. Though she stayed in Texas with Jason and attended the wedding with him, she broke off their engagement two weeks later.

She acknowledged, however, they continued to date off and on for another year or so.

Holt asked whether, during the altercation, Cargol had noticed anything unusual about Jason's face or his expression. She responded that Jason's "eyes were blank. There was no emotion there. I felt that his eyes were glazed over."

Eventually, Cargol testified, she moved to the Washington, D.C. area to attend graduate school. While living there, she received a group email—on which Jason was also included—about an upcoming Wolfpack football game at the University of Maryland.

Even though he knew she was in a committed relationship with her boyfriend Eric, Jason emailed Cargol separately prior to the game, propositioning her to spend time alone with him in his hotel room. She rejected his overture. The morning of the football game, Jason spoke with her by phone to let her know he would be attending the game with his girlfriend—Michelle Fisher—whom he had been dating.

Holt asked Cargol about her teaching job in Texas following the completion of her master's degree. She testified she taught at an elementary school in Austin for two years until June 2006.

The Assistant DA showed her the email Jason had written on September 12, 2006, addressed to her school email address. Cargol confirmed that the email address Jason had used was accurate. Yet she never saw the email, she said, because she had already stopped teaching by then.

Finally, Holt asked her if she had witnessed Jason engage in any other violent outbursts.

Cargol recalled two.

The first incident occurred after they attended an outdoor concert in Raleigh. Jason had become upset with her for allowing a male friend to walk her home from a bar a few days earlier. They were still arguing while sitting in her car in the parking lot. In anger, Cargol testified, Jason punched the windshield so hard he knocked it out entirely.

A similar incident occurred at his apartment in Charlotte. Cargol testified she had just arrived for a visit with Jason following a road trip from Raleigh and had to use the bathroom. While there, she noticed a letter from another woman sitting on the countertop. When she came out, she asked Jason about the letter. He became so angry she had read the letter, she said, that he punched a hole in the wall of his apartment.

Holt ended her questioning, stood up, and informed Judge Stephens the State's proffer of evidence was complete.

The judge asked to see a copy of Jason's September 2006 email and took the time to read it thoroughly. He then looked up, saw Klink on his feet, and asked him why the defense was objecting to the evidence the State had proffered.

Klinkosum's argument was simple. The State was seeking to prove Jason engaged in a deliberate, premeditated killing of his wife. In contrast, "Everything Ms. Cargol has related," he explained, "involved some type of heat of passion after drinking or anger or something of that nature." Her testimony was therefore not relevant, he contended, to the State's theory of the case.

Judge Stephens responded, as he understood it, the defense's theory was that Jason "certainly didn't commit this crime, that he loved his wife and he loved his child." Holding up Jason's email, the judge stated Jason apparently "loved Genevieve Cargol *powerfully*," sarcasm dripping from his lips. And it was certainly relevant, he concluded, that "when he was engaged in an act of violence in getting the ring back, his eyes were blank and he showed no emotion, basically indifferent to her pain."

He overruled the objection, telling the lawyers he would allow all of Cargol's testimony—as well as Jason's email—to be admitted into evidence.

When the jury reassembled in the courtroom, Holt took her witness back through much of the same territory she had just covered during the State's proffer.

This time, Cargol was more graphic in describing her fight with Jason in their Texas hotel room, telling the jury that Jason was "jumping on me with all his weight and pinning my arms, both of them, behind me so hard that I felt like my arms were going to come of the sockets of my shoulders." She testified the scuffle left her bruised on the inside of her arms and her rib cage.

Though Holt asked Cargol about Jason's contacts with her after she moved to the Washington, D.C. area, she neglected to ask a single question about Jason punching out the windshield of her car or punching a hole in his apartment wall. And for whatever reason, though Holt had Cargol confirm Jason sent his September 12, 2006, email to an accurate email address, she didn't seek permission to publish the email to the jury, who was left to wonder what Jason had said.

Clearly surprised Holt had omitted these important items from her questioning, Klinkosum asked Cargol only a handful of questions, and then came to an abrupt stop. In view of the damage her testimony could have inflicted, he and Collins felt like they had dodged a very dangerous bullet.

# 13

## CSI

David Saacks and Becky Holt were keenly aware that to prove Jason's guilt beyond a reasonable doubt, they would need to point to evidence establishing his presence at the crime scene. It would be an arduous task for sure.

Saacks had Detective Brent David testify about his initial observations of the crime scene, which he quickly turned over to CCBI Agent Mike Galloway for processing. Detective David testified about his repeated contacts with Meredith during the investigation—how she inquired nearly daily about new developments. He also told the jury about the extensive cooperation and assistance Linda and Alan Fisher provided. This testimony was clearly intended to contrast Jason's *lack of* cooperation.

During cross-examination, Klinkosum had Detective David confirm investigators were so concerned about the distance between Hillsville, Virginia and Raleigh—and resulting tight timeline for Jason to have committed the murder—that they considered the possibility Jason might have chartered a private plane to Raleigh. Detective David acknowledged he had contacted the Raleigh-Durham Airport Police to determine if a private plane had arrived from Hillsville on November 2 or 3. He was informed none had.

Agent Mike Galloway testified for nearly two solid days about the processing of the crime scene. Saacks walked him through the entire house, showing the jury video footage the agent personally filmed of each room. They projected onto a large screen numerous photos of the master bedroom, spending considerable time on the gouge mark on the wall near Jason's closet. Agent Galloway pointed out the blood that landed in that indentation. He showed the jury Cassidy's bloody footprints and two of Michelle's teeth on the closet floor.

Saacks then projected onto the screen several gruesome photos of Michelle's bloody face. Agent Galloway pointed out how her ear had almost been ripped off, the gash under her chin, and her torn and swollen lip and missing teeth. He also pointed to the spot where blood had dripped off the bed.

The prosecution witness told the jury he noticed something significant when he closed Jason's closet door—there was a continuation of blood spatter from the dresser to the left of the door onto the front of the door. The blood spatter went up as high as eight feet near the closet door and continued all the way to the lamp on the night table next to Michelle's side of the bed and above the bed's headboard.

He walked the jury through a series of photos of the pillows found on and near Michelle's legs, pointing out multiple shoe impressions made in blood. He also highlighted what appeared to be bloody shoe impressions on some Progress Energy paperwork found on the master bedroom floor.

Mike Klinkosum was determined to turn Agent Galloway into a star witness—for the defense. He began with 21 photos of Jason taken during his submission to the non-testimonial order. Agent Galloway agreed he and his fellow agents were unable to document any cuts, scratches, abrasions, or bruises on Jason's hands or face. He also confirmed Jason was forced to strip naked in front of investigators—and they were unable to locate any bruising, cuts, or abrasions on his entire body other than the bruise under his left big toenail.

Klink then placed before the witness another 27 photos, this time of Jason's Ford Explorer. He asked him to review the photos carefully.

"Now, Agent Galloway," Jason's attorney proceeded, "one

of the reasons you searched this vehicle, or the primary reason, was to uncover any forensic evidence, correct?"

Agent Galloway agreed.

"And by 'forensic evidence,' we're talking about blood, correct?"

Again, the witness agreed.

"Hair, saliva, things of that nature?" Klinkosum homed in.

"Trace evidence, fibers, yes, sir."

"Trace evidence that would perhaps link Mr. Young or this vehicle to the scene of that crime, correct?"

"Yes, sir," Agent Galloway replied.

"And you noted in the crime scene photos that this was a very bloody scene, correct?"

"Very. Yes, sir."

"Agent Galloway, you *scoured* this Ford Explorer for the presence of blood, correct?" Klinkosum inquired. Again, the witness agreed.

Klink then had him confirm his agents inspected the vehicle's driver's side, steering wheel, steering column, floor, passenger side, back seat area, and all of the items found in the car, including shoes and soda cans—as well as the entire exterior of the vehicle. He said chemicals such as phenolphthalein were used to enhance any traces of blood.

"Nowhere inside of that vehicle, on the doors or the passenger area or the rear area—nowhere in that vehicle did you find any blood, correct?"

"I collected no blood from that vehicle, sir," Agent Galloway agreed.

Klinkosum redirected the agent's attention to the Birchleaf Drive house. Agent Galloway conceded no blood was found in Cassidy's bedroom, on the garage door, fence gate, concrete walkway by the rear water spigot, or on any of the clothes in Jason's closet. The defense lawyer walked the witness through photos of the interior of Jason's closet and Michelle's closet, both of which were in complete disarray. But again, no blood.

. . . . .

Sergeant Al Sternberg of the Sheriff's Office was involved in a hodgepodge of activities related to the investigation. Among other things, he conducted a thorough search of Jason's black suitcase found in his Explorer, which hadn't been removed following his business trip to Virginia.

Saacks plopped the suitcase down in front of the prosecution witness and had him describe how he carefully documented each and every item it contained. The detective also testified about the items found in the rear cargo area of the Explorer—a pair of jeans, a pair of size 12 Kenneth Cole slip-on brown shoes, a second pair of shoes of a different size, the weekend edition of the *USA Today* newspaper, a travel atlas, and a Hampton Inn hotel directory.

Sergeant Sternberg also analyzed the eBay printouts found on the printer in the home office, and informed the jury they were made at 7:08 p.m., just before Jason left for his business trip. Another item he processed was an envelope that contained an anniversary card addressed to Michelle, bearing a postmark from Orlando, Florida, and a date stamp of October 7, 2006.

. . . . .

Agent Jennifer Remy, who specialized in hair and fiber analysis, was the first of several SBI crime lab witnesses to testify. She analyzed approximately fifty hairs found underneath Michelle's body and one found in her left hand—conclusively ruling out Jason's hair as a match.

She noted many of the hairs, including the one found in Michelle's hand, contained an "antigen root," indicating they had been forcibly removed. They were all sent off for DNA testing, as was another hair caked in blood on a pillow.

Agent Remy also analyzed carpeting that had been cut out of the Youngs' master bedroom. Despite her thorough analysis, she testified she was unable to detect a single trace fiber that originated from Jason's room at the Hampton Inn.

Klinkosum asked the SBI agent about a hair she analyzed that was stuck on the framed photo of Jason's and Michelle's wedding displayed on their dresser, near the bedroom's entrance. She agreed that hair wasn't consistent with Jason's.

Jason's lawyer also delved deeper into the hair and fiber expert's search for carpet fibers from the Hampton Inn. She testified she had taken trace samples from fibers on the fitted bedsheet and comforter in the master bedroom, a bed pillow, the sweatshirt and pants Michelle had been wearing, and Cassidy's pajama pants. Not a single fiber from the Hampton Inn's carpeting, she agreed, was detected on any of those items.

Next to testify was Special Agent Nancy Gregory, a forensic drug chemist. She had analyzed the medicine dropper from the hutch in Cassidy's room to determine the contents of the liquid residue. She testified that one of the compounds found in the liquid was dihydrocodeine, an opium derivative. Also included in the liquid were acetaminophen, or Tylenol, and pseudoephedrine, or Sudafed.

Agent Gregory conceded, upon cross-examination, she had no idea how long the liquid had been in the dropper, and the chemical compounds she detected could have been from the residue of different liquids present in the dropper at various points in time.

Special Agent Russell Holley, a serologist, took the stand next. He testified about his analysis of a portion of sheetrock removed from the wall adjacent to Jason's closet, as well as a large sample of the closet door molding.

The SBI agent noted there appeared to be a handprint or fingerprint on each sample, so he swabbed them in an attempt to collect DNA. The swabbings were then sent to the crime lab's DNA section. He also informed the jury he swabbed a rock found near the emergency exit door at the Hampton Inn for epithelial DNA—the DNA contained in skin cells.

Agent Holley also analyzed fingernail clippings removed from Michelle's fingers. The clippings, he told the jury, didn't include any skin tissue or foreign material and therefore had no "evidentiary value." He also analyzed a pair of blue jeans and a belt removed from the black suitcase found in Jason's Explorer, neither of which, he explained, contained any blood.

During cross-examination, the serologist confirmed none of the additional items removed from Jason's Explorer—Kenneth

Cole shoes, Rockport shoes, blankets, a water bottle, fleece coats, a suit jacket, a car seat, and several items of clothing and toiletries from Jason's suitcase—tested positive for the presence of blood.

Special Agent David Freeman, a forensic biologist who specialized in DNA analysis, took the witness stand next. He testified he had been provided blood stains from Michelle and Jason, which served as DNA "standards" or "profiles" against which to analyze swabbings taken from the crime scene.

He informed the jury the DNA profile from the swabbing taken from the sheetrock adjacent to Jason's closet matched Jason's DNA profile. So, too, did the DNA profile from the swabbing of the closet door molding, though there was also DNA in that profile that didn't match any known standard. "There's two donors," he testified. "We have Jason Young as the major and then someone else is the minor."

Agent Freeman analyzed the DNA profile obtained from the swabbing of the top of the jewelry box. He told the jury though Michelle could be excluded as a match, Jason couldn't because there were markers in that profile similar to his DNA profile.

He testified a "very weak DNA profile" was obtained from the rock found outside the Hampton Inn's emergency exit door that was "consistent with the mixture from multiple contributors and, again, no conclusion could be rendered as to the contributors of DNA on that item."

The forensic biologist also received cheek swabbings from Cassidy to create a profile of her DNA. Using that profile, he confirmed the medicine dropper found in her hutch contained her DNA.

Interestingly, her DNA was found not only on the tip of the dropper that would have been inserted into her mouth, but also on the bulb portion on the opposite end. But neither Michelle's nor Jason's DNA was detected on either end of the dropper.

Klinkosum began his cross-examination by focusing on the concept of population frequency data, which, in the world of DNA analysis, establishes the mathematical probability that someone else—other than the suspect—contributed to DNA found at the crime scene. In the typical case, Agent Freeman testified, the odds could be as high as one in "millions of trillions" that DNA found at the crime scene that fully matches a suspect's DNA profile could belong to someone else.

Jason's lawyer then asked him, "You did not run the population frequency data for the match to Jason off the sheetrock, correct?"

"That's correct."

"And that's because that was his house, correct?" Klink continued.

"That is correct," the SBI agent replied.

"Because you would expect to find Jason Young's DNA in Jason Young's house, correct?"

"That is true," the forensic biologist answered. "It's not uncommon to find your own DNA profile in your home or items that you've touched or been around." He also conceded there was no way to determine when any of the DNA material collected at the crime scene had been deposited.

Interestingly, on redirect examination, Holt asked Agent Freeman if he also had a DNA standard for Meredith at the time of his analysis. As it turned out, he did. The prosecutor asked whether Meredith's DNA profile matched any DNA found on the medicine dropper. He answered it did not.

Special Agent Michelle Hannon, another forensic biologist, took the stand next. She analyzed the DNA from the hair samples that contained antigen roots. She testified all of the samples found underneath Michelle's body, in her hand, and on the bloody pillow matched Michelle's DNA profile. But the sample taken from the framed wedding photo, she told jurors, contained a predominant profile from an unknown contributor.

During his cross-examination, Klinkosum asked the witness about her analysis of two cigarette butts found in the garage. The DNA extracted from each, she testified, came from a different, unknown male. That DNA didn't match the profiles of the more than twenty standards Agent Hannon had been provided from people known to have been inside the Youngs' home. The defense lawyer also had her confirm she ran the DNA profile from the cigarette butts, and from the hair found on the picture frame, through the Combined DNA Index System (CODIS) database containing profiles of convicted and suspected offenders—and no matches were found.

Finally, Klink asked Agent Hannon about DNA testing she performed on an Adidas sneaker found in Jason's closet in Brevard, which contained some blood in the toe area. Although there was a partial match to Jason's DNA, the predominant DNA profile, she explained, was from an "unknown contributor."

"So you found in this case DNA from two unknown males on two cigarettes butts, correct?" Klinkosum asked.

"That's correct," she answered.

"A hair that can't be identified, correct?"

Again, the agent agreed.

"And then on the toe of his sneaker, you found DNA from someone that can't be matched, correct?"

Once again, she agreed.

.....

The State wasn't content to rely solely on the SBI crime lab to analyze the DNA evidence. In late March 2011—two months before the trial began—the prosecutors engaged the private medical laboratory, LabCorp, to perform additional analysis. Shawn Weiss, associate technical director of LabCorp's forensic identity department, was called to testify about the lab's analysis and findings.

The SBI crime lab had provided LabCorp with "extract tubes" containing DNA material from the landscaping rock found outside the emergency exit door at the Hampton Inn as well as from possible prints found on the sheetrock next to Jason's closet door, the jewelry box, and a sprinkler water pipe near the hotel's western stairwell security camera. LabCorp also received blood samples for Jason and Michelle from which to create its own DNA profiles.

Weiss testified LabCorp was able to obtain only a partial

DNA profile of the genetic material found on the rock. Even though it was only a partial profile, he told the jury, "We cannot exclude Jason Young as the source of that DNA." Jason also couldn't be excluded as the source of the DNA material on the sheetrock next to his closet, he testified.

As for the DNA material from the top of the jewelry box, Weiss testified both Jason and Michelle could be excluded. That DNA profile, he explained, was consistent with a mixture from more than one person. Similarly, Jason and Michelle were both excluded as the source of the DNA material from the water pipe at the Hampton Inn.

Klinkosum was able to get the LabCorp witness to concede, during cross-examination, that one out of every 79 Caucasians possesses the same DNA markers found in the swabbing of the landscaping rock. Weiss elaborated that if a stadium were filled with 200 people, "you could have two or more individuals that could have the same partial profile that was obtained."

The DNA extracted from the swabbing of the sheetrock in the master bedroom, however, was very different. Only one in greater than 6.8 billion people on earth, he testified, would have matched that profile.

"Given the size of that number," Weiss quipped, "unless Jason has an identical twin, I would not expect another person to have that profile."

.....

Agent Andy Parker from the CCBI took the witness stand next. He specialized in footwear impressions and fingerprints. As to the former, he testified that, early on, a positive identification was made on one of the bloody footwear impressions on the embroidered pillow—it belonged to a cross-trainer type shoe manufactured by Air Fit, which was sold by Family Dollar Stores. It appeared to be a size 10. Agent Parker was unable, however, to determine the identity of the shoe that made the second footwear impression.

A total of 151 latent fingerprints had been collected at the crime scene, he testified. Michelle accounted for 19 of those fingerprints and Jason 21. Two prints belonging to Meredith were collected from the door handle on the outside of the home's front door. Carol Anne Sowerby's fingerprints were among those collected, as were Alan Fisher's, even though he hadn't been to the house for more than six months prior to Michelle's death.

Agent Parker testified a few of the prints collected at the crime scene couldn't be matched to a known standard — including a set of prints from the master-bedroom door frame and another set from a shoe-shine box in Jason's closet.

Holt handed the witness two "lift cards" of fingerprints collected from the interior side of Jason's closet door. He told the jury one print belonged to Jason's right thumb and the other belonged to his right index finger.

The prosecutor then asked about a series of prints found just to the left of Jason's closet door molding.

"In a nutshell," the fingerprint expert testified, "I couldn't identify these as Jason Young, but I could not eliminate him as the potential source to those items."

Holt asked whether any fingerprints or handprints were made in blood. Agent Parker responded none were.

During Collins' cross-examination, Agent Parker explained only 16 of the 151 latent prints collected "were of value." The prints were compared to 161 people who were known to have been in the house, including the investigators who processed the crime scene. Significantly, one of the prints that couldn't be matched with any of the 161 known standards was from the medicine cup that sat on top of the Tylenol bottle found in the hutch in Cassidy's bedroom.

. . . . .

With all of that tedious, forensic testimony out of the way, the stage was now set for the most important crime scene evidence of all — the second bloody shoe impression. Saacks called Michael Smith to the stand. Smith worked at the FBI lab in Quantico, Virginia, and specialized in footwear impression evidence. He testified that in December 2007, he received a call from SBI Special Agent Karen Morrow, who was looking for help identifying a footwear impression. She emailed him a photo of the impression that had stymied her.

Agent Smith testified the FBI lab maintained an extensive database of outsole designs, each of which captured all of the design elements from the bottom of a particular shoe. He studied the image Agent Morrow sent him and queried the database to find any shoes with similar design elements. He hit on a match quickly. The FBI's footwear expert recalled calling Agent Morrow and telling her, "Karen, I have your shoe." The outsole design that matched her image was a Hush Puppies Sealy.

With Judge Stephens' permission, Agent Smith stepped down from the witness stand and compared the Hush Puppies Sealy image from the FBI database with Agent Morrow's image, showing the jury the heart-shaped design elements that ran down the middle of both.

Agent Morrow took the witness stand next. She testified she had received the pillows and pillowcases from the crime scene. She used various chemical solutions to enhance the footwear impressions, which she then photographed. She ran those photos through two different databases, but couldn't find a match. At that point, she contacted Agent Smith and asked him to run one of her enhanced images through the FBI's footwear database. About six weeks later—in late January 2008—he called to inform her he had found a match.

The FBI agent then connected Agent Morrow with a Hush Puppies product specialist in Michigan, Tom Riha. Agent Morrow provided Riha the same image. Riha confirmed it appeared to be a Hush Puppies outsole design—either a Sealy or a Belleville brand shoe. He also told her both shoes had been discontinued.

Not long after that, Agent Morrow learned that SBI field agents had confirmed that Jason owned a pair of Hush Puppies Orbital brand shoes, size 12. Riha confirmed the Orbital had the same outsole design as the Sealy and the Belleville. That style, however, had also been discontinued.

But Riha told Morrow the factory in China still had the

original molds for the Orbital shoes and offered to have a pair made for her. The following month, a brand-new pair of size 12 Hush Puppies Orbitals appeared on Agent Morrow's desk.

Holt handed the witness a large box, State's Exhibit 84, and asked her if she recognized it. Agent Morrow testified the box contained the Hush Puppies Orbital shoes she received from China. She then cut the box open and pulled out the black, size 12 loafers.

She held up the left shoe, with the outsole facing the jury, and pointed out the heart-shaped elements running down the middle of the sole and other bar-shaped elements running along the perimeter. She explained how she used fingerprint powder and an acetate sheet to make a "known standard" of the outsole design of the two shoes.

Holt next handed the footwear expert an envelope containing the Progress Energy paperwork that had been found on the floor in the Youngs' master bedroom. The agent testified she was able to identify on the paperwork some of the same design elements from the outsole of the Orbital shoe.

The Assistant DA then approached the witness stand with two large brown paper bags. Agent Morrow told the jury that inside each bag was one of the pillows she had analyzed. She testified one of the pillows had shoe impressions from both a right and left Franklin shoe and a right Hush Puppies Orbital shoe. She also testified the Orbital shoes matched several impressions found on the Progress Energy paperwork as well as on the master bedroom's bedspread.

Collins handled Agent Morrow's cross-examination. More than any other prosecution witness, the Public Defender was fully aware her testimony came closest to connecting Jason to the crime scene. To obtain an acquittal, he knew it was imperative for him to sow seeds of doubt about her conclusions.

He first had her admit that in the typical case, she is provided the actual shoes in question—and makes known standards from those shoes—rather than brand-new, factory-issued shoes.

By making impressions from the actual shoes in question, Agent Morrow agreed, she could detect and analyze wear and tear, small cuts, pieces of rock, gum, and other items that would permit her "to effect an identification to include that shoe and only that shoe."

She conceded because she didn't have the actual shoes in question in this case, her findings were "only based on the 'could have been made by'" the Franklin or Orbital shoes.

"So you're not trying to tell the jury that there's a match in this case, are you?" Collins asked.

"No," the SBI agent acknowledged. She also conceded she couldn't conclude the Orbital impressions had been made by a size 12 shoe. All she could determine was the impressions found at the crime scene were the same physical size as the impression created by the Orbital shoes she received from China. She agreed the shoes that left those impressions could have been anywhere from size 11 to size 13.

Jason's lawyer next had the footwear expert admit she couldn't conclude the impressions had been made by an Orbital shoe—as opposed to a Belleville or a Sealy. Recognizing the limitations of the FBI database, she even conceded the impressions could have been made by a different shoe altogether, agreeing, "There could be something else out there. You're right."

Collins ended his questioning by focusing the prosecution witness on her seventh written report, pointing to the last sentence in ten different paragraphs. Incredulously, he stated, "They all say, 'Due to the limited detail, a more conclusive comparison cannot be made.' Ten times."

"Right," Agent Morrow responded.

On redirect examination, Holt asked her witness to clarify what she meant by the phrase "due to the limited detail, a more conclusive comparison cannot be made."

Agent Morrow told the jury she always used that exact same language—in every report—if she didn't have the *actual* shoe in question from which to make a conclusive match. That phrase, she testified, had no more significance than that.

.....

The final area of forensic testimony focused on computers, specifically, the home computer and Jason's work-issued laptop. First up was Agent Beth Whitney from the CCBI, who examined the home computer. She testified she discovered several phrases had been searched on Yahoo.com, Ask.com, and WebMD.com. They included "anatomy of a knockout," "head trauma," "head trauma blackout," and "head blow knockout."

Agent Whitney testified, however, she had no way to determine when the searches were conducted, whether they had been made close in time relative to one another, or who made them. The only time parameter she could provide was the day the computer was placed into service—January 2004.

Toward the end of her direct examination, Saacks handed Agent Whitney a printout of an email she found in the home computer's Microsoft Outlook sent folder, dated October 5, 2006. The subject of the email was an upcoming football game tailgate Jason planned to take Cassidy to. In the email, he told Michelle he didn't want a lecture about weather. He wrote:

*… I have always felt I am extremely cognizant of my daughter's health in EVERY [sense], even more so than you in most cases. I do not want to hear anything else on the subject, or we will have another disagreement.*

*You have trouble lying in the bed you make for yourself. You are the first person to gripe, complain and be very bitter about tailgates … When is the last time you had fun at a tailgate and didn't complain about me, my actions, your "friends," their actions, not drinking, the heat, the weather or any other thing you can. Yet ironically, you want to put yourself through all those negative things that you typically bitch about … I just don't get you. … you can't have it both ways.*

He ended the email by saying:

*Hopefully you will lighten up at some point in your life, but if not, don't try to bring me with you for I have no desire for that type of experience.*

Agent Whitney was then shown an email exchange between Jason and Michelle she found in a Yahoo Mail account, dated October 24, 2006. In that email, Jason expressed his fears and threats about Linda intruding on their Thanksgiving and

Christmas plans, as well as his mother-in-law's plans following Rylan's birth. He also discussed the "drama" Michelle created by telling her mother he put "'no thought' into our anniversary, not giving you a card and not getting you anything."

He continued:

*In reality, I HANDWROTE you a card, dropped it in the mail on 10/7 as it is postmarked and got you more than $25 worth of Starbucks cards. Have you gone back to your mom and told her all that yet??? All I've heard about is how I don't care b/c I didn't even get a card or anything for you ... heck, I actually did more than you ... you wrote "love, michelle" and I actually had a nice hand written note. In reality, does that bother me? NO, but I have to point that out as a defense mechanism since you came on so strong to me in front of your mom. Moral of the story—don't get so emotional over "spilled milk" and make sure your mom and WHOEVER else gets a picture of the GOOD as well as the bad.*

Saacks asked the CCBI agent if these were the only two emails between Jason and Michelle she had found on the home computer. Agent Whitney responded that there were actually hundreds of emails between the two, including ones that contained expressions of love between them.

During his cross-examination, Collins had Agent Whitney focus on the times both the laptop and home computers were in use on November 2 and 3. She testified the laptop had "user-generated activity" from 6:49 to 6:52 p.m. on November 2, and then not again until 11:38 p.m. Meanwhile, the home computer had user-generated activity from 5:42 to 5:45 p.m., 6:31 to 7:53 p.m., 10:48 to 10:58 p.m., and at 11:45 p.m. She agreed with Collins the activity at 11:45 p.m. was not initiated by Jason.

Next to testify was another gentleman named Michael Smith, an investigator with the SBI's computer crimes unit. He testified he performed a forensic examination of Jason's work-issued laptop. Among the items he found was the email Jason sent to Genevieve Cargol on September 12, 2006.

Collins lodged an objection to the introduction of the email, which Judge Stephens promptly overruled. The judge permitted Saacks to publish the email to the jurors, who had been eagerly waiting since Cargol testified to learn what Jason had said to her.

From the expressions on their faces as they read his email, they appeared to find his words—and confession of love for Cargol—of considerable significance.

# 14

## WRAPPING UP

The State called several more witnesses to help connect dots and fill in gaps. Among them was Jennifer Sproles, the Records Manager at Dickenson Community Hospital, who met with Jason in Clintwood, Virginia, the morning of November 3, 2006. She testified her meeting with Jason had been scheduled for 10:00 a.m., but he didn't arrive until after 10:30 a.m. She told the jury the meeting lasted 30 to 40 minutes.

When David Saacks asked her how Jason appeared that morning, she initially responded, "He acted just normal." She then clarified he "might have been just a little bit nervous, but that would just—to me, that was just him wanting to sell the product and demonstrating it to me."

Jason's leg was either shaking or trembling, Sproles said. She recalled him mentioning he had driven in from Galax that morning. During cross-examination, she agreed Jason had told her he had gotten lost on the way and would have called, but had no cell service, and apologized for being late.

Paul Matthews was Michelle's supervisor at Progress Energy. He told the jury she "was an outstanding communicator and a dedicated employee and a high performer."

Becky Holt asked him about Michelle's proposal to go part-time once Rylan was born. Matthews testified he understood Michelle was trying to create a "work/family balance" with the impending arrival of her son, and praised her for being a "very devoted mom" who "loved spending time with Cassidy and her family." Both he and his department head had approved the proposal.

The evening before the murder, Matthews told jurors, Michelle worked until about 5:30 p.m. She requested permission to bring home a binder of Progress Energy materials she planned to work on that evening. He knew she had a doctor's appointment the next morning, but was expecting her in at some point. Sadly, she never arrived.

The State also presented the testimony of Jason Fitzgerald, who had been Jason's friend since the two began serving as RAs at University Towers in 1995. Fitzgerald described Jason's and Michelle's relationship as "up and down." Though the couple had "public arguments," he testified, he and his wife also had "fun times" together with them at football games and other activities.

Holt had Fitzgerald describe what had happened the Friday morning before Ryan's and Shelly's wedding. He told the jury several of the men had driven together from Raleigh that morning to play golf in Winston-Salem.

They stopped at a gas station in Greensboro to meet up with Jason, who had driven with Michelle to that point. When Jason entered the guys' car, Fitzgerald testified, "he was upset about the argument that they were having." Jason told the guys, "He was up to his neck with the relationship" and was "not willing to deal with it anymore." He understood Jason to be saying he was done with his marriage and his relationship with Michelle.

During cross-examination, however, he agreed with Klinkosum that, despite that argument, Jason and Michelle appeared to be getting along just fine later that weekend.

"Like nothing had happened, right?" Klink asked.

"That's probably how I would describe it, yes," Fitzgerald agreed.

The defense lawyer also asked Fitzgerald about a visit he and a couple of Jason's friends made to the Youngs' Birchleaf Drive home after the crime scene had been released. Jason's sister Kim was also there at the time. Klinkosum asked if Kim had shared with him any information about what she had found in the house. Fitzgerald replied Jason's sister told him she had found what appeared to be a tooth in one of the bloody areas in the master bedroom.

"And this was after the crime scene had been released?" Klink asked, hoping the jury would recognize the apparent sloppiness exhibited by investigators.

"Yes," Fitzgerald replied.

.....

The time had finally come for Linda Fisher to take the stand. She had been fighting for justice for Michelle for more than four and a half years. It had been a long, frustrating journey. Above all else, she wanted the jury to get to know her daughter. Nearly as important, she wanted jurors to understand the deeply troubled nature of her marriage.

Linda described Michelle's childhood, her migration to North Carolina to attend N.C. State, her education, and her career in accounting. When she learned her daughter was pregnant, and Jason had asked her to marry him, Linda told him bluntly, she testified, "'If you don't love her, then don't marry her. She will survive.'"

By 2006, Linda was keenly aware of the difficulties in her daughter's marriage. She told the jury—in her thick New York accent—Michelle "seemed to be more unhappy than happy. She was always talking negative about things. Things weren't going right. And then, when a date came that something was good, she was just like, 'Oh, you should see how great it was.' And then it was gone."

Linda explained she and Alan were in marriage counseling for thirteen years, off and on, and she didn't want Michelle to have to go through that.

Jason and Michelle "were always arguing," she testified. "It felt like there was no sweetness between the two of them. Most of the time, you know, Michelle would call me and tell me about a different fight. But in terms of actually witnessing, you know, I did see them fight more than I saw them being nice to each other."

She told the jury she spoke with her son-in-law about the state of his marriage. "He had said to me that 'things aren't good because she doesn't want to have sex' … and I was telling him, you know, that you don't want to go down the path of having another woman on the side and, you know, it would definitely end the marriage; there would be no hope."

She also told him, "You can't just expect sex without, you know, love."

Michelle had confided in her mother that Jason didn't "make love" to her when they had sex, but "was rather perverted in his behavior."

Holt asked whether she had seen a change in Michelle over time. "She was defeated," the former schoolteacher replied, becoming increasingly emotional. "She had so much to offer. There was so much about Michelle that was just … She was an N.C. State cheerleader. I mean, she had that pep, that energy, that vivacious …" Her answer trailed off as tears began streaming down her face. But Linda wasn't just sad. She was angry. "She loved life and he took it away from her—*just took it away from her*," she sobbed.

The prosecutor asked Linda to describe how she learned of Michelle's death. She was driving home from getting her hair done, she responded, when Meredith called and told her Michelle was "D. E. A. D." She had spelled out the word because Cassidy was listening.

Sobbing once again, she continued, "And I'm like, 'What do you mean? That can't be. Did she just pass out? Maybe she just passed out.'"

But Meredith insisted that Michelle was in fact dead. Linda testified she caught the first flight out of New York and was at Meredith's home in Fuquay-Varina—which she had recently purchased for her younger daughter—when Jason and his family arrived.

"What do you recall about when he got there?" Holt asked.

"Like cold air," Linda answered, in a disgusted tone. "There was no hugging. There was no 'Oh my goodness, I'm so sorry.' There was no crying. It appeared to me when I looked at him, his head was down and he looked like a five-year-old boy."

"Did you try to talk with him or have any conversation with him?" Holt followed up.

Bitterness now rolling off her tongue, Jason's mother-in-law replied, "I tried to talk to him and he told me, 'My lawyer told me I can't talk to anyone, not even you.' And that's a quote. And he also said, 'I'm going to take a hit on the house.' Those are the two things he said to me. Period."

After the funeral, Linda testified, she invited everyone back to Meredith's house. Jason didn't accept the invitation. "I could understand them not coming back at that point to the house," she explained. "But just to take Cassidy away—like they just took her away. She was gone. That I couldn't accept."

Linda described the difficulties she and Meredith had visiting with Cassidy. While at Pat Young's home in Brevard one day, "we were given an ultimatum," she told the jury, "and what we needed to do was to stand behind Jason. And if we didn't stand behind him, they were going to cut off all visits with Cassidy."

From that point forward, Linda said, not only was Jason denying them visitation with Cassidy, so was Pat. "And anything that I ever asked of Pat was like, 'Well, I have to check with Jason first, you know. He is the parent.' I understand that but, you know, for another grandmother not to understand you want to be with your grandchild, my only grandchild, I can't understand that. I just can't understand how she could do that to me."

As she neared the end of her direct examination, Holt asked the former schoolteacher if she had discussed with her daughter the topic of divorce.

"Yes," Linda answered.

"And what did you tell her?"

"You know, she deserved to be happy and she was not. She just—there was a void in her and I hated seeing her like that. And I know, like, divorce is not the answer for, you know, right away, you know. You want to try to work on it. You want to try to make it better. But they've gone three years, and three years, they were not headed in the right direction."

"Did you express those feelings to your daughter?" the Assistant DA asked.

"Absolutely," Linda replied.

Collins cross-examined Linda for only a few minutes. He asked her whether she had told detectives Jason was a great dad. She responded by saying, "Jason loved to play with Cassidy. He was down on the ground with her or out with the swings or on a bike ride. Yes, he loved to play with Cassidy." But she wouldn't give Jason — or his family — the satisfaction of agreeing that made him a great dad.

Mike Schilawski, Linda and Meredith's family-law attorney, testified next. He told the jury about their numerous attempts to establish a schedule of visitation with Cassidy — all of which were unsuccessful.

Holt led him through the filing of the custody lawsuit and Jason's eventual agreement to enter into a consent order that transferred Cassidy's custody to Meredith.

She asked Schilawski whether, had no agreement been reached, Jason would have been required to testify under oath about the circumstances surrounding Michelle's death. And whether Jason could have been subjected to a psychological examination.

Schilawski testified that in the normal course of affairs, he would have pursued both avenues. Jason's agreement to give up custody of Cassidy, he explained, was conditioned on him not having to testify or be subjected to a psychological examination.

.....

Sergeant Richard Spivey was the State's 37th and final witness. Holt had him walk the jury through video footage obtained from the Cracker Barrel in Greensboro, Hampton Inn in Hillsville, and the various gas stations at which Jason purchased gas. The Cracker Barrel video was the only one in color. As that video proceeded frame by frame, the detective pointed to Jason's brown, slip-on, casual leather shoes.

Holt questioned him extensively about video footage from

the Hampton Inn. The first video segment showed Jason at the hotel's front desk just before 11:00 p.m. Sergeant Spivey pointed out that the clothes he had on then appeared identical to what he was wearing at the Cracker Barrel. At 11:58 p.m., however, Jason appeared at the front desk a second time, wearing different clothes. He had on some type of dark sweater with a thin, white stripe across the chest. He also appeared to have a bottle of water in his hand.

The next video segment showed a hallway leading to a glass exit door next to the western stairwell. Immediately to the right of that door was another door, which the detective explained was "like the fire door or a solid door there, and that's the door where people working at the hotel said they found a rock lodged in that door propping the door open."

Just a few seconds before midnight, Jason appeared in the video, in the hallway, headed in the direction of the two doors. Sergeant Spivey again pointed out his sweater—with the stripe across the chest—his shoes with a rounded toe, a bottle of water in one hand, and some type of open booklet in his other. He testified he believed the booklet was the road atlas found in Jason's Explorer.

The detective also testified about his analysis of Jason's cell phone records. He told the jury that during the evening of November 2, there were several phone calls between Jason and Michelle Money. Jason had also called his home phone at 10:59 p.m. That call lasted just under five minutes. His last call that night was at 11:43 p.m.—to Money—which lasted about two minutes.

The following morning, Sergeant Spivey told jurors, Jason's first call was to his mother's home phone at 7:40 a.m. At 7:49 a.m., Jason placed his first of several calls to Money. His phone records also revealed that between 7:40 a.m. and 1:37 p.m., there were 28 different calls between his phone and his mother's. They also reflected Jason's call to his home phone at 7:49 a.m.—while he was already on the line with Money—and to Meredith's cell phone at 12:10 p.m. and 1:37 p.m. After eliciting this testimony, Holt abruptly ended her direct examination.

Klinkosum picked up right where Holt left off. He first had Sergeant Spivey confirm that those same cell phone records established that Jason called Michelle's work number at 12:02 p.m. on November 3.

He then focused on the detective's analysis of the cell towers Jason's phone connected with each time he made a call. Klink asked whether Jason's 7:40 a.m. call to his mother pinged a cell tower near Wytheville, Virginia.

"Yes, sir. It shows that it's bouncing off that tower. Yes, sir," Sergeant Spivey replied.

Klinkosum circled back to the Four Brothers BP station—in particular, investigators' numerous interviews of Gracie Dahms. And in all those interviews, he asked the witness, there was only one time when she provided a description of the customer who threw the $20 bill and cursed at her.

"I believe so, yes, sir," the detective responded. "I don't know if she was actually asked any more, but yes, sir."

Jason's attorney asked him about the Tylenol bottle found in Cassidy's hutch. "It's one of those medicines where the cup comes with it and it sets over top of the actual cap of the Tylenol bottle, correct?"

"It appears so. Yes, sir," Sergeant Spivey replied.

"That medicine cap was actually tested for fingerprints, correct?"

"I believe it was. Yes, sir."

"And I believe you heard the testimony that the fingerprints on that cap didn't match to Jason Young, correct?" the defense attorney probed.

"Best of my recollection of the testimony, that's correct," Sergeant Spivey agreed.

"In fact, it didn't match to anyone for whom standards—known fingerprint standards were submitted, correct?"

The detective agreed no match had been made.

Klinkosum next focused on Meredith, asking Sergeant Spivey whether there were inconsistencies in statements she had made to investigators.

"Throughout the statements, there may have been some. Yes, sir," the detective agreed.

One significant inconsistency related to where Meredith left her car keys when she entered the Birchleaf Drive home on November 3. Sergeant Spivey acknowledged he and other investigators were trying to clarify where her keys had been placed, agreeing with Klinkosum they had been photographed on the hood of Michelle's Lexus.

"And Ms. Fisher had said that she had left her keys on the kitchen counter at 5108 Birchleaf, correct?" Klink inquired.

"Yes, sir," Sergeant Spivey agreed.

"But you later came to find out that the keys on the Lexus were actually Ms. Fisher's keys, correct?" Klinkosum asked, in apparent disbelief.

"The ones in the photograph, that was my understanding. Yes, sir."

Jason's lawyer also got the detective to acknowledge that, in September 2007, he observed Meredith through a closed-circuit TV while investigators interviewed her. Though he didn't ask the question, Klinkosum surely was hoping the jury would wonder why the lead detective was observing Meredith—without her knowledge—if he didn't consider her to be a suspect.

As Sergeant Spivey returned to his seat behind the prosecution counsel table, Judge Stephens asked whether the State had further evidence to present.

In response, Becky Holt uttered the three words the jury had been waiting to hear for two weeks: "The State rests."

# 15

## DEFENSE

Pat Young and Jason's sisters, Kim and Heather, endured the first two weeks of the trial as best they could. They bit their lips as Becky Holt portrayed Jason as a monster who bludgeoned his wife to death. They watched helplessly as witness after witness described Jason as a deeply flawed human being. They knew their turn would eventually come. And it finally had.

Bryan Collins called Pat as Jason's first witness. She testified she was a schoolteacher for over thirty years, though stayed at home to raise Kim, Jason, and Heather. She told the jury how her first husband, Robert Young, was diagnosed with Hodgkin's disease and died within just a few months, when Jason was only five. Gerald McIntyre, whom Pat would later marry, would become the father figure in Jason's life, she said.

When asked to describe Jason's personality, his mom responded, "He was always quite an imp" and teased his sisters incessantly. She would tell the girls, "That's showing how much he loves you … because if he didn't love you, he wouldn't fool with teasing and aggravating you." Pat told the jury Jason's sisters would get so angry with him, "they'd be ready to skin him alive and he would, of course, run off laughing."

Collins asked the former schoolteacher to describe her first impressions of Michelle. "I liked her very, very much. She was a beautiful young woman," Pat replied. "She loves to cook and

I love to cook so she sat in the kitchen while we were cooking and talked." When Michelle came up to Brevard, Pat would always fix her favorite foods for her. "She especially liked my banana pudding, so I would always try to have banana pudding for her," Pat added.

Michelle was interested in learning how to grow vegetables in the backyard of the Birchleaf Drive home, she testified. She gave Michelle advice on planting lettuce, radishes, and onions. Pat also brought her boxes of hostas, she told jurors, which they planted together in the backyard.

When Michelle visited Brevard, she and Pat would walk together, pushing Cassidy in the stroller. The pair would also take Cassidy to a nearby lake to feed the ducks, she recalled fondly.

Collins asked Pat share with the jury her feelings about her daughter-in-law. "I loved Michelle," she replied warmly. "I loved her very much. She was a *wonderful* mother. She was kind. She was always doing thoughtful things."

The Public Defender asked Jason's mother to share her observations of her son's relationship with Michelle.

"Well, I always thought that Jason loved her very much," she testified. "They would kid and go on with each other. Yes, they would argue some, but I haven't seen too many young people in life who don't argue some." They would become aggravated with each other for a little while, she acknowledged, "and then it would be all over and they were fine again." In Pat's opinion, they were both "strong willed" and "very stubborn and so each wanted their own way."

Pat made clear she didn't approve of Jason and Michelle moving in together before they were married, but that obviously didn't stop them. And then she learned Michelle had become pregnant. Collins asked her to describe Jason's reaction to that news.

"Oh, he was excited," she responded. "He was very excited to be a father. I mean, he had always loved children and animals and things like that. So he was very excited to be having the child."

Collins asked whether she believed Jason felt pressured

into getting married.

She didn't think so, Pat said. "I think he wanted to marry her ... I said, 'Do you love her?' and he said 'Yes,' and he seemed to be very excited about it. I don't believe she would have pressured him into marrying her. I think he wanted to get married."

Jason's attorney then showed the defense witness a series of photos from the couple's wedding, including one of them with their ring bearer—Mr. Garrison—and another of "Mr. G" giving Michelle a kiss on the neck. Pat chuckled at the sight. One by one, she held the photos up for the jury and described—with a bright smile and calm, ingratiating demeanor—different events from their wedding day.

They next discussed Cassidy's birth. Pat was actually in Raleigh when her granddaughter was born, but was out shopping with Kim for some baby clothes when Jason called. "And he let me hear her cry and then he was just so excited about holding her. And he was telling me how, what a little bundle she was all wrapped up, you know, in his arms and I think he called her his 'little glow worm,'" Jason's mom recounted. "She was just such a beautiful, sweet, good baby and she made him so happy." Jason "loved taking care of her," Pat told the jury, "helping bathe her, doing all the things. He was great with her."

Collins showed his witness—and the jury—photos of Michelle, Jason, and Cassidy the day they came back from the hospital, of their life together as a family, and of her son and daughter-in-law at the Biltmore House in Asheville and in Puerto Rico.

Pat told jurors she and Jason had arranged a trip to Puerto Rico with Cassidy after Michelle died. "When we were hiking up into the rain forest, Jason told her that this is the place that her mother loved to go."

Collins asked her to describe the sort of father Jason was to Cassidy. She lavished praised on her son, proudly declaring, "Cassidy was first in his life."

She told the jury Jason took his daughter to and from preschool, attended her programs there, and would teach her how to eat new foods, including edamame, which he told Cassidy was one of Michelle's favorites.

Pat shared with jurors how Jason played games with Cassidy to get her to eat fruit. "He would say, 'Now I've got seven blackberries,' and he would have them lying on his plate and he would glance off and Cassidy would sneak a blackberry and put it in her mouth. And he's like, 'What happened? I've only got six blackberries.'"

Collins asked Pat to describe how her son reacted after finding out Michelle was pregnant with Rylan. She responded he was very enthusiastic "because he wanted four to six children." He was even more excited, she said, "when he found out they were going to have a little boy" to carry on the Young name.

The former schoolteacher was next asked how she learned of Michelle's death. She recounted receiving a call from Michelle's mother at about 2:00 p.m. on November 3. "She was crying, and she said, 'My Michelle. My Michelle is dead.'"

Linda told her Meredith explained there was blood everywhere. "I immediately thought, had Michelle had a miscarriage?" Pat testified. "Because I have had miscarriages and I know that there can be a lot of bleeding involved when you have miscarriages."

She told the jury she and Gerald decided not to call Jason, because it would have been dangerous for him to learn the news while driving. Instead, they waited until he got to their house. In the meantime, she called her son's home number and was able to speak to Meredith. "And she told me that, you know, there was blood everywhere. She told me that Michelle had a pillow between her legs and I thought, 'Oh, then maybe she was trying to staunch the blood. Maybe she did have a miscarriage.'"

Pat described for jurors Jason's arrival at her home that afternoon. Their dog, Gypsy, ran out to greet him at his car. Jason crouched down to pet her.

But when he walked up to Pat and Gerald, he sensed something was amiss. "He said, 'What's wrong Mom?'"

Gerald delivered the news, bluntly. "Michelle is dead," he

said. "And Jason just went pale," she explained, "just went white and just went down to the ground, you know, just sank to the ground."

"'That can't be right,'" she recalled her son repeating.

Pat thought he was going into shock, telling the jury he was going from hot to cold, and sobbing.

At about 3:15 p.m. that afternoon, Jason placed a call to Meredith, she said. Pat recalled hearing him say, "Homicide, no, no, no." And also saying, "I not only lost my wife, but I've lost my son."

Pat recalled sitting beside her son on a couch at Meredith's home later that evening. She overheard Jason on the phone talking with someone from the Sheriff's Office. "I will talk to you when my attorney is present," she overheard him saying.

He then handed the phone to her, exasperated, saying, "Mom, they wouldn't listen to me."

"I took the phone," Pat testified, "and I said, 'My son has repeatedly told you that he will speak with you when his attorney is present. Have a good evening. Goodbye.' And I hung up the phone."

Collins asked what she remembered about Michelle's visitation and funeral. At the funeral, Pat recounted, "We were asked to come up, I guess for that last viewing." The whole family went up together so Jason wouldn't be alone at the casket. "And we sort of surrounded him," she told jurors.

"And what did he do?" the Public Defender asked.

"He touched Michelle's hand and then he reached over and he just rubbed his hand on that little mound that was that little baby and I felt—it was so sad."

"Was this his last moment with her?"

"Yes, as far as I know that was." As his mother answered these questions, Jason buried his head in his hands at the defense counsel table, sobbing. Pat, on the other hand, remained stoic and unemotional.

While the family said their goodbyes to Michelle, news crews hungry for footage for their broadcasts waited outside. Pat recalled camera crews in the bushes beside their motel. Collins asked her if the swirl of media attention raised concerns for Jason.

"He didn't want Cassidy exposed to the media," she responded. "He didn't want her picture plastered everywhere. He didn't, you know, he didn't feel like that girl needed to go through that." That was why Jason had Heather and Joe take Cassidy back to the mountains immediately following the funeral, she explained—so his daughter wouldn't be exposed to that atmosphere.

Collins then shifted his focus to Cassidy's third birthday party in March 2007. He placed photos of the event in front of Pat and asked her about them. In one of the photos, Jason was flying his daughter around on a "magic carpet."

In another, he was pictured behind Cassidy and next to his mother, who was scooping ice cream from a container. Jason was wearing a dark-colored sweater with a thin white stripe across the chest—strikingly similar to the shirt he was wearing when he was spotted behind the front desk of the Hampton Inn the second time.

Jason's lawyer asked Pat why Linda and Meredith had been cut off from visiting with Cassidy. She replied that the last time Linda had been at her home, she "became very hysterical, crying, loud." That behavior, Pat testified, occurred after she and one of her friends confronted Linda with newspaper articles in which Linda had said she hadn't been permitted to see Cassidy.

Pat told Linda what she told the newspaper wasn't true. Linda agreed and offered to correct it. But to Pat's knowledge, she never did.

"Jason and I felt that she didn't need to be—Cassidy did not need to be exposed to all the drama," Pat explained. "The, you know, hysterical crying, you know, those sorts of things. We had tried, Jason and I had tried so very hard to have a normal life for Cassidy, a happy life and let her be the little three-year-old that she was."

As fate would have it, Pat was present when Jason was arrested in December 2009. She told the jury Jason's Explorer hadn't been running properly, so she followed him in her car to the small repair shop where he took the SUV. As they were walking back to her car to head home, she testified, officers came out of nowhere and surrounded her son. They handcuffed Jason and quickly put him in a patrol car.

"I spoke to a couple of the officers," Pat recounted, "and then I said, 'Can I hug him? Can I tell him goodbye? Can I hug him?' And they opened the door and I—he had the cuffs [behind him] so I reached down to hug him."

"Is that the last time you ever hugged him?" Collins asked.

"The last time I ever hugged him," Pat replied, finally showing a hint of emotion.

"He's been in jail ever since?"

"Yes, he has."

Collins ended his direct examination by asking Pat about the testimony she heard from Michelle Money and Carol Anne Sowerby. She testified she knew nothing about Jason's relationships with either woman.

"Do you approve of that sort of behavior?" he asked.

"I do not approve," she answered.

"Was he raised better than that?"

"He was," Pat replied. "He was raised better than that."

Becky Holt handled Pat's cross-examination. She asked Jason's mother about the restrictions placed on Linda and Meredith during their visits with Cassidy.

"You've heard described by the Fishers that they weren't able to be alone with Cassidy?" Holt asked.

"Yes," Pat responded.

"And was that your decision or was that the defendant's decision?"

"It was probably a combined decision," Pat responded.

"And so you had friends and family members that would watch them such that they couldn't even go into the bathroom and be alone?"

"Yes," Pat agreed.

After Holt was done, Collins asked Pat why she and Jason didn't want Linda and Meredith to be alone with Cassidy.

Pat said, "By now we had seen how angry Linda was and accusing Jason, and that sort of thing. We had read those things and we did not know what, how they might—what they might say to Cassidy, what they might put into Cassidy's mind. Also, I believed that they might take Cassidy—take Cassidy away."

At that point, Judge Stephens interjected. "You mean you believed they might, if they weren't supervised, they might put her in the car and just leave with her? Is that what you mean?" he asked.

"Yes," Pat told the judge.

.....

Jason's stepfather, Gerald McIntyre, was the next witness for the defense. He testified he and Pat were devastated by the news of Michelle's death—especially considering she was pregnant with their grandson. "Jason was excited over it. And it just took something out of us. Even this breath I'm taking now, I haven't got over it because part of him died that day," he told jurors.

McIntyre recounted how when he shared the news with his stepson, "he just about went to the ground. If I hadn't have caught him, he would have went plum on the ground."

Though Holt's cross-examination wasn't long, she did elicit a couple of noteworthy admissions. When Sheriff's officers came to Brevard in February 2008 to execute their search warrant, McIntyre acknowledged, he called Jason just before the officers arrived at the park to meet with him.

"And you told him ... to keep his mouth shut?" Holt asked.

"I told him not to speak of the situation unless he had representation with him," McIntyre told the Assistant DA.

"Do you remember stating several times that you would stick with your family to the death?" she probed.

"That's what I meant. It's what I said," McIntyre agreed.

Jason's younger sister Heather testified next. She described Jason's relationship with Michelle during their courting days as "playful. You know, they flirted a lot and were sweet to each other. It was kind of nice because Jason teased me often, but now that Michelle was part of his life, she got that teasing as well, so it wasn't as much on me."

Heather recalled the scene at Meredith's home the evening

of Michelle's death. "It was just very quiet, very sad," she told the jury. "Jason and Meredith embraced. And they stood there and cried quietly with one another."

When she and her husband Joe went outside to retrieve their luggage, as Joe was opening the trunk of Jason's Explorer and placing his hand on a suitcase, Heather recounted, "The police cars came in quickly and stopped. And the officers got out and they told Joe to put the luggage back and that they had a search warrant for the vehicle and that we were not to take anything out of the car."

She testified she "was just in disbelief. And the police officer asked us who we were. And I said, 'I'm Jason Young's younger sister.' … And he said, 'Where is your brother now?' I said, 'He's inside with his daughter.' He said, 'Is there any way he can leave or escape from the back?' I said, '*He's with his daughter.*' And I couldn't believe he was asking me that question."

. . . . .

Jason's friends and former N.C. State classmates Brian Ambrose, Josh Dalton, and Demetrius Barrett were also called as defense witnesses. Ambrose and his wife and children, who lived near Charlotte, had planned to travel to Raleigh to attend the Wolfpack football game with Jason and Michelle on Saturday, November 4, 2006. Earlier that week, Ambrose had discussed with Jason the possibility of spending that Friday evening at the Youngs' Birchleaf Drive home.

He testified he informed Jason during a phone conversation that Friday morning he had decided instead of coming to their home that night, his family was going to spend the evening at his wife's parents' home in Sanford.

They planned to meet up with Jason and Michelle at their home the next morning before heading to the stadium to tailgate.

During their conversation, Ambrose testified, Jason told him that because Ambrose's family wasn't going to spend the night at his house, he was going to head to his mother's home in Brevard, spend the night with her, and then meet up with them the next morning.

During cross-examination, Saacks asked Jason's friend if he knew of anything unusual Jason would sometimes do at parties. Klinkosum objected to the question's relevance, but Judge Stephens overruled the objection.

Ambrose responded, "I mean, it was pretty common knowledge that Jason, you know, was known to get naked and I guess, do genitalia tricks, I guess is the way I'll put it. You know, I'd say he—he was always the life of the party and he would do whatever it took, you know, to get the attention and to make sure people were laughing."

Josh Dalton testified detectives were at his house the afternoon of the murder, subjecting him to "very direct questioning" about Jason and his relationship with Michelle. He told the jury he could tell very quickly they considered Jason a suspect. He and Ryan Schaad discussed the matter and agreed Jason needed to get a lawyer. Ryan, he testified, called Jason to deliver that message.

Dalton also testified that, at the visitation at the funeral home, Jason went off to the bathroom by himself. When Dalton went to check on his friend, "he seemed to be pretty upset, like he had just either thrown up—pretty white, you know, pretty pale."

During cross-examination, Holt asked Dalton to describe Jason's relationship with Michelle. He responded, "It could be volatile," and they had "very heated arguments," which they weren't afraid to have in public. Their arguments, he testified, "ran the gamut." He also told the jury most of Jason's friends didn't believe they would have gotten married had it not been for Michelle's pregnancy.

Dalton also acknowledged Jason had confided in him about his trip to Florida that October to see Michelle Money. "He basically told me that he thought he was in love with her," he testified. Dalton added Jason had also mentioned Money hoped to have another child and they "had joked wouldn't it be funny—because she was trying to get pregnant again—if it was his kid."

Holt also questioned Jason's friend about the weekend of Ryan's and Shelly's wedding. Dalton testified he and his wife Julie, together with Jason and Michelle, were walking across the street from the hotel prior to the rehearsal dinner. "And on the way over, Jason just kept berating her and berating her," Dalton told jurors, about why she wouldn't admit that she had erased a message on their answering machine from Dalton's wife Julie. Both he and Julie told Jason to let it go. "He wouldn't stop and so Michelle turned around and went, 'Fine. I'll go back to the hotel.'"

The Assistant DA's final set of questions was on the topic of divorce. She asked the witness if he and Jason ever discussed that subject. Dalton responded that Jason "had made a statement at one time that he was afraid that if he ever got a divorce, Michelle would take Cassidy and move back to New York." Further, he said Jason didn't know if he would ever get to see Cassidy again.

Demetrius Barrett testified he was Jason's supervisor at University Towers and the two remained friends after college. He recalled calling Jason the evening of November 2 to discuss a home warranty. Though Jason didn't answer his phone, he called back just a few minutes later.

Barrett stated that Jason had just arrived at his hotel room in Virginia and that he could hear the Thursday night football game in the background as they spoke. Jason told him he was going to spend the following night at his parents' home, but would be back on Saturday morning to tailgate before the football game. They spoke for about five minutes. Barrett didn't recall anything unusual about the call.

.....

The defense also called Terry Tiller and Cindy Beaver as witnesses. Tiller testified the Youngs' home was "lit up" and "brighter than ever" when she passed by it on her *New York Times* delivery route between 3:30 and 4:00 a.m. on November 3. It "jumped out" at her because it was normally so dark. She thought there must have been some kind of party going on.

Tiller also noticed a light-colored SUV parked in front of the house and a blue minivan parked across the street.

Cindy Beaver was the ninth and final witness to testify on June 21. She testified she had a vivid recollection of driving by 5108 Birchleaf Drive on her way to work at about 5:30 a.m. that morning. Not only were the lights on inside and outside the house, she recalled a "soccer mom" type vehicle coming down the driveway in her direction.

"And the thing I remember so vividly," she told the jury, "was that I had my bright lights on—I had a lower car at the time and the bright lights were pretty bright. And the bright lights hit the automobile and I'm first concerned, I've just blinded somebody at 5:15, 5:20 in the morning. And there were two people in the car. And since the car was coming out of the driveway, you know, my lights hit them first, right in the face, basically."

Beaver testified her lights hit the passenger's face, causing that person to turn toward the driver. She then saw the passenger talking to the driver and noticed that the driver was a Caucasian man whose hands were gripping the steering wheel. She assumed the passenger was a woman because she had thick, bushy hair.

As she continued down Birchleaf Drive, Beaver testified, she noticed a delivery-type van parked to her right on a side street, with its lights crossing her path. As she drove by it, she could see that the vehicle's dome lights were on and that there were newspapers in the van—she then realized the person at the driver's seat was a delivery person.

Recognizing that Beaver's account was wholly inconsistent with the prosecution's theory and timeline, Holt subjected the defense witness to an aggressive cross-examination. She asked her whether she had told detectives in January 2008 she wasn't sure what she had seen and when she had seen it. Beaver denied saying that.

Holt pressed her: "Do you recall telling the agents that, 'It's possible it could have been the previous Friday or another Friday prior to November 3?'"

"I told them it was possible," Beaver replied. "I was being

interviewed somewhat frequently—I mean, not like day after day. But no, about the time you try to forget about the situation and move on with your life, someone would call or it would all be drug up again. And I was really getting tired with it."

She explained she told the detectives she was "ninety percent sure it was the Friday of the murder. It's possible it could have been the Friday before."

# 16

## SURPRISE WITNESS

Becky Holt spent the evening of June 21 preparing intensely for her closing argument. Without question, this would be the most consequential closing of her career. She wanted to make sure the jury understood each piece of evidence and how it all fit together to convincingly establish Jason's guilt. Above all else, she wanted her argument to cry out for justice for Michelle Young.

She and David Saacks were convinced Terry Tiller and Cindy Beaver would be the final witnesses to testify for the defense. Though, in the back of her mind, Holt never ruled out the possibility Jason might take the witness stand in his own defense, the approach his attorneys had been taking throughout the trial signaled they had no such intention.

For a defendant accused of murder, there is no more important strategic decision during trial than whether he will testify. Defense attorneys often begin their representation of a murder defendant with that very question at the forefront of how they will proceed.

Because the burden to prove a defendant's guilt beyond a reasonable doubt is so high, defense attorneys often conclude their best chance of winning a favorable verdict is to shine a spotlight on the gaps and deficiencies in the prosecution's evidence, rather than on their own client. Throughout the trial, Bryan Collins and Mike Klinkosum had been doing exactly that. They hammered home with witness after witness the absence of forensic evidence that pointed at Jason—or in the case of the Franklin shoe impressions and eyewitness testimony from Cindy Beaver, the presence of evidence that pointed elsewhere.

Calling a murder defendant as a witness is fraught with enormous risk. For starters, it shifts the jury's focus away from any gaps in forensic evidence back to the defendant. Jurors naturally focus on whether they believe the defendant—almost to the exclusion of all other evidence. The entire case tends to devolve into a single question: "Is the defendant telling the truth?"

It is a rare criminal defendant who can successfully withstand a withering cross-examination by a skilled prosecutor. By calling the defendant as a witness, defense attorneys provide prosecutors a grand stage to dismember their client by forcing him to confront the very worst aspects of his life and the most damaging evidence against him.

In addition to any inconsistencies or evasiveness in the defendant's answers, jurors may perceive dishonesty from body language, facial expressions, long pauses, or emotions that don't seem genuine.

With all eyes and ears on the defendant, prosecutors have a golden opportunity to persuade the jury, "He did it. You could just sense it from the way he testified." That is why so few murder defendants take the witness stand in their own defense.

So, as the bailiff called the courtroom to order the morning of June 22, Holt was focused intently—and exclusively—on the closing argument she believed she was moments away from delivering.

Directing his attention toward Collins, Judge Stephens asked if there would be further evidence for the defendant.

Collins jumped to his feet and responded, "Yes, sir, there will," much to Holt's surprise.

"Okay," the judge said, "call your next witness."

"*We call Jason Young,*" Collins announced.

"Mr. Young, come around and be sworn please," the judge

directed. Jason, wearing a gray suit and light blue shirt with a dark, patterned tie, walked toward the jury—sure to make eye contact—and stepped up to the witness stand to take the oath.

Holt and Saacks were blindsided. Ambushed. They didn't see this coming. Mild panic set in. It was only 9:40 a.m. What if the direct examination concluded midday, requiring cross-examination to be formulated on the spot, rather than with the evening to prepare? They were about to hear, for the first time in the four and a half years since the murder, Jason's account of his marriage to Michelle and his every step the evening before, and day of, the murder. How on Earth would they be able to question him effectively without having any time to prepare?

The reaction of jurors was quite the opposite. They had been sizing up Jason for weeks as they watched the testimony of countless other witnesses, none of whom were as significant as the defendant himself. Instead of observing him from afar as he sat by his defense team, they would now be almost close enough to touch him as he testified from the witness stand. They would be able to hear his voice, look into his eyes, and decide for themselves if he was the cold-blooded killer who bludgeoned his beautiful wife to death.

Jason clasped his hands on the desk in front of him and stared at Collins confidently, his high cheekbones and angular jaw line combining to convey a deadly serious expression. Collins began with short, crisp questions:

"State your name, please."

"Jason Young."

"Jason, did you love your wife, Michelle?"

"Yes, sir, I did."

"Were you a proper husband to her?"

"No, sir, I was not."

"Do you love Cassidy?"

"Absolutely, yes sir."

"Are you a good father to her?"

"Yes, sir, I am."

"Did you kill your wife, Michelle?"

"*No, sir,*" Jason replied emphatically.

"Were you there when it happened?" Collins asked.

"No, sir."

"Do you know who did it?"

"No, sir, I do not."

With Jason's forceful denial now before the jury, Collins took a step back and began leading his client through his courtship of Michelle. Jason appeared tender, thoughtful, and charming as he described the early days of their relationship. He reminisced about how Michelle seemed "a little out of my league" and how he was "overwhelmed at first."

"We always were jokey with each other and cutting up and being silly," he testified. "I think she was more of the serious type and I kind of was the loosener-up type, so she was always the planner and the really, the person who would take things really, really seriously, and I think sometimes she liked it because I could come in and say, 'Oh, that's not a big deal.' So, we kind of equaled each other out in that regard."

Jason recalled how he learned of Michelle's pregnancy with Cassidy. He was upstairs in their bedroom at the Arete Way townhome, he said, when Michelle came home to deliver the news. "We were both very shocked, like eye-opening, like whoa, it was, you know, a surprise, it wasn't planned ... but it was a good surprise."

Collins asked if her pregnancy caused them to get married. Jason responded it didn't, but it accelerated the process. He conceded on his schedule, the timeline probably would have been "stretched out a little more."

At his lawyer's prompting, Jason acknowledged his weaknesses. He procrastinated on doing household chores. He gambled on sports, though only with his own money and never went into debt. He and Michelle had many arguments while she was pregnant with Cassidy—he described his wife as being very emotional at the time, with frequent mood swings, and how she could "cry at the drop of a hat."

They would get angry at one another. There was a lot of yelling, Jason testified. "It would go both ways. And then sometimes I would pout and not talk."

Jason became particularly animated as he described what he saw while peering over the curtain during Michelle's

C-section:

"Cassidy was covered with this kind of like white, I didn't know what she was supposed to look like, but I didn't think she was supposed to look like *that* ... Then we heard that cry and we both smiled and they immediately did whatever they need to do. They got her bundled up and cleaned up and they took her in the same room under a little warming lamp and finished up with her there ... I hadn't gotten to hold her yet or see her, I just got to see the process of birth, but it was awesome."

In testimony that appeared both loving and sincere, Jason explained he was the first person to change Cassidy's diaper and see how her poop went from a tar-like substance to a mustard color and consistency. He told jurors his wife was an "absolutely amazing mother."

After the miscarriage in May 2006, Michelle quickly became pregnant again. They were both overjoyed, Jason testified, to learn that, this time, they would be having a boy. Having both a girl and a boy "couldn't have been more storybook," he told the jury. "That's just up Michelle's alley, just how she would have wanted it." Fighting back tears, he said having a boy was the only way he could carry on the Young name. He choked up again describing how he learned of that pregnancy—with Cassidy toddling into the den wearing a shirt saying, "I'm going to be a big sister."

Collins then led his client through his difficult relationship with Linda. "A lot of what Michelle wanted to do was to bring her mom in and have her live with us to help out with child care and I didn't want to be living with my mother in-law," Jason said. He explained they had significant differences in personality, "culturally maybe a little bit of difference, just me coming from the mountains in the south and her being from Long Island and New York. I think she could be a bit domineering."

"I was adamant about Linda not living with us," he acknowledged. "Yes, I was."

Jason also lamented how, during Michelle's pregnancy with Rylan—especially during her mood swings—she would instinctively reach out to Linda whenever she was upset. And that would only compound the problem, he testified. "Her mom would get Michelle sobbing and in tears." Moreover, Michelle herself could be overly dramatic and exaggerate problems, he said, which would cause the problem to grow further.

"Did you ever get physical with her?" Collins asked.

"*Absolutely not,*" Jason replied forcefully. He denied ever hitting her. He denied throwing a TV remote at her. He testified they didn't fight more often than most people, but acknowledged they were more open about it.

Michelle had been pushing for them to see a professional marriage counselor, he said, though he was more hesitant. They had seen a counselor when Michelle was pregnant with Cassidy. He wasn't particularly comfortable with that experience, he testified. He was much more comfortable with Meredith playing that role.

The defendant told the jury he was working on the issues in his marriage, but felt Michelle had her own, personal issues from her past—her darker side. Some things she shared with him, he said, and some she didn't. He wanted her to work on those issues before they worked on their issues together.

"Did you want to stay married to Michelle?" Collins asked.

"Yes, I did. I wanted to have another child and I wanted the family to grow," Jason responded. He denied ever thinking seriously about divorce.

"Did the two of you ever discuss it?"

"Yes, when we were angry," the former salesman answered. "I think it was a fair assessment that out of anger the divorce card might be played. Out of anger, I might say, 'Well just divorce me then.'"

Jason testified he never thought about going to a lawyer to pursue a divorce and didn't believe Michelle had either. Collins showed him his email exchange with Michelle from October 24, 2006, and had him point out to the jury where he told his wife, "I do love you too and want it to work out."

The Public Defender then shifted gears to the other women in Jason's life. He started with Genevieve Cargol. Jason admitted to pinning her down in a hotel room in Texas and forcibly removing her engagement ring. He testified he was intoxicated when that incident occurred and was only 25, though conceded that was no excuse for what he had done.

"Since that incident, have you ever put your hands on a woman in anger?" Collins asked.

"*No, sir,*" Jason replied firmly.

Collins then asked his client if he had learned anything from that incident with Cargol.

Now contrite, the defendant responded, "It's completely wrong to physically do anything to anyone like that when you're angry with someone just because you're bigger than them or stronger than them. It's wrong." He testified that he ultimately lost his relationship with Cargol because of what he had done to her.

Jason acknowledged that Carol Anne Sowerby had testified truthfully, admitting they had sex in the home he shared with his wife just a few weeks before the murder. He confirmed Michelle Money was also truthful in her testimony about their extramarital affair. But he denied having any plan to leave his wife for Money.

He explained he and Money had been confiding a lot in each other because they both felt they were missing intimacy in their relationships. He readily agreed his relationship with Money was "wrong."

"I don't think either one of us dreamed that it would ever be found out," he testified. "We both even knew that there was no way anything would ever come from it. And we—we really knew we had to stop." He admitted, though, they had been speaking to each other "a lot" just before the murder.

With that difficult subject out of the way, Collins pivoted to the events of November 2 and 3. Jason testified that he knew he had a very long drive to Clintwood, Virginia and decided instead of waking up at 4:00 a.m. on November 3, he would break the trip into two legs. Because he was a diamond member of the Hilton Honors Club, he planned to stop at a Hampton Inn to earn hotel points. He told the jury he and Michelle had been saving up their points, hoping to earn enough to one day vacation in Hawaii.

Jason explained he had taken a lot of grief from Michelle and her mom about not giving his wife an anniversary gift and confessed he and Michelle had a "pretty lousy" anniversary dinner. To make up for it, he testified, he wanted to surprise her with something that was "pretty non-typical for me," and planned to spend a lot of money on a Coach purse. It was actually Money who had given him the idea to search for a purse on eBay, he noted.

Jason offered a simple explanation about why the eBay printouts he left on the printer were for auctions that were about to expire—he was only using those particular purses to get an idea on pricing, he testified. He had no intention of bidding on anything that evening.

Instead, he said, he planned to seek Meredith's assistance later about what kind of purse to get for his wife. He had meant to place the printouts in his laptop bag, he testified, so he could have them with him during his business trip. Michelle loved surprises, he told the jury, which was why he was so determined to keep his shopping for a Coach purse a secret.

In contrast to Shelly Schaad's testimony, Jason testified he actually knew before leaving his home on November 2 that Alan Fisher wouldn't be coming to Raleigh that weekend. He told jurors Michelle was upset her dad wouldn't be able to visit with Cassidy. That was the reason why he called his mom shortly after leaving the house, Jason said, as he now could spend the evening of November 3 in Brevard, rather than rushing back to Raleigh to be with his father-in-law.

After eating dinner at the Cracker Barrel in Greensboro, Jason recounted, he drove to the Hampton Inn in Hillsville. He parked his Explorer at the side of the hotel, gathered his luggage, and went to the front desk to check in. He then took the elevator to the fourth floor and used his keycard to enter his room. After getting into the room, he called Michelle to say "good night" and, after concluding that call, spoke with Money, he acknowledged.

When that conversation ended, Jason testified, he wanted to review the electronic medical records software he planned to demonstrate the next day because he was nervous about his first solo sales call for ChartOne. He then realized he had left his laptop charging cord in his Explorer. Before heading downstairs and out to the parking lot, he told jurors, he pulled the hotel room door to the point just before it locked "to be cognizant of neighbors, 'cause I've been woken up before plenty of times." He left his keycard in his room, he said.

He then walked down the hallway, he testified, descended down four flights of steps, and headed toward the side exit door. Without his keycard, however, he realized there would be no way to get back in if he allowed the door to close. While holding the door open, he told jurors, he noticed some shrubbery nearby he was able to grab.

He recounted breaking off a twig and placing it between the door and the jamb to keep it cracked open. He then retrieved the charger from his Explorer, went back inside through the cracked-open door, and went upstairs to his room.

Just before midnight, the defendant testified, he decided to smoke a cigar, which was also outside in his Explorer. But he also wanted to see if he could get a *USA Today* newspaper to review sports schedules and standings. Because the front desk was on the other side of the hotel, Jason explained, he took a different stairwell down to the first floor. He walked up to the front desk and asked the attendant if he had a newspaper Jason could borrow. The attendant went back into his office and came back out with that day's newspaper.

Jason told the jury that he was carrying a bottle of water—as the surveillance video revealed—because his mouth tended to get dry when he smoked cigars. He left the hotel through the same exit door he had used earlier, he testified, and, once again, propped the door open with a twig.

He then went outside to the parking lot and grabbed a cigar out of his SUV. Because it was so windy, he recounted, he lit the entire book of matches to get a big enough flame to light the cigar. The windy conditions made it impossible to look at the newspaper while he was smoking. After finishing the cigar, he said, he went back inside through the exit door he had propped open.

Once again, Jason explained, he had left his room door

unlocked, which allowed him to get back in without using his keycard. He then brushed his teeth, set the alarm clock for either 6:15 or 6:30 a.m., and went to sleep. He told the jury he remained in his room until leaving the next morning for the final time, eating breakfast in the hotel lobby before driving off for his business meeting.

Jason emphatically denied he was the man Gracie Dahms saw pumping gas at the Four Brothers gas station that morning. Unlike the man she described as being about her height—five feet tall—Jason told the jury he was six foot one. At the time Dahms saw that man, he insisted, "I was in my hotel room."

Collins asked his client to explain why the SBI computer forensics examiner had found searches for "knockout blow" and "anatomy of a knockout" on his home computer.

Jason said just a few months before Michelle's murder, he had been the first to arrive at a horrible car accident. One of the drivers had been knocked out. He felt helpless. He wanted to know if there was anything else he could have done to administer first aid. He performed those computer searches, he said, to learn the answer.

Jason described the route he traveled to Clintwood, Virginia, and how he got lost on the tricky mountain roads, making him thirty minutes late for his appointment. Because the cell phone coverage was so spotty, he explained, he couldn't even call the hospital to let his contact there know he would be late.

As he was putting his laptop in its bag following the unsuccessful sales meeting, Jason recounted, he realized he had left the eBay printouts at home, rather than taking them with him. He worried they would spoil the surprise he was planning for Michelle if she found them.

He acknowledged he and his wife had a pretty big fight a few days earlier—"the one where she said that I threw the remote, and on top of that, I was getting, you know, and you have heard testimony about, I kind of got scolded from Linda and some people about not doing enough for the anniversary and the anniversary meal didn't go right, so I really was wanting to kind of make up for a lot in a big way, and I really wanted it to be a surprise. A surprise to Michelle means so much more than anything."

Collins then asked Jason about the anniversary card postmarked from Orlando. "Were you visiting Michelle Money at the time?"

"Yes, and that's what I went to Orlando for," he confessed.

"Was that part of the reason why you felt so bad about it?" Collins asked.

"Yes, sir. I was—I have a lot of guilt for that," Jason responded, trying his best to convey remorse.

He testified he tried to catch Michelle at the house the morning of November 3 before she went to her doctor's appointment and took Cassidy to her daycare. When she didn't answer, he left a message on the answering machine. He knew she was heading into work after her appointment, so he tried calling her there as well. When she didn't answer that time, he told jurors, he tried her cell phone, thinking she must have been at lunch. But she didn't answer that phone either.

When he arrived at his mother's home in Brevard, Jason recounted, he saw her and Gerald standing in the yard. They were holding each other and walking toward his car. He realized his mom was upset and something was wrong, he told jurors. That's when Gerald told him, "Michelle is dead."

For the first time since taking the witness stand, Jason began to cry, struggling to get the words out. "I just—I just fell. I just—I broke on the inside, I just broke, and I didn't believe it," he told jurors between sobs. "It was—it just didn't feel real, it didn't feel like it was—it didn't feel like it was happening. I just didn't believe it and I didn't understand it."

Though Jason remembered crying inside his mother's home, he confessed to not being able to remember much else from that afternoon. He did recall that when he, Pat, Heather, and Joe stopped at the Applebee's near Meredith's home that night, his mother indicated Ryan Schaad and Josh Dalton were saying he needed to get a lawyer and to not speak with law enforcement until he did.

When he met with his lawyer the following week, Jason testified, he was advised not to talk to the police or even his family and friends "about anything." And he took his lawyer's advice "to the letter."

Collins asked him about the Hush Puppies Orbital shoes he had purchased from the DSW Warehouse. He wore them a lot, Jason testified, both for business and casually. Because of that, he said, they had become worn out. He told the jury he wasn't wearing the Orbitals on November 2. He explained his wife constantly went through their closets to gather things to take to Goodwill—he believed she had donated the shoes before her death.

Next, Collins showed his client the photo of Cassidy's third birthday party Pat had testified about—the one of him standing behind his daughter as his mom was scooping ice cream. Jason confirmed the photo was taken on March 29, 2007, Cassidy's birthday.

Collins asked his client to focus on the shirt he was wearing in the photo. Jason pointed out the thin, white stripe across the chest. Though his lawyer didn't specifically ask Jason if that was the shirt he had been wearing the second time he appeared at the front desk of the Hampton Inn, just before midnight, that is precisely what they were hoping the jury would believe.

The next topic was Michelle's funeral. Jason testified he had picked out the colored daisies that adorned the top of her casket. When he described how he had placed the small piece of paper containing the words to the song, *A Bushel and a Peck,* into Michelle's hand, Jason grabbed his face, sobbing.

"Did you say goodbye to Rylan?" Collins asked him.

Jason nodded his head up and down.

"How did you do that?"

"All I could do was just put my hand on her stomach," he responded, and then broke down, sobbing uncontrollably.

When he was finally able to regain his composure, the former salesman explained that Cassidy wasn't at the funeral because he didn't want her around all of the media. "It was terrible, you know, hiding in the bushes, and they were relentless … I wanted her away from that, I wanted her away from all of it." That is why he had Heather and Joe take her back to Brevard, he testified.

His lawyer then shifted gears to Jason's interactions with

his sister-in-law and mother-in-law in the months following the murder, and their visits with Cassidy. The defendant explained that, initially, he did permit them to visit with his daughter. That changed, however, when Linda "had gotten really, really loud and really dramatic" in front of Cassidy. At that point, after talking with his mother, he decided, "I didn't want Cassidy around that." So he cut off contact between Cassidy and her aunt and grandmother.

After receiving a letter from their lawyer and retaining Alice Stubbs to represent him, Jason testified, he concluded he couldn't afford a full-blown custody fight. He had lost two jobs due to all of the media coverage surrounding Michelle's murder. He agreed to give up custody of Cassidy, he explained, because he simply didn't have the resources to fight. Plus, he knew custody is always subject to change. But, "it still was very hard," Jason said, trying to convey to the jury his anguish over that difficult situation.

Collins then began his final series of questions. "How has your life been impacted by the death of your wife?"

"I've lost everything," Jason answered. "I've lost family, friends, jobs. I've lost everything."

"Jason, have you ever intentionally, physically harmed somebody?"

"No, sir."

"Do you have a memory of the last time you spoke to Michelle?"

"It would be wonderful for me to say I remember what we talked about that night on the phone," he responded, "but I know it was a normal 'good night, I made it up here safely,' a normal conversation, and I don't remember."

"Do you know of any reason why someone would want to kill your wife?" Collins asked.

"No, sir."

"The State contended in their opening argument that you went there to strangle her. Is that true?"

"No, sir."

"And that you hit her on the head thirty times. Did you do that?"

"No, sir."

"Were you there when it happened?"

"*No, sir,*" Jason replied emphatically.

"Do you know who did it?" Collins asked.

"No, sir."

"Did you have anything to do with killing her?"

"No, sir."

"That's all the questions I have," Collins said, passing the witness to the prosecutors for cross-examination.

For three solid hours, the jury—indeed, the entire courtroom—was mesmerized by Jason's testimony. It was compelling. He seemed genuine and sincere—heartfelt even—as well as contrite and humble in admitting to his failings. His denial of any involvement in Michelle's murder was direct and forceful. Jason had clearly moved the needle in the direction of acquittal.

Collins completed his questioning at 12:52 p.m. "At least we've got a lunch break," Holt thought to herself. She would have all of an hour to prepare the most important cross-examination of her career. On an empty stomach, no less.

It was apparent from the outset of her cross-examination, however, that she didn't have adequate time to prepare. The Assistant DA meandered from topic to topic, with no obvious organization, long pauses separating one subject from the next. Her questioning was slow and devoid of rhythm. She confronted Jason with seemingly trivial points and details. At times, it was hard to understand where she was going.

Holt began her questioning by focusing on Jason's unfaithfulness to Michelle—*before* they were married. She asked him about a trip they had taken to Puerto Rico and the questions Michelle had for him after they returned.

"Michelle had found a pair of panties in your suitcase, isn't that right?" the Assistant DA asked.

"No, ma'am, that's not right," the defendant responded.

"You don't recall her getting upset about finding a pair of panties and asking you about where they had come from?"

"Yes, ma'am."

"And what you told her was that the maid had probably

put them in your suitcase in Puerto Rico. Isn't that right?"

"No, ma'am, that's not right."

"You had a sexual relationship with Julie Tyndall during the time you were supposedly dating Michelle Fisher, who later became your wife. Isn't that correct?"

"Yes, ma'am, that is correct."

The prosecutor asked whether he and Michelle had disputes over financial matters and about his online gambling. He agreed they did. She re-plowed with Jason his friction with his mother-in-law, which he readily admitted—again. For the second time, he told the jury he was adamantly opposed to Linda moving into his home, and wanted to minimize the time she spent with his family over the 2006 holidays. Yet Jason adamantly denied telling Michelle, after he learned she was pregnant with Cassidy, that if she didn't abort the baby, he would hold it against her and the baby for the rest of their lives.

Finally, Holt began focusing on the events of November 2 and 3, suggesting that Jason had fabricated his testimony about leaving the hotel to smoke a cigar. "Isn't it true, Mr. Young, that you, on occasion, would take a strong stand against smoking and argue with people about smoking, that that was one of the things that you did not like?"

"Cigarette smoking I think is very bad," Jason said. But he didn't feel the same way about cigars, which he had been smoking since working for Black & Decker before he and Michelle met, though he agreed he didn't smoke them often.

Jason's testimony about smoking a cigar in the Hampton Inn parking lot highlighted an important clue the prosecution team had missed during Klinkosum's opening statement. There was only one witness in the entire world who could have established he had smoked a cigar at the hotel: Jason Young. Thus, Klink's reference—weeks earlier—to his client smoking a cigar telegraphed that Jason would testify in his own defense. Having failed to pick up on that significant clue, it was Jason who was now getting the better of Holt during his cross-examination, rather than the other way around.

The defendant also denied having a four-hour counseling

session with Meredith the Friday before the murder. He testified he couldn't imagine what Cassidy would have been doing that length of time and that, to the best of his recollection, such a lengthy session with Meredith never occurred.

Holt then shifted her focus to Genevieve Cargol, asking Jason whether he had been violent with her prior to the incident in Texas. He denied he was, though admitted striking the windshield of her car hard enough that it had to be replaced. He denied ever punching a hole in the wall of his apartment in Charlotte in reaction to Cargol finding and reading a letter Carol Anne Sowerby had written him. But he did admit it made him mad she had read that letter.

The prosecutor next focused on Jason's argument with his wife about how she was getting to Ryan's and Shelly's wedding, as well as their belated anniversary dinner. Michelle was upset the night of their anniversary dinner, the former salesman testified, because he was on the phone with a co-worker during the entire car ride to Bella Monica, not because of their travel plans to Winston-Salem.

Shifting gears again, Holt asked, "You made it well-known, you told friends, didn't you, that you didn't have enough sex in your marriage?"

Jason admitted he told friends, family members, his mother, and even co-workers he didn't have enough sex in his marriage. "Intimacy was a problem," he agreed.

"In fact, you told your wife that maybe she should let you have a girl on the side, didn't you?" she asked.

"I think I said that in jest one time, being angry and saying it in a sarcastic way. Yes, ma'am."

"Mr. Young, you have told this jury that you loved your wife. Did you love your wife when you were having an affair with Michelle Money?"

"Yes, ma'am."

"Did you love your wife when you were having sex with Carol Anne Sowerby in her home on the couch with your daughter upstairs?"

"I didn't have sex with Carol Anne in *her* home."

"How about in your wife's home?" Holt asked, correcting

her mistake.

"Yes, ma'am. I did love my wife."

"Did you love your wife when you wrote Genevieve Cargol an email and told her that she was the love of your life?"

"Yes, ma'am. I did."

Jason agreed he was not "working on" his marriage when he was having sex with Sowerby two weeks before Michelle was murdered. "That was not the way to work on a marriage," he admitted, seemingly contrite. "That was very detrimental." He conceded the email he sent to Cargol that September was also not "working on" his marriage.

The Assistant DA asked whether Jason was "working on" his marriage when he communicated with Money more than 400 times in the month before the murder. He acknowledged he and Money "confided a lot in each other and we talked about my issues with my wife and she talked about her issues with her husband and we both tried to kind of help each other in regards to things we could do to make the other person more loving towards us."

"So is the answer, 'yes,' when you had an affair with Michelle Money, that you were working on your marriage?" Holt asked, this time unable to control her scorn and derision.

"No, ma'am," Jason responded with apparent regret. "Having the sexual intercourse and having the intimacy was very detrimental to that." He also admitted telling Josh Dalton—"in jest"—he was hoping to get Money pregnant, "but I absolutely did not mean that."

"Mr. Young, you've told this jury that you love your daughter Cassidy. Is that right?" Holt asked.

"Yes, ma'am."

"And this is the same daughter that, rather than answer any questions, you signed over custody to Meredith Fisher?"

"Yes, ma'am, that is exactly what happened. I had to sign over custody. I couldn't financially fight that battle," Jason reiterated.

Holt asked Jason whether, as part of the custody case, he would have been required to sit for a deposition and to answer questions. "Isn't that right?"

"Yes, ma'am. From what I understand."

"Your attorney told you that?"

"Yes, ma'am."

"But instead of doing that, you signed over custody of your child. Is that right?"

"Yes, ma'am. I did sign over custody of my child," Jason agreed.

"You understood that you were giving up physical custody in exchange for not having to sit for a deposition, not having to answer questions, and not having to undergo a psychological evaluation."

"That was all part of the agreement. Yes, ma'am."

After a lengthy pause, Holt pivoted to Jason's refusal to cooperate with law enforcement. He agreed he decided on November 3 not to talk to the police, not to provide any information about his wife, his home, or even to listen to what they had to say. He also acknowledged that he decided not to talk to his friends or his family, testifying, "I followed my legal counsel's advice to the tee."

The Assistant DA asked Jason to describe what he said to his attorney when he finally met with him. Collins objected on the basis of the attorney-client privilege. Judge Stephens overruled his objection, likely because the defendant had waived the privilege by testifying that he was not speaking with the police, or his friends or family, because that is what his attorney told him to do.

Forced to answer, Jason responded, "I told the attorney what I'm telling the people here today. I told the attorney about my experience riding up to the house and the car being seized. I told the attorney about where I was, that I was away on a business trip. I told my attorney that I was alone and by myself. I told my attorney that my wife was pregnant. I told my attorney that I was having an affair. I told my attorney a lot, and my attorney said, 'I don't think you should talk to law enforcement.'"

"So you continued to follow the advice to keep your mouth shut, to not say anything, even after you were arrested?" Holt asked.

Collins again lodged an objection, which Judge Stephens promptly overruled.

"Yes, ma'am," Jason responded.

"You never yourself, or anyone acting on your behalf, contacted investigators to find out about the investigation into your wife's murder, did you?"

"I didn't," Jason conceded.

"Did you ask anyone to contact law enforcement to find out what was going on?"

"I didn't talk about it with anyone. No, ma'am."

Holt then paused and began ruffling through her notes. After about four minutes—which seemed more like an hour—she looked up at Judge Stephens, sheepishly, and said, "That's all I have. Thank you."

Her cross-examination lasted all of 52 minutes. During that time, she didn't ask Jason a single question about the murder or murder scene. She didn't press Jason on his story about why he used his Hampton Inn keycard only a single time, yet admitted to leaving his room at least twice. Or what happened to the shirt he was wearing when he appeared at the hotel's front desk just before midnight. Or his account of smoking a cigar in the parking lot—with no coat or gloves—in the bone-chilling cold and wind. The defense team had presented her a golden opportunity to forcefully attack Jason on those subjects. Yet, for whatever reason, she didn't seize it.

In view of the brutality of the murder, most prosecutors would have subjected Jason to an aggressive, confrontational cross-examination. For instance, Holt could have asked Jason, "You bludgeoned your wife to death by repeatedly striking her in the head with a blunt object, didn't you? You hit her forcefully enough to expose her skull and jawbone, knock out her teeth, and cause her blood to splatter all over the walls, didn't you?"

Jason didn't have to answer those questions and have the jury scrutinize his facial expressions, demeanor, and body language while doing so. Nor was he forced to look at the gruesome photos of his wife's disfigured and bloody face or of her dead body lying amidst pools of blood and Cassidy's bloody footprints. The jury would never see his reaction to those photos—because he was never confronted with them.

He also wasn't asked whether it had been a mere coincidence that, on the very night his wife was murdered, the surveillance camera at the Hampton Inn was tampered with—not once, but twice. He wasn't forced to deny he printed out the eBay auction items, and left them on the printer, to have a reason to send Meredith to the house to find Michelle's body and Cassidy. Or to deny that he called Michelle three times on November 3 to make it appear he didn't know she was dead. Or that he knew full well before his stepfather told him that Michelle was dead—*because he had killed her.*

Holt also neglected to confront the defendant with the July 2006 email in which he angrily lashed out at Michelle: *I could kill u for not letting me finish the yard this morning.* Or the lengthy email he wrote to Cargol 52 days before the murder professing his love for her. Or his email exchange with Money just six days before the murder in which he professed: *i feel lucky just to know you, much less love you, but i do.*

Jason wasn't even asked about the $2 million life insurance policy on which he was the sole beneficiary. Or the double-indemnity provision that would have led to him collecting a payout of $4 million. Holt didn't ask what efforts he had made in the years since the murder to find the "real killer." The prosecution team had been caught so off guard that these questions never made it into the outline they had hurriedly prepared during the lunch hour. Jason therefore didn't need to address any of these difficult subjects. He was basically given a free pass.

Collins and Klinkosum couldn't have been more pleased. Considering the enormous risk they had taken by calling Jason as a witness, he had left the witness stand virtually unscathed. Hardly anything Holt had gotten him to admit was important and most of it merely rehashed answers he had already provided in response to Collins' questions. More importantly, her questions didn't rattle him or make him appear defensive or combative. He was polite and respectful from beginning to end, with appropriate body language and emotions. Even likable, they believed.

Their gambit had paid off. Given the absence of forensic evidence linking Jason to the crime scene and his strong performance as a witness, acquittal now seemed to be a very legitimate possibility. They just needed to close the deal with a strong closing argument.

# 17

## CLOSING ARGUMENTS

In a criminal case, if the defense presents any evidence at all, the State gets the last word. And if the prosecutors desire, they can force defense counsel to make their closing argument first, without the benefit of hearing a single word of the State's argument. That way, they can listen carefully to the defense team's arguments and respond to each and every point they make.

In contrast, the defendant's attorneys are forced to guess what the prosecutors will argue and attempt to respond based on their guesses.

That is precisely how the closing arguments proceeded on June 23, 2011, before a packed courtroom at the Wake County Courthouse. At Judge Stephens' prompting, Mike Klinkosum rose and walked toward the jury, a discernible spring in his step. He placed his notes on the lectern, looked up, and focused the jurors on their task.

"Any time another human is killed, is murdered," he began, "it is a natural human reaction to want to punish, to want to blame. That's a natural human reaction. But in our society, we say that is not done unless and until the government proves beyond a reasonable doubt that the person they accuse of murder actually committed that murder. We do not convict, we do not punish, except by proof beyond a reasonable doubt."

He framed the remainder of his argument around the

forensic evidence—"circumstantial evidence," as he called it—
that "shows that Jason Young did not kill his wife, could not
have killed his wife, and that this case is not solved." Klink
discussed seven such circumstances, labeling the first, "the
fight."

"All of the evidence in this case in that crime scene, in that
bedroom, indicates there was a fight," he argued. "Ladies and
gentlemen, there was hair pulled out, there was blood all over
the walls almost up to the ceiling, papers strewn everywhere,
pillows strewn on the floor—there was a fight."

He focused on the scratch marks on Michelle's neck "from
where she was trying to pry her attacker's hands off of her
throat." But four days later, when "Jason Young was made to
strip naked before the CCBI," he reminded jurors, "there was
not a mark on Mr. Young." Logically, he explained, if Jason
had been Michelle's attacker, "you would have seen scratches
on his neck, at least on his arms, at the least on his hands where
she was trying to pry hands away from her neck."

But there were no marks on his body—anywhere.

Klinkosum labeled the second circumstance "the blood."
He pointed to the crime scene photos. "There was blood all
over one side of that bedroom. It had soaked into the carpet. It
had pooled between the wall and the molding at the bottom of
the floor. It was all over the walls."

He reminded the jury that Jason's Ford Explorer had been
seized the minute Jason got back to Raleigh, without even
allowing his family to remove their luggage. "They not only
looked for blood in his car, ladies and gentlemen, ... they
scoured that vehicle, the outside of it and the inside of it for
blood, and didn't find one drop of blood anywhere in that
Ford Explorer. Not one drop." How could Jason have "killed
his wife in one of the bloodiest ways possible," gotten back into
his Explorer, and driven all the way back to Virginia without a
single drop of blood winding up in his vehicle? Jason's attorney
asked.

The blood evidence related to Cassidy, he argued, pointed
away from his client, not toward him. "You saw her bathroom.
You saw how much blood was in that bathroom, how she

tracked it in on her feet, how she smeared it on the walls, how she had smeared it behind the bathroom door." That had to mean someone had placed her in the bathroom and shut the door. But when Meredith found her, Klink reminded jurors, she was "shockingly clean." Someone had to have cleaned her up. But Jason wouldn't have had the time to do so, he insisted.

The defense lawyer then transitioned to the third circumstance: "no fiber transfer." He noted investigators had taken carpet samples from the Hampton Inn and had scoured the Birchleaf Drive home for any similar fibers. Not a single one had been found. "The State wants you to believe that Mr. Young committed this crime, killed his wife and got out without any blood on him and somehow managed to not track any fibers from the hotel room into that house. Not possible, ladies and gentlemen," he argued. "It's not possible because Jason Young did not murder his wife and this case is not solved."

The fourth circumstance was DNA. Two cigarette butts had been found, which contained DNA traced to two unknown males. Klinkosum argued two unknown males must have been in the house. In addition, a hair was found on the wedding photo whose DNA didn't match Jason, Michelle, or anyone connected to the case. That hair, Klink reminded the jury, contained an antigen root—meaning it had been forcibly removed—which suggested it had been pulled out during the attacker's fight with Michelle.

The DNA on the jewelry box was particularly noteworthy, he argued, because it was swabbed before the house was ever released. The State considered those swabs so important, they sent them not to the SBI lab, but to LabCorp, which found a mixture of DNA belonging to more than one individual. "And the important thing, ladies and gentlemen," Klinkosum reminded them, "is that DNA didn't match Michelle Young and it doesn't match Jason Young."

He then transitioned to the fifth circumstance: fingerprints. Fingerprints were found, he told jurors, which didn't match Jason, Michelle, or anyone else who was known to have been in the house. "That means there were some strangers in that house at some point, ladies and gentlemen, and those prints were collected before this house was released."

Most importantly, the medicine cup that rested on top of the Tylenol bottle in Cassidy's room contained a fingerprint that didn't match anyone connected with the family. "Think about this, ladies and gentlemen," Klink continued. "If the State is right and someone tried to drug Cassidy Young to make her fall asleep and used the Tylenol and they mixed it with the Pancof or something else ... they had to take the medicine cup off the Tylenol bottle." And that person left behind a fingerprint that did not match Jason's—because he didn't kill his wife and this case is not solved."

The sixth circumstance involved Jason's phone calls the evening before the murder. During his drive to Virginia on November 2, Klinkosum acknowledged, his client was "burning up the cell phone, talking to Michelle Money." He was talking to her "about everything under the sun." He was talking to his mom about picking up some furniture. "Does that sound like a man who's got a plan and who is trying to pull off a murder and get away with it?" he asked rhetorically.

When he saw that Demetrius Barrett had left him a message, Klink continued, Jason called him back and talked about a home warranty on a heat pump, of all things. They talked about a football game on TV Jason was watching. "Does that sound like a man who is actively plotting to kill someone and try and get away with it? If that's the case, ladies and gentlemen, he would have been in deep thought planning this out. He wouldn't have called Demetrius back or he would have called him back and said, 'Look, I've got a lot on my mind. I can't talk to you right now. We'll talk later. Bye,' and would have hung up."

The defense attorney then turned to the seventh and final circumstance: "The Hampton Inn itself."

"The State wants you to believe that Jason Young somehow climbed up and messed with the camera, disabled the camera on the western end of the hotel. But what do we know about that?" Once again, Klinkosum reminded jurors, the fingerprints pointed to someone else—the prints on the camera didn't match Jason. "Why? Because he didn't jump up there to disable it." He noted how observant investigators were to notice the water pipe above the camera and swab it for DNA. Once again, no match—the DNA was from an unknown male.

But even assuming it was Jason who pushed the camera up toward the ceiling, he argued, "Why in the world, if he did that, why, if he figured out that camera was the one he needed to take out so he could get away with the murder of his wife, did he go back to the front desk at midnight, at 11:59, in full view of the camera at the front desk" without disguising himself or covering his face or head?

The circumstantial and physical evidence, Klinkosum insisted, didn't add up. Rather, the prosecution was seeking a conviction because of his client's behavior toward Michelle. "I told you in opening and I say to you again," he told jurors, "he has acted like an immature jerk. And I say that to you, ladies and gentlemen, because I can't think of a stronger word that is acceptable to say in a court of law." But that was not a basis to convict his client of murder, Jason's lawyer insisted.

"They have spent three weeks bringing in all this information about his bad behavior, about how he and Michelle fought, about how he was cheating on her, about things he's doing with wedding rings. But they haven't presented one piece of concrete evidence, either direct or circumstantial, that Jason Young killed Michelle. Not one."

He then pivoted to Gracie Dahms's testimony. "She was only shown one photograph. In six or seven interviews, they only showed her one photograph and they never bothered to test her memory by giving her a photo lineup," Klink protested. "They never bothered to do that even though she could not describe to them his face or his height or his weight or any detail of what he was wearing."

And just a few weeks before the trial, at a pre-trial hearing, when asked to describe the person who threw money at her early that morning, "she said, 'Well, he was a little bit taller than me and had a little bit of hair.'" "Ladies and gentlemen," Klinkosum reminded jurors, "she's five feet tall. A little bit taller is five one, five two. Jason Young is six feet one inches tall

… The person she saw is a *short, bald guy,* not someone who's six feet one inches tall and has a thick head of hair."

Finishing his argument, Jason's attorney implored the jury to look at the circumstantial evidence. "Please look at it. *Look at it hard.* Because when you look at the seven circumstances in this case, when you look at the physical evidence, ladies and gentlemen, Jason Young did not murder his wife and his unborn child and this case is not solved, ladies and gentlemen. And the only just verdict in this case is to find him not guilty."

With that, Klinkosum took his seat at the defense counsel table.

Collins then rose to deliver the final closing on Jason's behalf. He began by introducing the jury to the concept of confirmation bias, musing, "Sometimes you find what you're looking for." It was completely understandable, he said, that the police began their investigation thinking Jason was the attacker.

"They should have been suspicious of him," Collins acknowledged. "He's the husband. He's not there. He won't talk. You always suspect the husband. Then Keith Hicks, the young man at the Hampton Inn, finds a rock in the door and then the camera is moved and Keith Hicks thinks that's important and he reports that to the police. And then they find out that he's having an affair. Of course they suspect him. Nobody blames the police for suspecting him."

Collins made clear he wasn't suggesting there was a "rush to judgment"—borrowing the phrase from the O.J. Simpson case—recognizing the investigation lasted three years. "But I think it is fair to say," he continued, "that they jumped to some conclusions. And they went looking for things. But then the physical evidence didn't make sense, as Mr. Klinkosum has very aptly told you." That was true despite "all of the resources that the State of North Carolina has poured into the investigation of this case," including the FBI, SBI, Medical Examiner's office, DNA experts, blood experts, a fiber expert, shoeprint experts, a computer expert, and hundreds of interviews.

"They tried to solve this case for three years and you have seen the totality of what they have found. That's because you can't find evidence of guilt when your suspect is not guilty, no matter how hard you try."

It was notable, Collins suggested, that his client's arrest wasn't triggered by any particular finding, conclusion, or discovery. "It just came after a time. And it looks like they just gave up and decided to arrest him because they had found all they could find."

The Public Defender then turned to a litany of evidence the prosecution wanted the jury to find significant even though "if you didn't know that somebody had been murdered," he told jurors, it would all be "completely innocuous." Falling into that category were Jason's internet searches for head traumas and knockouts. "If his plan was to strangle her, what difference does that make?" he asked incredulously. Further, did Jason really need to research "head trauma," he asked rhetorically, to know that beating someone in the head with something heavy thirty times is going to kill them?

The garden hose by the back walkway was equally unimportant, Collins argued, even though there was a little bit of water trickling out the end. So was Jason's search for a Coach purse via eBay auctions that were about to close. Even more insignificant was the discovery "that some of his DNA was in his own house and his fingerprints were in his own house."

"We've learned that … he didn't want his mother-in-law to live with him. That he and his wife argued a lot and that he made 28 phone calls to his mother on November 3. None of those things have any significance in and of themselves," he insisted.

"And I'm arguing to you," Collins continued, "that the State is stringing together a bunch of innocuous events and trying to tell you that they mean something and that we somehow have convenient excuses for them. That's what you do when you don't have physical evidence. It's called hindsight, and it's not 20/20 in this case."

He suggested what the prosecutors had done was akin to taking video footage of Michael Jordan and stringing together his worst moments on the basketball court. "What if you put together a highlight reel of every time Michael Jordan missed a shot? Or every time he dribbled the basketball off his foot, or missed a pass, or fell out of bounds, or fouled somebody, and that's all you showed somebody who has never met Michael Jordan. You'd think he was a terrible basketball player, 'cause you hadn't seen the whole picture."

Michael Jordan also became famous for his shoes, and, perhaps for that reason, Collins next transitioned to the shoe evidence. He suggested that Agent Morrow was actually a great witness. "You have to give her credit for her honesty because she admitted to you that the quality of the footwear impressions that she found that have anything to do with the Hush Puppy type shoe were poor."

He noted she had conceded the print could have been made by a Sealy, a Belleville, an Orbital, or "none of the above." Its size could have been 11, 12, or 13.

"She just doesn't know and admitted, 'I was not able to make a match.' As she said ten times in her report, Collins reminded jurors, "Due to the limited detail, a more conclusive comparison could not be made. Limited detail, according to her, means no match. No match, I argue to you, is no evidence."

The defense lawyer then pivoted to his client's decision not to cooperate with the police or talk with anyone. He argued Michelle's death "broke him on the inside." And when a traumatic event like that happens, he suggested, you rely on friends and family for guidance. Ryan Schaad, one of Jason's best friends, told him the police were pointing a finger at him and that he needed to get a lawyer. "And then the lawyer said, 'Don't talk to anybody,' and that's what he did. And that's all that evidence means."

Turning to the confounding enigma of Cassidy's appearance the afternoon of November 3, Collins told the jury it was an "unanswered question that I don't guess we'll ever have the answer to."

She was two years old and "yet she was shockingly clean. She wasn't wearing a diaper. No diaper for nine and a half hours and yet she did not have urine on her, she didn't have any fecal matter on her, there was no urine in the bed, there was no fecal matter in the bed."

There "was blood all over that child at some point and yet she's shockingly clean."

"How long must it have taken for someone to clean her up," he asked, "and how many times must someone have changed her diaper and taken care of her? And how could that have possibly been Jason Young in the time he had to do that?"

Collins connected Cassidy's shockingly clean appearance to the different vehicles spotted at the house that morning. One between 3:00 and 4:00 a.m. Another between 5:00 and 5:30 a.m. And a third as late as 7:30 a.m., which was the account of Fay Hinsley, whose testimony was submitted to the jury through a written stipulation.

Did the presence of those vehicles explain how Cassidy was cleaned up? Collins reminded the jury the last two vehicles clearly had nothing to do with Jason, who was in or near Wytheville, Virginia at 7:40 a.m. that morning.

He then focused on the other enigma—Mr. Garrison. "The dog could have come and gone at will and yet that dog was clean as a whistle, and even more importantly, there's no sign inside that house anywhere that a dog was in any blood … How can that be? Think about how long it would take a person to clean a dog up who had all that blood. Who took care of Mr. Garrison?" he pondered. "What happened to Mr. Garrison? How can that be? Think about that circumstance."

Collins then guessed the State would argue his client had help in pulling off the murder. "I argue to you that that borders on the ridiculous based on the evidence that you've heard, based on their forecast of the evidence about how he had this plan and he went in there and strangled her and then beat her to death."

There was all kinds of evidence, he insisted, that Jason was alone—at the Handy Hugo, the Cracker Barrel, and the Hampton Inn. There were no unexplained phone calls, emails, or texts. Was he acting in concert with his own mother—or with Meredith? Collins asked facetiously.

He then pulled up a PowerPoint presentation on a TV monitor to walk the jury through Jason's travels on November

2 and 3 and his use of gas.

"I've thought about this for a long time," Collins said.

Pointing to the screen, he traced Jason's travels from the Handy Hugo in Raleigh, to the Cracker Barrel in Greensboro, and to the Hampton Inn in Hillsville and calculated the mileage.

"Gets up to the Hampton Inn, he heads to Clintwood, he gets turned around a little bit, and then he gets to Clintwood. The actual distance between the Hampton Inn and Clintwood is 145 miles. I'm guessing—estimating—that it was twenty miles that he got lost." Following his meeting he stops in Duffield and purchases 19.452 gallons of gas. "So in that trip, correct my math if I'm wrong, but I think that's right: 380.3 miles on 19.452 gallons of gas. That's 19.55 miles per gallon."

He then traced his client's travels on his second tank of gas—to the Transylvania Regional Hospital, his mother's house, and then to Burlington, where his brother-in-law Joe purchased 18.441 gallons of gas after traveling 359.8 miles. The gas mileage on that tank of gas—amazingly—was 19.54, almost identical to his first tank. Collins acknowledged this was Jason's version of events, but suggested the exact match had to make his version of events correct.

He then pulled up slides tracking the prosecution's theory about Jason's gas usage. "We start at Handy Hugo's with a full tank of gas. We go to the Cracker Barrel. We go to the Hampton Inn ... We go back to the house ... and then we head back to the Hampton Inn to try to cover ourselves with this alibi and we get to Four Brothers."

He calculated 458.7 miles on that first tank of gas. "That's 20.386 miles to the gallon, and that doesn't seem like a whole lot more than 19 and a half until you do this math: he would have run out of gas 18.8 miles before he got there and been sitting on the side of the road. Okay?"

Collins calculated that under the State's theory, Jason would have purchased 6.944 gallons of gas at the Four Brothers gas station, based on a $15 purchase at the price that day of $2.16 per gallon. From that point, Jason would have traveled another 260.6 miles until he filled up again in Duffield "on less than seven gallons of gas. That's 37.53 miles a gallon. That's not what happened. There's *no way* that that happened," he argued.

Content he had disproven the State's theory about Jason's travels, Collins put the PowerPoint aside and, one by one, addressed arguments he expected the prosecutors to make.

"You're likely to hear how beautiful and how smart and how wonderful, caring, and great a mother Michelle Young was and we agree with that—all of that. You may hear that she was a shining light that's been brutally extinguished. That's true. You may hear how tragic and how sad all of this is and that's true." He agreed, "This case is awful. It's sad and it's awful and that doesn't have anything to do with who killed her."

He predicted the prosecution team would ask what happened to the Hush Puppies Orbitals. "To that I say to you, where's the blood in the Ford Explorer?" And if they were to raise the missing shirt from the Hampton Inn, Collins continued, "To that I say to you, where's the blood on the blue jeans? You may hear about Gracie Dahms Bailey. To that I say to you, Cindy Beaver. Cindy Beaver, the neighbor who saw two people leaving the Youngs' home at 5:30 that morning and who was relentlessly challenged for her statement."

"You may hear, 'Use your common sense,'" he told jurors. "I invite you to use your common sense. I practically *beg you* to use your common sense. But that doesn't mean fill in the gaps. That doesn't mean, 'Help us with the evidence that we don't have.' That's not like winking at you and saying, 'Well, you know, who else could have done it? Use your common sense.' That's not what 'use your common sense' means."

Nearing the end, the Public Defender's passion reached a crescendo: "You may hear that these lawyers represent the People of the State of North Carolina. They really represent the Government of the State of North Carolina. You are the People of the State of North Carolina. As taxpayers, you pay for this courthouse. You pay for the chair you're sitting in. You don't owe your government anything other than to follow the law, which you have sworn to do."

Collins recognized jurors might have "unanswered questions. You might not be convinced that he's innocent." For that reason, he drilled home the State's burden of proof, noting they could find Jason guilty only if they were "fully satisfied" and "entirely convinced" of his guilt. "That's following the law, as all of you promised that you would do. It's your duty. It's that law that will let you come back in here and render your verdict with your head held high, not owing any person an apology. You can do that proudly and with confidence that you have done your duty and done it right, and no one will fault you."

With that, he paused, and with a solemn expression, uttered the final words the jury would hear from the defense, "We will never know what happened at 5108 Birchleaf Drive that night. We're just never going to know. This case is not solved. The evidence is not clear. Do your duty and find Jason Young not guilty. Thank you."

Collins sat down. Together he and Klinkosum had covered a lot of ground, raising doubt after doubt about the State's evidence. They had done their level best to push the needle toward acquittal. The prosecutors had their work cut out for them if they were to convince all twelve jurors that there was no reasonable doubt—that Jason was the one who had killed his beautiful wife.

David Saacks went first, beginning his argument by displaying an enlarged photo of Michelle—with her radiant smile—on the TV monitor.

"Michelle is no longer with us," he said, in a somber tone. "She can't tell us anymore what happened to her on that night. She was taken from us. She was taken from us way too soon in a truly brutal and vicious way. There will be no football games for Michelle Young. There will be no McBroads' trips. There will be no more megawatt smile from this beautiful young lady."

He argued the case was "exponentially worse" because Cassidy was in the house, found her mother in a pool of blood, and walked through her blood. He tugged on jurors' heart strings when he described Cassidy laying her baby doll next to her mom to comfort her. And even more, when he reminded them Michelle was five months pregnant with Rylan.

Saacks focused next on the autopsy results. "Dr. Clark told you it had to be at least, at least thirty different, distinct blows. *Thirty* ... And that there had to be a weapon used, the skull fractures, back and the side—that couldn't be caused except for a weapon being used. You saw when they shaved her head, the nature of a lot of those wounds, and some of them cutting down all the way to the skull."

To him, Michelle's jaw fracture was "absolutely amazing"— she had been struck with such force the bone had come through her skin, making it appear as if she had been stabbed from the bottom of her face. "There was a weapon used and she was beaten mercilessly," the prosecutor asserted.

The brutality of the crime, the Assistant DA contended, made clear that it wasn't a robbery. "This crime speaks of a personal and passionate nature." It was "clear overkill" by an assailant who wanted Michelle dead. "What intruder," he asked rhetorically, "would come in and continue and continue and continue to beat on her when she's down on the floor by that closet?" What intruder, he pondered, would leave a witness in the house completely unharmed? This "was a targeted killing. This was a planned and intentional murder. Whoever did this, just from seeing Michelle in that room, you know wanted Michelle dead."

Saacks then addressed each of the key points Klinkosum and Collins had made. The blood evidence actually pointed to Jason's guilt, he argued. He reminded the jury how the blood spatter in the bedroom established that Jason's closet door was closed during the attack, but had to have been opened afterward.

"What killer would have a reason to go into that closet?" he asked. The answer was obvious: Jason. The defendant, he posited, would have had blood all over his clothing following the murder and therefore needed to get into his closet to change into clean clothes. An intruder, on the other hand, wouldn't have needed to get into Jason's closet.

The prosecutor turned Collins' focus on Mr. Garrison on its

head, asking, "What unknown intruder would come into the house and do all this with a big Labrador just sitting there?" The killer must have known the dog personally, he argued, so that it "would not go crazy, would not be barking, would not be trying to protect Michelle, would go into a room when asked or ordered to, would not be walking around in this pool of blood and making tracks all over the place." The killer, he insisted, had to be someone Mr. G knew and trusted.

Saacks then pivoted to the absence of blood in Jason's Explorer, suggesting he had gotten clean clothes from his closet. He reminded jurors Michelle's blood was found on the kitchen doorknob and that garbage bags were conveniently located in the garage on the other side of that door.

He pointed to the running garden hose found by the back deck. Saacks theorized Jason had washed his hands, shoes, and perhaps even Cassidy's feet with the garden hose, and the blood on the ground would have washed away during the nine plus hours the hose was left running.

He disagreed with Klinkosum's contention Jason's body bore no evidence of a struggle, pointing to the bruise on his left big toe. Because the bruise was at the base of the toenail, it was new, Saacks asserted, and is exactly what would be expected if Jason had been using a weapon to beat Michelle and had inadvertently struck himself on the way down.

The absence of scratches or bruises on Jason's arms and legs, he suggested, was easily explained by his clothing. "The only thing not covered are face and hands, okay?" Since he was using a weapon, rather than his fists, there was no reason for his hands to have been scratched or bruised. And he certainly could have been wearing gloves, Saacks argued. "Yes, there are no marks but the one on the defendant. Does that mean he could not have done it? Absolutely not."

The prosecutor next addressed the enigma of Cassidy's shockingly clean appearance, first noting she was potty trained and knew how to take off her own diaper. He hypothesized the smearing of blood on her bathroom walls likely was from her feet, not her hands. "Nobody's saying she's Spiderman, right. She's laying on her back and just hitting her feet on the wall or playing, messing around. That's what's on the wall. It's not hands," he contended. "It's feet."

Responding to Klinkosum's argument about the lack of carpet fibers from the Hampton Inn at the murder scene, Saacks told the jury, "There's a common saying in the forensic world that says 'absence of evidence is not evidence of absence.'"

Hotel carpet fibers, he asserted, wouldn't have been transferred into the house because hotel rooms are cleaned and vacuumed daily. Fibers would therefore not collect on a guest's shoes. But even if they had, once the guest walks outside, across the parking lot, and into his car, he argued, the chances of the fibers being transferred to another location were actually quite small.

He attempted to explain away the mysterious DNA on the jewelry box, noting LabCorp was provided only two known standards to test against—Jason's and Michelle's. And it found a mixture that didn't belong to either. LabCorp didn't try to determine if the DNA belonged to anyone else. Saacks told jurors they could ignore the DNA on the cigarette butts and hair on the picture frame because not a single witness told them when or where those items were collected. The DNA on the jewelry box could have been from the salesman who sold it, the cigarettes from a repairman, and the hair from a party-goer, he argued.

Turning to evidence from the Hampton Inn, the Assistant DA speculated the DNA on the water pipe and camera probably came from Elmer Goad, the maintenance man who got on the ladder to fix the camera and had to steady himself while doing so. LabCorp, he reminded jurors, didn't have Goad's DNA to test against. More importantly, however, and not mentioned at all by Jason's lawyers, was the landscaping rock from near the emergency exit door. That rock was also sent to LabCorp—and it had DNA on it matching Jason's—Saacks contended, embellishing the forensic testimony on that point.

The prosecutor shifted his focus to Jason's testimony that he left his room door open—with his keycard in his room—when he left the hotel to go to his car. He argued that was "amazing in and of itself for someone who is such a frequent traveler such as he, to walk out of a hotel room, knowing that you had your computer and your phone and your clothes and everything else in your room not to take your key with you and close the door."

Equally incredible, Saacks contended, was his story about grabbing a twig from a nearby bush to prop the door open. In a mocking tone, he suggested Jason was "Mr. Fantastic" to have stretched that far. "Wouldn't it be easier, and wouldn't it be quicker, if he did what the evidence shows, and that is, come through this door and just grab a loose rock and catch the door before it closes back to hold it open?"

As for Jason's testimony he was eating breakfast in the lobby that morning, Saacks asked, incredulously, "Where on Earth in any of the surveillance footage that you saw did you see him coming out a second time or eating breakfast in the lobby area?" And if he had left the hotel twice, as he testified, why was there security camera footage of him leaving just one time?

Saacks suggested Jason was lying about going out to the parking lot to smoke a cigar. "What do you need to smoke a cigar? You need a cigar, right? You need lighters, matches. What else do you need? Don't you need little clippers, right, you got to cut off the end of the cigar before you start smoking it." None of those items were found in his Explorer when it was searched. "He wants to tell you that he's been smoking cigars for years. *For years*," Saacks said sarcastically. "Yet no one else has said that."

He then turned to the shoe impression evidence, describing it as "huge." Holding up one of the Hush Puppies Orbital shoes entered into evidence, he stated, "This sole does match, is consistent with, the bloody prints in that scene."

Even though Jason wasn't the only one who had a pair of Orbitals, Sealys, or Bellevilles, it was an "awfully big coincidence," he argued, that the bloody print next to Michelle just happened to be of the type of shoe her husband had purchased one year earlier.

"And just to direct the point home, just to drive it home, four days after Michelle is dead, where is the defendant found?

He's at DSW buying another pair of shoes that are awfully similar to these Hush Puppy Orbitals."

Just as Collins had predicted, Saacks asked, where were Jason's Hush Puppies? Where was the shirt Jason was wearing when he was seen at the front desk of the Hampton Inn at midnight? It couldn't have been the same shirt Jason was photographed in at Cassidy's third birthday party, he asserted, because it wasn't in any of his luggage or in his Explorer when investigators searched it the day of his wife's death.

Finally, Saacks turned to the most difficult subject confronting the State: the Franklin size 10 shoeprints.

"What does it mean? Does it necessarily mean that there had to be another person in there? No. The defendant could have changed into another pair of shoes," he suggested, reminding the jury that the assailant went into Jason's closet. "This was a pair of shoes that was found for about ten bucks at a Dollar Store. So a cheap pair of shoes that might have been laying around, needed to use to get away, would fit, would fit with what was going on at that time."

And then, despite any evidence at all that Jason conspired with someone else, Saacks suggested perhaps he did. "If that does mean another person is in that house, does that excuse the defendant?" If Jason did commit the murder with someone else's assistance, he argued, "it doesn't matter, because he doesn't personally have to do everything to constitute the crime. This tells you that the one mystery that really might be out there doesn't make a difference."

As Saacks neared the end of his argument, he asked the jury to assume Jason wasn't the killer. "I invite you to do what some of those crime scene technicians do—flip it. They change the contrast, right? Sometimes they darken photographs to make something, they put chemicals on something to make it seen. Flip it and let's say the defendant is not guilty, somebody else did this. How do you then explain all this other stuff that points to the defendant?"

"When did you realize that this was not a coincidence any more?" the prosecutor asked the jury. "Was it after the no forced entry to the house? The nature of the assault? Or the rock and the camera at the hotel? When did you know beyond any reasonable doubt that the defendant did this? Was it after the Hush Puppy shoeprint? Was it after his motive is played out? Was it after all the ring incidents? Was it after he gave up Cassidy before answering any questions about this case?"

As he began wrapping up, Saacks told the jury Jason had "a very twisted definition of love. He claims that he loved his wife and loved Cassidy during this whole time. You have to wonder how much he loved Michelle as he was bludgeoning her to death on the floor of their own bedroom. Michelle Young had no other enemies but the one she shared her bed with. You have to wonder how much he actually loved Cassidy when he gave her up for his sake."

He closed by suggesting the question before the jury wasn't whether Jason did this, but whether jurors had enough evidence before them to say he did. "All we ask is you answer that simple question. And we look for justice for Michelle, for Cassidy, for Rylan, and, frankly, for all of us in that simple answer. Thank you."

Holt then stood up to deliver the final argument of the trial. She began by focusing on Jason's failure to cooperate with investigators, noting that he had no fewer than 1,693 days "to come up with the story that he told you in court yesterday. From November the 3rd of 2006 until June the 22nd of 2011." And that was after he had the opportunity to review all of the investigative reports and listen to every other witness testify.

After all that, "he took the stand to tell you that on the night that his wife was murdered, he was asleep in a hotel room in Hillsville, Virginia," the Assistant DA told jurors, incredulously.

"He didn't tell that to investigators on November the 3rd of 2006," she continued. He didn't tell that to his family and friends on November the 3rd, 2006, or in the days, weeks, months, years that followed. He didn't discuss his wife's murder with his friends, with his family, or even Michelle Money, the woman with whom he was having an affair. ... He expects you to believe the story that he told you from the witness stand 1,693 days later," she told jurors, in a mocking tone.

Holt then walked the jury through the timeline of key events, with digital photos displayed on a large projection screen behind her: Jason and Michelle's August 2003 civil ceremony; their formal wedding on October 10, 2003; Cassidy's birth on March 29, 2004; and the purchase of their home at 5108 Birchleaf Drive in the summer of 2005.

She paused to discuss the email Jason sent to Genevieve Cargol in September 2006 and how, in that email, "He basically told her that he loved her and has always loved her and would love her forever."

She recalled Cargol's testimony of the incident in Texas, when she confronted Jason about his drinking and how he responded by wrestling her to the ground, pinning her arms behind her, and forcibly removing her engagement ring.

"What you know," the prosecutor continued, "is that that was not the first incident of violence between Genevieve and Jason, that there had been a prior event where he took his hand and punched her windshield with such force that it broke."

Holt reminded jurors of Jason's intimate weekend with Michelle Money in early October 2006 and the heated argument between Jason and Michelle during and after their belated anniversary dinner, leading him to angrily tell his wife the next morning, "'I'm done. I'm through with this.'" She also highlighted Jason's infidelity with Carol Anne Sowerby the following weekend and yet another ring incident with her. And then the November 1 TV remote incident, leading his wife, this time, to say, "I can't do this anymore."

She then turned to the evening before the murder, showing the jury the still image of Jason checking out at the Cracker Barrel wearing a cream-colored, Henley-type shirt, dark pants, and dark brown shoes. The projection screen then displayed several images of Jason at the Hampton Inn: his check-in at the front desk at 10:54 p.m. wearing the same clothes; his second appearance at the front desk at 11:59 p.m., this time wearing a dark sweater-type shirt with the thin, white stripe investigators would never find; followed by still images of Jason walking down the western hallway toward the exit. He left the hotel,

Holt argued, to travel to Raleigh to kill his wife.

She contended Jason drugged Cassidy with a combination of adult strength Tylenol and Pancof PD because he planned to leave her in the house and didn't want to harm her. "What robber, what intruder," she asked rhetorically, "would have taken the time to deal with the child?" It made no sense for Jason to print off the Coach purses from eBay, Holt argued, because their third anniversary had already passed. Rather, he printed them off—and left them behind—she asserted, to have a reason to call Meredith to get her inside the house.

Holt recounted Jason's "unfortunate mistake of getting mad and getting angry and cussing out a clerk. Why is that important? That is important because she remembered him, Gracie Dahms Bailey at the Four Brothers Amoco in King, North Carolina, remembered the defendant coming in." Jason paid in cash, she suggested, so no one would know about the purchase. "He didn't want you to know about the cash purchase in King, North Carolina, and you probably never would have, had he not yelled at that clerk and made such an impression."

The gas purchases revealed on Jason's credit card, she argued, were merely the ones "he wants you to know about." But that didn't mean he hadn't made others, including during the time he supposedly got lost on his way to his sales meeting in Clintwood, Virginia—which was how Holt responded to Collins' contention Jason would have run out of gas long before stopping to refuel in Duffield, Virginia.

Working her way through the timeline on November 3, the prosecutor stopped to play Jason's voicemail message to Meredith at 12:14 p.m., in which he asked her to stop by the house to retrieve the eBay printouts; and then his second message to Meredith at 1:37 p.m. to make sure she had done so. It was clear, she told the jury, Jason was "desperate to make sure someone has gone and recovered Cassidy."

By that evening, she continued, Jason was already refusing to speak with the police. "And in the days, weeks, and months that follow, the defendant doesn't call the investigators, he doesn't ask questions, he doesn't talk to his friends and family."

Having completed the timeline—which occupied the bulk of her closing argument—Holt turned her attention to motive. Why did Jason want Michelle dead? She suggested to jurors he didn't want his mother-in-law moving into the house after Rylan was born. "He didn't want to be pinned down," but rather, "wanted to live as a single person and you know that because of his actions."

"He has taken the stand and told you that he loved his wife and that he was working on his marriage," the Assistant DA said, in utter disbelief. "Everything that you have heard is contrary to that. How are you working on your marriage when you're contacting old girlfriends and telling them that they're the love of your life and you're having sex the week before in the same house, when you're involved in an affair, where you talked more than 400 times in a month?"

Jason killed Michelle—rather than divorcing her—Holt argued, because he concluded "it would be worse to be divorced from Michelle than to be married."

"He told Josh Dalton," she reminded jurors, "'If I divorce her, she will move to New York and take Cassidy.' He couldn't have that." And even if Jason did love his daughter, he "loved Jason Young more than Cassidy because when it came down to it, rather than answer questions, rather than submit to a sworn statement, he gave up Cassidy. And in those 1,693 days, he didn't tell anybody that he was at the hotel sleeping … but he expects you to believe that because now it is contrived so that he can take care and explain away every piece of evidence."

Turning to Jason's shoes, she argued, "Don't you know that he knew he had to answer where those Hush Puppy shoes were? Don't you know he knew that was coming? But what was his answer to that? 'I'm pretty darn sure that Michelle either threw those away or gave them to charity.'" She told the jury Jason knew "exactly where they are 'cause he threw them away. … He had to get rid of those Hush Puppies. He had to get rid of that shirt. He had to dispose of them and then he had to make sure that someone came to discover Cassidy."

As she began wrapping up, Holt implored the jury not to believe Jason's eleventh-hour testimony: "Tell Jason Young by your verdict that you're not buying what he's trying to sell. Tell Jason Young that his story and his tears on this witness stand were too little, too late."

Working herself up to a fever pitch, she ended with a cry for justice: "Tell Jason Young that there will be justice for Michelle. Tell Jason Young that there will be justice for Cassidy. That there will be justice for Rylan. Tell Jason Young that he is guilty beyond a reasonable doubt of the first-degree murder of Michelle Marie Fisher Young. Thank you."

With that, Holt took her seat, leaving Jason's fate in the hands of twelve complete strangers. Had she and Saacks done enough to convince them to return a verdict in their—and Michelle's—favor? Or had Jason, Collins, and Klinkosum been more persuasive? The next few days would answer those questions—as well as determine the fate of Jason Lynn Young.

# 18

## JURY

Jury deliberations represent an abrupt reversal of the trial process. The jury suddenly assumes control of the case the moment it is set free to deliberate, while the judge and lawyers relinquish control.

For the first time, jurors get to speak and have their voices heard, while the activity inside the courtroom comes to a screeching halt. For the defendant, lawyers, and families waiting on the other side of the jury room door, time seems to stand still. The anxiety and tension are often so palpable, they are almost debilitating.

In a trial involving one spouse accused of killing the other, the anguish experienced by both sets of families reaches a crescendo at the precise moment the defendant's fate is placed in the jury's hands. Linda and Meredith had waited over three years for Jason's arrest and another eighteen months for him to be brought to trial. Their quest for justice had been arduous and at times excruciating. And here they were, moments away from what they hoped would be closure. And justice. But the fear that haunted them was that they would get neither.

Meanwhile, Pat Young and her daughters Kim and Heather clung to the hope that the jury would set Jason free. That he would finally have his life back. And that he would once again be part of their birthday and holiday gatherings at Pat's home in Brevard. With luck, they hoped, Cassidy would be able to join them as well. But by the same token, they knew there was every possibility the jury's verdict could result in Jason spending the rest of his life in prison. The difference between those two possibilities could hardly have been more extreme.

It wasn't just Jason Young and the two families whose fate was hanging in the balance. Sheriff Donnie Harrison and his team of deputies and detectives—most notably Sergeant Spivey—had invested tremendous time and resources into the case for nearly five years. So, too, had the CCBI and virtually every section of the SBI crime lab. Sheriff Harrison, Sergeant Spivey, Agent Galloway, and every law enforcement officer and crime lab agent who testified at trial had their reputations riding on the jury's verdict as well.

.....

Jury deliberations began in earnest just after 3:00 p.m. on Thursday, June 23, after Judge Stephens recited some seventeen pages of instructions. The jury deliberated for about two hours before retiring for the day. When jurors returned that Friday morning, the judge had a dry erase board, flip chart, and plenty of markers deposited into the jury room to assist them with their task. With the weekend quickly approaching, there was great hope on both sides that there would soon be a verdict.

That hope was dashed at 1:30 p.m., just before the jury went to lunch. At that time, the bailiff handed Judge Stephens a lengthy note, penned by the foreperson, which contained nine separate requests. The jury asked to be provided still frames from the surveillance videos of Jason paying his bill at the Cracker Barrel in Greensboro as well as when he was walking down the western hallway at the Hampton Inn. Jurors asked to be provided still frames that clearly showed the shoes Jason was wearing.

They also asked for the photos of Cassidy's third birthday party, which showed what Jason was wearing; crime scene photos of Cassidy's bathroom; and photos of the exterior side of the emergency exit at the Hampton Inn, showing what was to the right of that exit door. They asked to review the transcript of Meredith's call to the 911 dispatcher; LabCorp's DNA analysis; the eBay and MapQuest printouts; and Jason's September 2006 email to Genevieve Cargol.

Just before 3:00 p.m., the jury was ushered back into the courtroom. One by one, each item requested, except one, was either projected onto a large screen or passed through the jury box for jurors to examine individually. Because no photo had been entered into evidence showing what was to the right of the Hampton Inn emergency exit door, however, Judge Stephens informed jurors he couldn't accommodate that request.

After they had reviewed all the requested items, the jurors went back into the jury room for about ninety minutes, before indicating they were ready to go home for the weekend—without a verdict.

Jason, his family, Linda, and Meredith would have to wait at least another three days for their decision.

·····

Monday, June 27, 2006, would prove to be a momentous—albeit heart-wrenching—day for everyone involved in the trial. After less than two hours of deliberations, the foreperson had the bailiff deliver another note to Judge Stephens.

The judge quietly reviewed the note and then invited all four lawyers to join him in chambers to discuss it. After about thirty minutes, the lawyers reemerged. As he was nearing his seat at his counsel table, Collins glanced at the gallery's first pew and, spotting Pat Young, gave her a wink.

"Good news?" she wondered.

Judge Stephens then took his seat at the bench and read the jury's note aloud:

"Your Honor, over the weekend I have looked up the responsibilities of a jury foreperson. One that stuck out was to act as a mediator and manager of this group of jurors. Unfortunately, at this time, we are at an impasse and appear to be immovably hung. We currently sit at a 6/6 ratio and do not appear to be able to make any further movement. Where do we go from here?"

Upon hearing the content of the note, Pat instantly understood the reason behind Collins' wink. A sense of relief began washing over her. On the other side of the courtroom, Linda and Meredith were bewildered. They hadn't fully considered the possibility of a hung jury. The anxiety they had been feeling since Thursday afternoon was quickly replaced by a sense of doom and despair.

Becky Holt rose to her feet and asked Judge Stephens to deliver the "Allen charge," more commonly referred to in legal parlance by its nickname, the "dynamite charge."

True to its nickname, the Allen charge is designed to provide a significant jolt to a jury seemingly on the verge of a deadlock. Its use had been sanctioned not only by the North Carolina Supreme Court, but by state and federal courts throughout the country.

Judge Stephens told the lawyers he would give his own version of the Allen charge. The bailiff then led the jurors back into the courtroom to their seats in the jury box. In his brief instructions, the judge told them it was their duty "to do whatever you can to reach a unanimous verdict."

He instructed them to act "together as reasonable men and women in an attempt to reconcile your differences, if you can, without the surrender of conscientious convictions." But he also told them, "No juror should surrender his or her honest conviction as to the weight or the effect of the evidence solely because of the opinion of your fellow jurors or for the mere purpose of returning a verdict."

The judge also informed the jury if it did not reach a verdict, a retrial would likely be necessary, and that it was unlikely a subsequent jury "will be in any better position to resolve these difficult questions. It is equally unlikely that any other future jury would be any better qualified than you are to return a unanimous verdict, if that can be done without violence to individual judgment." He asked the jury to return to the jury room, considering what he had just said, in an effort to reach a unanimous verdict.

While jurors continued their deliberations, Pat and her family huddled with Collins and Klinkosum around the defense counsel table while Linda and Meredith huddled with Holt, Saacks, and Sergeant Spivey around the prosecution's. Their parallel discussions focused on precisely the same question: What would happen if the jury couldn't reach a unanimous verdict?

At their table, Collins and Klinkosum explained there could be a second trial, though that was entirely up to the District Attorney. If the DA concluded a second trial wouldn't increase the likelihood of a conviction, they said, he might offer Jason a plea bargain to significantly reduced charges—or even dismiss the charges altogether. There was every reason for Pat and her family—and Jason—to consider a hung jury a victory. With that understanding, optimism was on the rise around the defense table.

The mood was decidedly more somber around the prosecution table. Holt and Saacks couldn't provide any certainty to Linda and Meredith as to what might happen in the event of a hung jury. They would have to let matters play themselves out. Michelle's mother and sister took little solace in the prospect of a second trial. Their quest for justice for Michelle had gone on long enough already.

At 1:30 p.m., the jury indicated that it was ready to take a lunch break. Before letting jurors leave, Judge Stephens asked the foreperson whether they had been making any significant progress since he had provided his additional instructions.

"No, Your Honor, we are not," the foreperson replied glumly.

The judge asked if they were still divided six to six. The foreperson confirmed they were. He indicated he didn't believe further progress could be made.

But rather than giving up, Judge Stephens asked them to step back into the jury room to determine if there was agreement they were "hopelessly divided," such that further deliberations wouldn't lead to a unanimous verdict no matter how long they continued.

The judge told jurors if they unanimously agreed that they were, in fact, hopelessly at an impasse, he would declare a mistrial and let them go. He asked them to focus on only that question and then report back to him. With that admonition, they retired once again to the jury room.

Six minutes later, the jury once again assembled in the jury box. Judge Stephens asked the foreperson if he felt there was a consensus on the jury's inability to reach a verdict. To everyone's surprise, however, the foreperson reported, "The jury feels that the seriousness of the consequences here, we owe it to the Court, that we have a little bit more work to do."

Relieved he wouldn't yet need to declare a mistrial, Judge Stephens released the jury for a late lunch. Jurors returned at 2:45 p.m. and resumed their deliberations.

Unfortunately, what little hope there was that a verdict might still be reached was short lived. At 4:00 p.m., Judge Stephens received another note. This one read:

*Your Honor, we have made some progress, however the current 8 (NG)-4 (G) situation that we find ourselves in leads us to believe that we will make no further headway in this matter. We find ourselves deadlocked and at this time the decisions of the parties that feel the defendant [is] guilty or not guilty will not change. We are deadlocked.*

When the jurors came back into the courtroom the final time, their collective frustration was evident on their faces and in their body language. One last time, Judge Stephens asked the foreperson if he was sure the jury couldn't make any more progress.

"I believe we're done, Your Honor," he replied. The judge asked for a show of hands of all jurors who agreed with that sentiment. All twelve raised their hands.

"Let the record show," Judge Stephens stated, "that all twelve jurors indicated to the Court that they agree. Therefore, the Court will order that the case be mistried." The judge told the jurors that he sincerely appreciated their efforts. "You can't put a price on the value of this part of what we do in our society being a part of your own democratic way of life," he added.

He then excused them and formally declared a mistrial, indicating there would be a status conference on July 20 to discuss whatever next steps might occur. With that, he adjourned court.

Pat, Kim, and Heather were permitted to give Jason a hug

before Sheriff's deputies led him away, headed again for the jail cell that had been his home since December 2009.

Linda and Meredith stood up, visibly shaken, Linda clutching an oversized photo of Michelle and Cassidy. She walked to the other side of the courtroom—in Pat's direction. Through her tears, she asked Pat, "Isn't she beautiful?" though it wasn't clear if she was referring to Michelle or Cassidy. Pat smiled awkwardly, not sure how to respond to the first words Linda had spoken to her in years.

Slowly, the courtroom that for a solid month had been the epicenter of the Young and Fisher families' world emptied out. Left behind in its wake was an uncertain future—for Jason, his family, and for Linda and Meredith's quest for justice. It would take some time to sort through what had just taken place. And what might happen next.

. . . . .

July 20 couldn't come soon enough. Jason was led into the courtroom in a fresh, dark suit and took his seat beside Collins and Klinkosum. Sitting next to Holt at the prosecution table was Howard Cummings, Wake County's first Assistant DA. Though he had no involvement in the trial, it was clear he was back at the helm now.

Judge Stephens asked Cummings if the State intended to retry the case.

"Yes, sir," Cummings responded resolutely. He told the judge the State could be ready for a new trial as early as the middle of October.

The judge stated if the court reporter was able to complete all transcripts from the first trial in time, the case would proceed to retrial on October 10. Though Judge Stephens likely didn't realize it at the time, that date would have marked Jason's and Michelle's eighth wedding anniversary.

The status conference then transitioned to the subject of a bond—as Jason had been held in jail pending the first trial without bond. Collins argued forcefully that Jason should have the opportunity to post a bond. He told Judge Stephens his client had a total of one infraction in the nineteen months he had been in jail—for hoarding food. "I think that says something about the way he has comported himself since he's been in custody. As you know, he has no availability to pay a bond at all. Any bond that he might make would be posted by family."

In view of the result of the first trial, the Public Defender suggested, Jason had "every reason to come back, no reason to flee. If he was going to flee, I argue to you that he would have done that while he was under investigation."

He noted that Jason was in Puerto Rico while the case was being investigated, but ultimately was back home where investigators knew he lived.

Cummings argued against any bond. "Your Honor heard all the evidence," he stated. "I would just like to point out to you that this is a very brutal murder of a fine person, and that it's the State's contention in this case that some of the evidence that was involved has been disposed of, either by the defendant or persons on his behalf."

Judge Stephens ruled swiftly, declaring, "Certainly a bond is appropriate, and in my discretion, the Court sets the bond at $900,000 secured. That's the ruling of the Court. The case is set for trial October the 10th."

.....

The mid-afternoon sun was shining brightly on downtown Raleigh on July 28, 2011, as Jason Young walked out the doors of the Wake County Public Safety Center and took his first steps of freedom. His mother Pat had posted his bond by offering five pieces of property as collateral.

For the first time in nineteen months, Jason was no longer confined to the tight spaces of the county jail. He left the building wearing the same Nike T-shirt he had worn when he first entered it.

News crews followed Jason as he and Mike Klinkosum strode side-by-side to Klink's office a few blocks away. Reporters shouted questions at the newly liberated defendant—not one of which received any response.

"Jason, are you innocent?"

"Where will you go, Jason?"

"Are you going home to Brevard and your family?"

"How does it feel to be out in fresh air?"

"Jason, are you glad to be out?"

"Do you have anything at all to say to your family?"

The reporters should have known better. In the nearly five years since Michelle's murder, Jason hadn't uttered a single word to law enforcement officers or the media. That strategy had worked well enough to win him eight votes in favor of acquittal. With a second trial looming on the horizon, he certainly wasn't going to abandon that strategy now.

*Court-exhibit photos of public record.*

Pictured with their ring bearer, Mr. Garrison, Michelle and Jason were all smiles on their wedding day, October 10, 2003 (top). In happier times: Puerto Rico (bottom).

*Court-exhibit photos of public record.*

The light of both Jason's and Michelle's life: Cassidy Elizabeth Young. The bond between mother and daughter was undeniable.

Jason at the front desk of the Hampton Inn upon check-in
at 10:49 p.m. (top), wearing a different shirt at 11:59 p.m.
(bottom left), and walking toward the exit door seconds later
(bottom right).

Michelle was found lying facedown in pools of blood, with her head pressed against Jason's open closet door (top). Blood spatter nearly reached the ceiling, covering the walls and exterior side of the closet door. DNA collected from the jewelry box, and from a hair found on the picture frame (bottom), didn't match Jason's or Michelle's DNA.

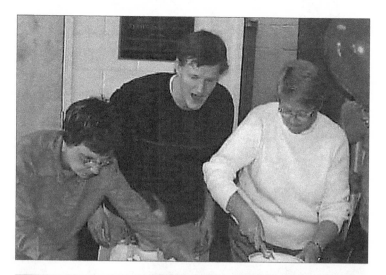

*Court-exhibit photos of public record.*

Jason lived in the North Carolina mountains with Cassidy for more than two years before agreeing to transfer custody to Meredith. The picture taken at Cassidy's third birthday party (top) featured prominently at both trials.

*Photos courtesy of WRAL News.*

Linda and Meredith's raw emotions were on full display at the March 2009 wrongful death hearing (top). Even though Jason hadn't yet been charged with Michelle's murder, Sergeant Richard Spivey told the presiding judge the evidence pointed directly at him (bottom).

*Photos courtesy of WRAL News.*

Following their December 2009 drive across North Carolina,
Sergeant Spivey escorted Jason to his new home at the
Wake County Public Safety Center (top), the same place
he and Michelle were married. The striped jumpsuit
(bottom) was standard issue at the county jail.

Meredith and Linda fought for twelve years for justice for Michelle (top row). Pat Young (bottom left) was her son's biggest supporter, standing by his side through a custody battle and two criminal trials. Jason's testimony at the first trial (bottom right) was convincing enough to win him eight votes in favor of acquittal.

*Photos courtesy of WRAL News.*

The State's star witness—a convenience store worker in King,
North Carolina, who claimed Jason cursed at her when she
refused to turn on the gas pump—appeared to have had a
complete makeover between the first and second trials.
Testifying at the first (top left), her name was Gracie Dahms.
At the second, she was Gracie Calhoun (top right). The defense challenged her relentlessly. Cindy Beaver (bottom), a
postal worker who lived on Birchleaf Drive, was the defense
team's answer to Gracie Dahms. She actually witnessed
two people in the Youngs' driveway just before 5:30 a.m. the
morning of the murder. The State challenged her relentlessly.

Jason was actively involved in an affair with his wife's sorority sister, Michelle Money (top left). While Michelle was in New York less than two weeks before the murder, he had sex with his old friend, Carol Anne Sowerby (top right), with Cassidy upstairs. In an email investigators discovered on his work-issued laptop, Jason had also professed his eternal love to his former fiancée, Genevieve Cargol (bottom), just seven weeks before the murder.

*Photos courtesy of WRAL News.*

The prosecution team: Becky Holt (top) was the lead prosecutor at the first trial and "second chair" at the second. David Saacks (bottom left) was a last-minute substitute at the first. Howard Cummings (bottom right), who had been in charge of the prosecution from the very beginning, took the lead at the second trial.

*Photos courtesy of WRAL News.*

The defense team: Jason was very fortunate to be represented by two excellent lawyers—Public Defender Bryan Collins (top) and Mike Klinkosum (bottom). He didn't have to pay a penny for either.

Judge Stephens

*Photos courtesy of WRAL News.*

Judge Donald Stephens (top) held his tongue throughout both trials. Once the second jury found Jason guilty, the judge's lengthy speech eloquently expressed his belief that Michelle had succumbed to an all-too-predictable incident of domestic violence. After listening to the judge's soliloquy, Jason is sentenced to life in prison (bottom).

*Photos courtesy of WRAL News.*

Jason enters the courtroom for the June 2017 hearing on his
ineffective assistance of counsel claim (top). His five years
in prison had aged him considerably. The star witness at the
hearing was none other than Bryan Collins (bottom right), now
a superior court judge.

# Part III
# Take Two

# 19

## RESET

The retrial presented numerous difficulties and challenges—to Judge Stephens, the prosecution, and the defense. For the judge, ensuring the selection of a fair and impartial jury was complicated significantly by the extensive media coverage of the first trial.

Not only was there almost daily newspaper and television coverage, the entire trial was streamed live across the website of Raleigh's WRAL television station.

In addition, there was widespread blogging about the trial as well as copious information available on the internet and in social media prospective jurors were likely to have encountered.

For these reasons, jury selection for the retrial was painstakingly slow, lasting twelve court days—one day longer than the entire first trial. Judge Stephens even found it necessary to disqualify two prospective jurors for misbehavior—one who had been posting information about the proceedings on an internet message board and a second who was overheard discussing the case at a restaurant. Finally, though, on February 1, 2012, a jury of eight women and four men was impaneled.

The biggest hurdle facing prosecutors, of course, was to figure out how to transform a near acquittal into a unanimous guilty verdict.

The first jury had been so unconvinced of Jason's guilt, it

had nearly set him free. The State was quite fortunate four jurors had held out and hung the jury. With this second bite at the apple, the prosecutors knew they had to do better. Though they couldn't manufacture new evidence, they definitely needed to develop some new ideas and a more coherent trial strategy. Replacing David Saacks with Howard Cummings provided a fresh perspective to do just that.

Cummings, who had spent 23 of his 32 years in law practice at the Wake County DA's Office, served as second in command to District Attorney Colon Willoughby. He had been the lead prosecutor in numerous high-profile cases—including the Brad Cooper murder trial that ended with a guilty verdict shortly before Jason's first trial began.

Like Collins, the first Assistant DA spoke with a thick Southern drawl, delivered in a painfully slow—almost hypnotic—cadence. Cummings' was more of an Eastern North Carolina accent he had developed growing up in Kinston, not far from the coast.

Thus, at this new trial, the seats behind the prosecution table belonged to lawyers reared near the beach—just like the victim for whom they were fighting. Fittingly, the seats at the counsel table across the room were filled by lawyers and a defendant who grew up in the mountains.

The second trial provided Cummings and Becky Holt the opportunity to correct the biggest mistake the prosecution team had made in the first trial—when Holt had a mere sixty minutes to prepare for Jason's cross-examination after being caught completely off guard by him taking the stand in his own defense. In preparation for the retrial, she and Cummings had more than seven months to parse and fact check every word of his testimony. Were he to testify again, they would be more than ready to cross-examine him.

The prosecution team also had the luxury of interviewing jurors from the first trial to learn what led two-thirds of them to vote in favor of acquittal. Those interviews allowed them to retool their case and to focus on new themes and new witnesses who could support them.

Cummings and Holt decided they needed a more detailed,

methodical presentation of evidence, and to call additional witnesses to help establish Jason had the evil mind and depraved heart possessed by the monster who had so savagely beaten Michelle.

With a longer witness list and a greater focus on detail, the second trial would ultimately last nearly twice as long as the first. The prosecutors believed jurors would appreciate the depth and breadth of their presentation and would be more likely to return a guilty verdict.

Meanwhile, Bryan Collins and Mike Klinkosum understood all too well establishing reasonable doubt this time around would be significantly more difficult. They no longer had the tactical advantage of holding their cards close to the vest—as they did when they surprised prosecutors by calling Jason to testify in his own defense.

The risk of calling him to the stand in this trial would almost assuredly be too great. In all likelihood, therefore, Jason wouldn't be able to look these jurors in their eyes and emphatically deny his involvement in the murder.

If there were one advantage for the defense, it was that—unlike during the first trial—Jason was now a free man. He wouldn't be locked into his jail cell following each court session. This time, the defense team could strategize with him during lunch, in the evenings, and over the many weekends the trial was likely to last. That was as liberating for Collins and Klinkosum as it was for Jason himself.

. . . . .

On Monday, February 6, Holt rose from her seat at the prosecution table to reprise her opening statement. Yet this version was notably different. Not only was it more than double the length as in the first trial—nearly an hour—it included several new themes and far greater detail.

She began by focusing on Jason's and Michelle's marriage, rather than his so-called "plan" to kill her. As she described it, it was a "marriage in trouble." Jason "felt pressured into the marriage," she told jurors, due to Michelle's pregnancy. He was "stuck in the college life," and would go to parties, tailgates, and football games and get drunk. While Jason wanted to live the college life, Holt said, his wife wanted to focus on family life. But he wasn't ready for that or for the responsibilities that came with it.

The prosecutor described the "friction" between the pair. "They argued often. They argued in public. So much so that some of their friends would say they really didn't want to be around them as a couple much."

There was also friction between Jason and his mother-in-law, Holt noted, who wasn't afraid to tell him how he was shirking his responsibilities. And friction regarding Linda's plans over the holidays and her plans to move into their home after the baby was born.

This time around, the Assistant DA was more explicit about Jason's involvement with other women. She told the jury that in September 2006, Jason "reached out to an old girlfriend, someone he hadn't seen in years, describing her as the love, his one and only, the love of his life." In that email, she stated, the defendant indicated the biggest mistake he had made was proposing to Cargol before they were ready.

Holt next discussed Jason's relationship with Michelle Money, which started as "flirtations" and developed into an "affair." She told the jury about his October 2006 trip to Orlando to be with Money and how he told at least one friend he believed he loved her.

Following his trip to Orlando, and then a business trip to Denver, Jason returned home, Holt recounted, and had a belated anniversary dinner with Michelle. Their argument that evening was "like World War III," she said, continuing right through Ryan's and Shelly's wedding in Winston-Salem.

The week following the wedding, she noted, Michelle went to New York on business. Meanwhile, Carol Anne Sowerby, who had been Jason's friend when he was a camp counselor, came to stay at the couple's home. In a disgusted tone, Holt told the jury Jason and Sowerby "engaged in sexual relations in the Young residence with Cassidy Young present upstairs."

Later that week, she said, while Sowerby was having dinner

with Jason and Michelle, the defendant swallowed their guest's wedding ring, causing her to delay her trip back to Montana until he could pass them.

Hinting at new evidence prosecutors would introduce, Holt told jurors that in that same time period, Michelle visited with a counselor because she was distraught about the state of her marriage, and cried during their session. She tied that visit together with the four-hour counseling session Meredith mediated for her sister and brother-in-law later that same day. The jury also heard about the argument Jason had with his wife on November 1, and Michelle's claim her husband had thrown a TV remote at her.

Finally, the Assistant DA turned to the events of November 3, telling the jury about the voicemail Jason had left for Meredith about the eBay printouts, and how Meredith went to their home to retrieve them. "What she discovered when she got to the Birchleaf house was horrific. She found her sister in her bedroom having been beat to death. She found her niece hiding under the covers in the master bedroom ... She found little footprints by Michelle Young as she lay facedown on the floor of her bedroom, little footprints in blood. She found them around Michelle's head. She saw them as she was coming up the stairs in Cassidy's bathroom. She found baby dolls, a baby doll by Michelle's head, another baby doll in the bed, a blanket, and she heard Cassidy say, 'Mommy got boo-boos.'"

Holt told jurors the Medical Examiner found evidence of strangulation, and that Michelle's face and head had been struck with an object at least thirty times. "The blood in that bedroom, in the area where Michelle Young was found, goes almost to the ceiling," she explained. "It was a brutal, personal beating." Investigators, she said, also discovered the diamond engagement and wedding rings Michelle always wore had been removed from her finger.

The prosecutor next told the jury about "some awfully strange events" at the Hampton Inn, forecasting evidence about Jason's change of clothes, the use of his room keycard, the rock that propped open the exit door, and the tampering with the security camera. She also told jurors they would be hearing from a convenience store employee in King, North Carolina who would testify the defendant was pumping gas outside her store at 5:30 a.m. on November 3.

"What you will learn about the events of November 2 and November 3 throughout this trial," Holt said, "will have lots of pieces, a lot of pieces to the puzzle."

She described Jason's journey back to Raleigh on November 3 and how he learned from his friends the police wanted to talk to him. From that day forward, she told the jury, he refused to talk with investigators, his family, or his friends about what happened. "In the days, weeks, months, years that followed, a man whose wife has been brutally murdered in his home does not call to say, 'What does your investigation reveal? What is going on?'"

In the meantime, the Assistant DA recounted, rather than having to answer questions about where he was and what he was doing that day, he turned over physical custody of his daughter to Meredith.

At that point, Holt dropped the biggest bombshell of her opening statement—signaling a major shift in strategy from the first trial: "You will learn that there was a civil suit, a wrongful death suit filed in which the allegations were that the defendant murdered Michelle Young. And you will learn that instead of responding to that lawsuit, instead of responding to those allegations, the defendant defaulted. He didn't answer because that would have required him to submit to a deposition, to answer questions. So instead of doing that, he gave up his daughter. He allowed publicly [the] allegations to be admitted."

Belatedly, Klinkosum jumped to his feet to object. Judge Stephens sustained the objection. But Holt continued to tell the jury about the wrongful death case, prompting Klink to object again. This time, the judge asked the lawyers to approach the bench, where they hashed out the objection.

After the sidebar, the prosecutor stated—for the third time, "Instead of responding to those allegations, he allowed a civil judgment to be entered against him." The first jury hadn't heard anything about that judgment. This jury, however, would hear about it in great detail.

Holt ended her opening statement by pointing to Jason's testimony at the first trial, telling jurors he had first answered questions "1,693 days after his wife's murder." And all he said at the time, she stated, was that he propped open the hotel's exit door and went outside to smoke a cigar. "1,693 days later. That is what he tells. How in any way would that have been incriminating?" she asked incredulously.

Then, in a solemn tone, she concluded, "The evidence in this case will convince you, each and every one of you, that Jason Young is responsible for the murder of Michelle Young, that he is guilty of murder in the first degree."

Once again, Klinkosum delivered the defense opening. It was short and crisp, just as it had been in the first trial. As he did then, he focused largely on the forensic evidence. "It's no coincidence," he said, "that, in the State's opening statement, they didn't mention anything about any physical evidence linking Jason Young to the murder of his wife."

He alerted the jury to the two different sets of bloody shoeprints found in the bedroom and "fingerprints that remain unidentified." And that LabCorp had found DNA on the jewelry box that didn't match anyone.

He used maps of Virginia and North Carolina to demonstrate the long distances Jason needed to traverse to have committed the crime, leaving precious little time to clean himself up.

Yet, Klinkosum continued, he had supposedly "killed his wife in the most brutal and in one of the most bloody ways possible and somehow got back, got out of the house, without getting any blood downstairs, and not one drop of blood in his truck, in his Ford Explorer, not one drop of blood back in his hotel room."

Once again, Jason's lawyer conceded his client wasn't a good husband. "He was far from it. He wasn't ready to get married. He was not ready to have a child." He engaged in "juvenile behavior" and acted like an "obnoxious jerk." Klink even told jurors about the incident in which Jason got drunk at Ryan's and Shelly's home, urinated on their rug, and then sat down on the sofa completely naked. He also agreed Jason and Michelle fought often, including at Ryan's and Shelly's wedding. "But you'll also hear that, after it was over, he hugged her at the reception, kissed her, and told people, 'I love my wife. She's crazy, but I love her.'"

Though Holt didn't mention it, Klinkosum told the jury about Jason's violent outburst toward Genevieve Cargol: "You're going to hear about how they had a physical altercation at a wedding reception where he pulled an engagement ring off her finger." But even though he behaved like "an obnoxious, juvenile jerk," he continued, "we don't convict people of murder just because they sometimes act like jerks."

Like Holt, the defense attorney discussed the Hampton Inn security camera, but told jurors this wasn't the first time a camera at the hotel had been tampered with. Also, fingerprints found on the camera didn't match Jason's, nor did the DNA collected from a water pipe above the camera. He also wondered aloud why his client would have gone to such great lengths to disable that security camera only to walk directly in front of two other cameras and a hotel employee at the front desk just before midnight.

All Jason did that evening, Klinkosum contended, was go outside the hotel, smoke a cigar, and come back to his room to go to bed. And by 7:40 a.m. the next morning, he was calling his mother from near Wytheville, Virginia. That timeline was inconsistent with the prosecution's theory, he suggested. "The puzzle the prosecution talked to you about—Jason does not fit into it."

During the ride back to Raleigh on November 3, Klink said, Jason heard from his friends, "The police think you did this. This is serious. They are after you and you need to talk to a lawyer before you talk to them."

"The police kept focusing on him like a laser," he told jurors, "even though there was evidence of someone else's DNA in the house, unidentified fingerprints, different feet."

It was important, Klinkosum suggested, that it took more than three years for authorities to charge Jason with the murder, noting, "in that intervening time period, there was nothing, no physical evidence that was developed that linked

Jason to this murder. Nothing." He agreed with Holt that the murder scene was very bloody. "And what they also want you to believe, ladies and gentlemen, is that Jason Young did this with his daughter, Cassidy, in the house and then somehow had her walk around in the blood, get blood on her and clean her up and put her back to bed and left her there."

As for his client's decision to give up custody of Cassidy, Klink explained his original lawyers had told him, "'You don't say anything about this unless you go to trial on this.' It was a hard decision for him to make, but he did it because he was told that once it was over he could come back and get custody of his daughter back. But they want you to believe that this man, that was a good dad, that loved his daughter, let his little girl walk around in her mother's blood."

Noting that Cassidy was found by Meredith to be "shockingly clean," Jason's lawyer contended that "the time that it took to do this and clean her up and clean up this house and clean himself up if he did it—which he didn't—the time it would have taken to do that and again get back on the road to Hillsville, Virginia, and then make a call to his mother at 7:40 a.m., you will see that it does not add up. And the reason, ladies and gentlemen, is because Jason Young did not commit this murder."

"The physical evidence in this case points to other people," Klinkosum argued, as he began wrapping up. "The amount of time it would have taken points to someone else doing this. Jason Young did not kill his wife and his unborn child, and this case, ladies and gentlemen, you will see, has not been solved."

Thus, he told jurors, "The only verdict in this case that is proper to find is that Jason Young is not guilty."

. . . . .

It became evident with the State's first witness—Meredith Fisher—this trial would last considerably longer than the first. She was on the witness stand for portions of three days. Holt's questioning covered significantly more territory, and explored details in far greater depth, than in the first trial. There were also more demonstrative exhibits to help focus the jury's attention, including large, blowup floor plans of 5108 Birchleaf Drive.

Unlike in the first trial, Holt had Meredith describe in detail how Jason and Michelle plunged into the French Broad River during their trip to Brevard over Memorial Day weekend in 2006.

Meredith testified her sister had informed her that while she and Jason were on the road to Starbucks, he thought the back hatch of his Mitsubishi Endeavor SUV had come open, which made him turn toward the rear of the vehicle. When he looked back through the windshield, he was drifting off the road. He apparently overcorrected, resulting in them descending down the embankment. According to Michelle, Meredith testified, water started filling the vehicle to the point she began to panic. But they were both ultimately able to escape and make their way up the side of the mountain as the SUV sank into the river.

The Assistant DA asked Meredith whether her sister was wearing her seatbelt at the time Jason veered off the road. She responded Michelle had told her she had unbuckled her seatbelt to grab some lotion in the backseat the moment before Jason veered off the road. She also testified that for Father's Day that June, Michelle had purchased a tool for Jason that could be used to crack a window open if something similar ever happened again.

Holt had her first witness go into much greater detail about Jason's refusal to speak with the police. "I asked him countless times," Meredith testified, "if he had spoken to the police … When he indicated 'no,' I continually asked him why he wouldn't do that."

"And what was his response to you?" the prosecutor asked.

"His attorney told him not to."

"Did you try, attempt to have conversations with the defendant about information he might have, where he had been that night when Michelle was murdered? Did you attempt to yourself elicit information from him?" Holt asked.

"Yes," Meredith answered.

"And what was his response to you?"

"He would not say one word unless his attorney was there and his attorney told him not to speak. So he wasn't going to speak to anyone. Not me. Not anyone."

Meredith recounted in detail the difficulties she and Linda had in arranging visitation with Cassidy, including the incident that precipitated Jason and his mother cutting off visitation altogether. She testified one of Pat's friends was at her Brevard home having a "heated conversation about us supporting Jason publicly and contacting the newspaper, the media, and saying that we support him publicly, and if we weren't willing to do that that contact with Cassidy would end." At the time, Meredith responded she wanted Jason to talk to the police, "but until he did that, until he answered questions, I wasn't willing to do that."

"What happened after that visit?" the Assistant DA asked.

"Shortly thereafter, any attempts to talk to Cassidy on the phone, schedule a visit, cards that we sent, gifts that we sent, were returned to sender. Completely cut off. No contact whatsoever."

Noting the custody order she and Jason signed included restrictions on Meredith's smoking, Holt had her discuss what she knew about her brother-in-law's attitudes about smoking—foreshadowing how the prosecution intended to rebut his testimony that he left his room at the Hampton Inn to smoke a cigar.

When she first moved to North Carolina and didn't have a car, Meredith said, she had been borrowing one of brother-in-law's cars. "I would smoke cigarettes in there to or from work and he was not happy about that," she told jurors. "I had never seen him smoke and, you know, family functions that people go outside and smoke a cigarette or a cigar or whatever, he had never joined anyone that was smoking."

Returning to the custody situation, Holt asked what efforts the defendant had made to contact and visit with Cassidy since he had been released from jail in late July 2011. Meredith testified Jason first spoke with Cassidy by phone at the end of August. His first supervised visit with her, she said, didn't occur until October 16. Eight such visits had occurred—every other Sunday afternoon for one hour.

During his cross-examination, Collins asked Meredith if her sister made it a practice "to gather up old clothing and donate it to charity" — an attempt to bolster Jason's testimony that his wife had probably donated his Hush Puppies Orbital shoes prior to the murder. Meredith agreed it wasn't unusual for Michelle to bag up and donate old clothing.

The Public Defender asked her about the custody lawsuit she and Linda had filed against Jason. Surprisingly, he read aloud the complaint's allegation that, "In the early morning hours of November the 3, 2006 the defendant brutally murdered Marie Fisher Young at their residence."

"You swore that was true in 2008, right?" he asked.

"Correct," Meredith answered.

"And he wasn't even charged with the murder at that time, was he?"

"Not yet, no," the prosecution witness agreed.

Collins pressed her. "You knew he wasn't going to answer this lawsuit, didn't you?"

Meredith responded she really didn't know if he would, but had "a feeling he wouldn't."

Jason's lawyer also pushed back on Meredith's testimony that his client had little contact with his daughter after being released from jail. He got her to agree that, as part of his conditions of release, Jason was ordered not to have any contact with either her or Linda.

She agreed if Jason had called them, he would have gone back to jail. And in contrast to the picture she painted during her direct examination, Collins had Meredith confirm Jason actually asked to visit with Cassidy every Sunday, rather than every other Sunday.

"And you said no?" he asked.

"We kept with the custody order as close as we could. Every other weekend," she responded.

Collins spent considerable time going through Meredith's 911 call to emergency dispatchers, pointing out several answers she provided that didn't directly address the questions she was being asked. Picking up on that topic, on redirect examination,

Holt focused Meredith on her statement to the dispatcher that Cassidy was "very smart for her age. She's two and a half, but I think that she's saying that there was somebody in the house."

"What was going on that led you to say that?" the prosecutor asked.

In a brand-new revelation, Meredith responded that while she was on the phone with the dispatcher, Cassidy "referenced her father and then, when I asked her further questions, she was saying 'he.'" As they sat together in the fire truck that afternoon, Meredith testified, she asked her niece additional questions, and Cassidy "continued to talk about her father."

.....

The first few days of the retrial also included testimony from Hampton Inn employees, who provided the second jury similar information as in the first trial, including about the rock that propped open the emergency exit door and the tampering with the western stairwell security camera. But the new jury also heard, from Howard Cummings' direct examination of the hotel's general manager, that November 3, 2006, wasn't the first time that camera had been tampered with. The general manager said sometime before then, the camera had been "knocked up" when some people were sneaking in and out of that hallway exit door.

Shelly Schaad testified about her interactions with Michelle—and Jason—the evening before the murder, as well as the weekend of her wedding a few weeks earlier. Under Holt's questioning, she also provided some interesting new details. The evening she learned of Michelle's death, Shelly testified, she and Ryan had gone over to Meredith's house to comfort Jason and his family. When she entered the bedroom where Jason was lying in bed with Cassidy, Jason got up and hugged her. His words, though, were peculiar.

"I'm so sorry," he told her.

As in the first trial, Shelly testified that when she went to Jason's hotel room a few days later, he asked her whether his living will would stand up. Holt asked her what the context of that discussion was. Shelly replied, "Like if he goes to jail, will Cassidy still go to his sister and Joe?"

The Assistant DA also asked Shelly whether she continued to maintain contact with Jason following Michelle's funeral.

She didn't, Shelly responded. "When this first happened," she said, "I told myself that, you know, there was, I think, very quickly speculation, I think. Even my husband's first words were, 'I hope to God he didn't do it,' which never even crossed my mind at the time." Rather, she decided to support Jason, telling herself that "in time his true colors will show and it will become apparent. And just over time, there's just a lot of things that happened the day his wife was murdered that he can't explain. I mean how unlucky can one man be to have a series of events …"

It wasn't until Shelly was mid-sentence that Klinkosum realized she was about to tell the jury she believed Jason had killed Michelle. He jumped to his feet and objected. Though Judge Stephens sustained the objection, the bell the jury had just heard was unlikely to be un-rung. And to make sure it wasn't, Holt asked the witness what happened thereafter.

She responded that she cut off all contact with Jason. "I just personally withdrew myself," Shelly told jurors. "My husband remained in contact, but I personally didn't want to speak to him or see him."

.....

The last witness to testify that Wednesday afternoon was Gracie Dahms. The former convenience-store worker appeared to be a completely different person than the woman who had testified back in June. Her hair was significantly shorter and was professionally styled. She was wearing makeup, dangling silver earrings, a long silver necklace, and silver bracelets. A sharp-looking checkered dress coat covered her black blouse. It looked as if she had received a complete makeover. She even had a new name—Gracie Calhoun—which she acquired upon her recent remarriage. Yet her testimony on direct examination was largely the same, both in substance and delivery—

monosyllabic, poor grammar, and little observable emotion.

Though there were no new revelations during Calhoun's direct examination, her cross-examination was a different story entirely. For starters, when Klinkosum asked her about details of her meetings with law enforcement officers, she volunteered, "I have been through a lot of stuff myself ... So my brain—I can't remember half of what went on and then I can sometimes ... Because I've been through a lot with myself since '06."

But that wasn't the only significant testimony about her brain. Klink asked whether she had been hit by a truck when she was six years-old.

The prosecution witness acknowledged she had, and her parents later said her brain "was laying out on the street." But she denied suffering a brain injury, testifying, "They told my mama I'd be about like two years-old when I'm 22 years old and I'm not even that far off the bench."

Calhoun agreed with Jason's lawyer, however, that she had been collecting Social Security disability benefits since she was a little girl because of her disability, which she described as "slow normal." Though she conceded she had memory problems, she attributed them to problems she had been having with her ex-husband and children since 2006, rather than her brain having fallen out of her head as a child. "I'm going through a hard time myself," she explained.

On redirect examination, Holt tried her best to rehabilitate her star witness. She asked Calhoun if she had received any medical treatment in the 29 years following the truck accident.

"As far as I can remember, no," she responded. She acknowledged, though, she couldn't remember half of her childhood because of the accident.

The Assistant DA also asked Calhoun about her testimony that the man who cursed at her was just a little bit taller than her.

"And what do you mean when you say 'a little bit taller' than you?" Holt inquired.

"On that, 'a little bit taller than me,' anybody that's about as tall as me is just a little bit taller than me," Calhoun responded.

"I can give a sample. My son's about 5'11" and that's about I'd say about how tall the guy was."

"And so would you describe your son as being 'a little bit taller' than you?"

"Yes, ma'am."

Klinkosum wasn't about to let the witness—and Holt—get away with their attempt to turn 6'1" Jason Young into someone just "just a little bit taller" than Calhoun's five-foot-tall frame. On re-cross examination, he asked her to focus on the May 2011 pretrial hearing.

"And you didn't say anything about actual height like 5'11" or anything, correct?" Klink asked.

"Correct," she responded.

"Okay. You didn't say anything about your son being 5'11", correct?"

"Correct," she agreed.

"And then you were asked that question again at last year's trial and you said the person was a little bit taller than you, correct?"

"Correct."

"And I asked you how tall you were and you said five feet tall, right?"

"Yes," Calhoun replied.

"And at that time … you didn't say anything about being five—the person being 5'11" or compare them to your son, correct?"

"Correct," she acknowledged.

"You really didn't—you didn't say anything about the height of the person until you were interviewed last Friday? Is that correct?" Klinkosum asked.

"Correct."

Smelling a rat, he asked, "And that interview last Friday was with Sergeant Spivey, correct?

"Correct."

"Who's sitting here now. He's in the back right there. And Ms. Holt and Mr. Cummings, correct?"

"Correct."

"And that was after you had testified twice about the person being a little bit taller than you, right?"

"Yes," Calhoun agreed.

With that, Jason's lawyer was satisfied he had made his point. Holt, Cummings, and Sergeant Spivey may have succeeded in dressing up their star witness and adorning her with fancy jewelry, but they couldn't change the basic facts: the third-shift convenience-store worker had indeed testified the man who threw the $20 bill at her was just a little bit taller than five feet—not someone over six feet tall, like Jason. And by her own admission, her memory wasn't very reliable.

. . . . .

Once again, Dr. Thomas Clark, the Medical Examiner, testified about Michelle's autopsy. Cummings had him describe in meticulous detail the thirty or more wounds she sustained to her face and head. Dr. Clark told the jury about the bruises and abrasions on the victim's hands, which he explained had likely resulted from her efforts to defend herself. He also shared his opinion that most of Michelle's injuries had been inflicted by a heavy, blunt object.

Although his testimony included no new revelations, Cummings broke some new ground by having Dr. Clark display the clothing Michelle was wearing at the time of her death. The Medical Examiner first held up for the jury her white sweatshirt, which was covered in her own blood. He then showed the jury the bloody T-shirt she had been wearing underneath, and her black sweatpants.

It was almost as if Michelle's badly beaten body were being reconstructed before the jury's eyes. This display left jurors with a deeper sense of the beating she had sustained than the two-dimensional autopsy photos could ever convey. Just as Cummings had planned.

. . . . .

Terry Tiller found herself back on the witness stand early in the second trial—this time as a prosecution witness. Though her testimony was largely the same as in the first trial, she did provide a couple of interesting new details. First, she testified she drove by 5108 Birchleaf Drive not once—but twice—between 3:30 and 4:00 a.m. the morning of the murder.

Holt asked her to describe the SUV she saw parked at the home. Tiller described it as a "medium-sized" SUV. The prosecutor asked the witness if she was familiar with a Ford Explorer. Tiller indicated she was. Asked to describe the size of a Ford Explorer, she replied, "I would classify that as medium."

With the exception of Calhoun's testimony, the prosecutors had to be pleased with how the retrial had begun. They had been more focused, more detailed, and—most importantly—more aggressive. This time, they would leave nothing to chance in their quest for justice for Michelle.

# 20

## PARADE OF WOMEN

Linda Fisher didn't need to wait nearly as long for her turn in the second trial. The State called her to the witness stand early on, before any crime scene or forensic evidence was presented. Her testimony about her son-in-law was more direct and forceful than it had been in the first trial.

She told the jury she found Jason to be "very immature." During her month-long stay at the Birchleaf Drive home in the summer of 2005, Linda testified, he was in a basketball league and a softball league and actually wanted to play in two leagues of each. In view of the responsibilities he should have been shouldering for his one-year-old child, she found that selfish and irresponsible.

Howard Cummings discussed with her at some length her visit to Raleigh in October 2006—which began the day of Michelle's and Jason's third wedding anniversary. He asked her where Jason was at the time. "Well, I thought he was on a business trip," Linda responded.

The Assistant DA followed up, asking if she had heard his testimony at the first trial about being in Orlando at the time and whom he was with.

"Right. He was having an affair," Linda retorted, in utter disgust.

Cummings then asked her about the evening of October 12, when her daughter and son-in-law went out for a belated anniversary dinner. Linda told jurors Michelle was the only one who entered the house when they returned that evening. Her daughter was crying and was very upset. The couple's fight, Linda testified, had apparently begun when Jason told his wife she would have to find her own ride to Ryan's and Shelly's wedding because he was going to play golf with the guys.

According to her elder daughter, Linda said, "By the time when Michelle walked out of Progress Energy and got into the car, Jason was on the telephone and stayed on that telephone until they drove to the restaurant, got seated at the restaurant, and then once they were seated he finally hung up."

When he was back in the house later that evening, she told the jury, there was a full-on "screaming match," with doors slamming throughout the house.

During the evening of November 3, Linda said, she and her son-in-law were seated together in Meredith's living room and began a conversation. Jason said "two things that I can clearly remember," she told jurors. "He said, 'My lawyer told me I can't talk to anyone, not even you,' which what do you mean, your lawyer? Here we are and he's got a lawyer? ... And then the other statement was, 'I'm going to take a hit on the house.' And that was another, 'Like what? What do you mean, you're going to take a hit on the house?' And all I'm thinking about is Michelle's dead."

Cummings pivoted to the difficulties Cassidy's grandmother and aunt had trying to visit with her following Michelle's death. The prosecution witness claimed—in contrast to what Jason and Heather had each said during the first trial—that Cassidy had been whisked away to Brevard *before* her mom's funeral. And after a couple of initial visits, Linda testified, Jason and his mother were never allowed additional visitation. "Whenever I asked Pat, she would always say she'd have to ask Jason. And it would never happen."

She described the confrontation at Pat's home that led to Jason and his mother cutting off visitation, conceding, "I got loud to say the least. And I was disagreeing with a comment about Jason having an affair."

Pat and a friend of hers had apparently remarked, "'You don't know that he had an affair.' And I said, 'Yes, I do,' and so it was getting a little loud ... And Meredith continued the conversation with some girl that was there who told us that if we didn't stand up behind Jason publicly," visitation with Cassidy would be cut off. And then it was, Linda said.

When Cummings completed his direct examination, Collins told Judge Stephens—unlike in the first trial—there would be no cross-examination. Relieved to hear that, Linda stepped down from the witness stand and resumed her seat in the front row of the gallery. This time, she hoped, her testimony would help convince all twelve jurors of her son-in-law's guilt.

.....

The State called three women to the witness stand who hadn't testified during the first trial: Valerie Bolick, a coworker of Michelle's at Progress Energy; Jennifer Powers, one of her best friends from New York; and Kimball Sargent, a mental health counselor Michelle had seen a week before her death. Each provided powerful new evidence.

Bolick got to know Michelle at Ernst & Young in 2001, where she was an intern and Michelle was a junior accountant. By 2003, they were working together again at Progress Energy. Bolick testified they had become good friends, and would often socialize together, both at and outside of work. Just before Memorial Day weekend in 2006, Michelle told her she was pregnant. The following Tuesday, when her friend didn't report to work, Bolick learned she and Jason had been involved in a car accident in the mountains.

Later that week, Michelle discussed with her how the accident happened. She told Bolick, "Jason had insisted on getting coffee before they actually got on the road to come back to Raleigh." Michelle said, "Jason thought he saw the interior light of the car on so he turned towards it, and she said that right before that had happened she had taken off her seatbelt to reach her makeup bag that was on the floorboard. So the wreck happened right after she took her seatbelt off." Bolick made no effort to hide her suspicion that Jason had swerved off the road *because* Michelle had taken off her seatbelt.

A short time later, the witness told jurors, Michelle informed her she was pregnant again and how she planned to share the news with Jason—by dressing Cassidy in a T-shirt saying, "I'm a big sister." The next day, Bolick discussed with her friend how Jason took the news. Michelle, she stated, "specifically said that she did not get the reaction out of Jason that she had hoped to get."

Finally, Holt asked Bolick to describe her interaction with Jason at Michelle's pre-funeral visitation. She told the jury everyone had to pass him on the way out of the funeral home. When it was her turn, Bolick said to her friend's husband, "'I'm sorry for your loss,' and his response was very odd. He said, 'Cassidy's been a real trooper.'"

Jennifer Powers provided even more damning testimony about Jason. She and Michelle had attended high school together in Sayville, Long Island. They became close friends and remained in regular contact as adults, even though they lived some 500 miles apart. They emailed and spoke by phone frequently and visited each other in New York or Raleigh as often as they could—including at each other's wedding.

The most stunning revelation during Powers' testimony was about a phone call she received the day Michelle learned she was pregnant with Cassidy. Michelle was crying hysterically, she told the jury. "She said to me, 'You have to promise to keep this a secret for the rest of your life. I have to tell you something. I'm pregnant and Jason *wants me to abort the baby* or he said he will resent me and the baby for the rest of our lives.'"

Considering Jason's testimony at the first trial that Michelle's pregnancy with Cassidy was a "good surprise"—that he was happy about—Powers' testimony about her friend's desperate phone call was quite startling.

She recalled speaking with Michelle a couple of days after that phone call, explaining to jurors her friend was "still working on the situation. There didn't seem to be any progress." But she then heard from her a week or two later "and her news was, 'I'm engaged. We're getting married.' And there was no further discussion."

Holt also raised the topic of smoking. Powers told the jury Michelle was a social smoker during high school and college. But after meeting Jason, she testified, her friend had to quit smoking because he hated it so.

Toward the end of Powers' testimony, Holt introduced an October 4, 2006, email exchange between Jason and Michelle about the upcoming Thanksgiving holiday. Michelle had forwarded the email to Powers, seeking her advice and guidance.

In the email, Jason stated that Linda: *has got to start realizing that seeing us as often as she does creates an imbalance in our relationship and I've told you that from the start.*

He continued: *I could NOT even count on one hand the WEEKS that your mom has spent with us in less than three years of marriage! I am sorry, but that is EXTREME. I would love for you to have found a guy out there that would be thrilled to be in that same boat as I in regards to time spent with [your] mother in law....GOOD FREAKING LUCK! It is not easy, and I don't appreciate being deemed the "jerk" who has to make a stand simply [because] you either don't have the balls to stand up, or it just doesn't bother you and you simply don't hold your husband's opinion very high.*

In that same email, Jason expressed his adamant opposition to Linda spending the Thanksgiving holiday with his family in Brevard.

*If you want your mom to come to Brevard for the whole weekend, that's fine. Bring her on. I'm just telling you that our marriage has seen better days and I don't see it trending up.*

He even suggested that his wife stay behind in Raleigh and not come with him and Cassidy to Brevard:

*YOU can stay here with your Mom and have your own Thanksgiving.*

The notion of his mother-in-law spending the entire holiday in Brevard, he made clear, was *too EXTREME!*

In her forwarding email to Powers, Michelle stated:

*So this is the issue — you can pretty much figure it out from Jason's rant below ...We obviously had a huge fight about it this morning. As you can see, Jace thinks mom visits too much (I think she's a big help!!) So I either have to make some excuse to tell my mom no she can't come or have Jace think that his opinion doesn't matter.*

Toward the end of her email, Michelle asked her friend:

*What is the big deal about having 1 more person—my mom!! … But he is making a big stink.*

Clearly frustrated, she wrote:

*AHHHH!!!! I just don't know what the 'right' thing to do is??? Please help. And PLEASE don't share this with anyone, I think Mom's feelings would be really hurt. … Welcome to my world of fighting with Jason. He loves to go below the belt.*

Though Powers wasn't on the witness stand very long, her testimony packed a powerful punch. So too did the testimony of the State's next witness, Kimball Sargent. She provided counseling to Michelle through Progress Energy's employee assistance program.

She testified Michelle had set up an appointment for October 19, but for some reason, came to her office a day early. Seeing that Sargent was tied up, Michelle realized she had written down the appointment date incorrectly. Sargent testified Michelle was very upset. "When she walked in and found out I couldn't see her, she burst into tears and so I actually came out and talked with her."

Her next available appointment wasn't until October 27, so they set up an appointment for that day.

Cummings asked the counselor to describe what happened when they finally met on October 27—one week before the murder.

Michelle started crying from the moment she sat down, Sargent responded, and cried for the entire one-hour session. Her new client told her she was there "to get her life and herself straightened out. She was pregnant with a baby that was due in March and she had a very conflicted relationship with her husband." She told Sargent she needed to figure out what to do so she could "fix herself and make things better."

Michelle said she was "stressed out with her marriage" and she had a big fight with her husband that morning. She explained she really wanted to be in marital counseling but that Jason "was resistant because he felt like the problems were her … She was very anxious over the fact that she was pregnant and their marriage was in some real trouble." Michelle told Sargent how Jason would get drunk at football games—sometimes staying out in the parking lot drinking rather than even going into the stadium.

They also discussed Jason's complaints about their sex life. Michelle explained they used to have sex about twice a week "and now it was down to about once a week and he didn't feel like it was enough." That very morning, Michelle told her, "they'd had a big fight because he wanted to have sex and she didn't, and she said there was a lot of storming out."

During their session, Michelle revealed she had been sexually assaulted when she was in college "and one of the issues that she was having with Jason at the time was that when she had sex with him she felt like he was forcing himself on her." His approach to sex evoked in her the same feelings she experienced, Michelle explained, when she was assaulted. She had sex with other boyfriends before Jason, Michelle told the counselor, none of whom made her feel that way.

In addition, their communication had been so bad, Sargent testified, "it had gotten to the point they could not talk at all." They were only able to communicate through emails.

Cummings then showed Sargent her notes from her October 27 session with Michelle, which she read aloud for the jury's benefit. Significantly, toward the end of her notes, she had written that another therapist had indicated that Jason "had anger issues. Says if she—you try to joke on him he will get revenge. He gets angry and she can't tell him something that hurt her feelings. He leaves the bedroom and gets angry."

Sargent told the jury her assessment was her new client "was being verbally abused." Michelle planned to make another appointment to take place within one to two weeks, she testified. But she never heard from her again.

Despite the gravity of Sargent's testimony, Klinkosum asked her just seven questions, the last of which was whether Michelle had reported "anything about any type of physical violence in the marriage."

Michelle "never reported any physical abuse," Sargent

acknowledged.

.....

Once again, the prosecution team put on several days of testimony regarding the crime scene, Jason's Explorer and luggage, and forensic evidence. Though most of that evidence was essentially identical to the first trial, Sergeant Al Sternberg shared an interesting new detail: within Jason's luggage, there was a pack of four to five condoms.

That scintillating tidbit provided a good transition for jurors to hear about the other women in Jason's life. In rapid succession, the State called Genevieve Cargol, Carol Anne Sowerby, and Michelle Money to the stand.

One question Cargol was never asked directly at the first trial was how Jason's personality would change when he drank. Holt asked her to share her answer with this new jury.

Cargol explained, "His behavior would change so drastically and he typically got real angry with me usually over just nothing and he would do things like leave me alone in the dark after a football game with no way to get home. And there was even a time—he did that multiple times. There was even a time where I was left alone at a bar downtown … and I didn't have a way home."

Cargol described the fight in their Texas hotel room in more vivid detail than she had at the first trial, testifying that "something inside of him snapped like I've never seen before and he physically came after me to get the ring off of me … He grabbed me by the arms and threw me down onto the bed but with such force that it just stunned me, and he grabbed my arms so tightly that it ended up leaving bruises in the shapes of his fingers. Later he was pinning my arms behind my back with such force I felt like my shoulders were going to pop out of the sockets."

She told the jury that Jason jumped on her with all of his weight, straddled her, and held her down with his arms and his knees until he was finally able to yank the engagement ring off of her finger.

"And I wanted to state this," the witness continued. "The fight was so scary not just because of the violent part of it, but I had never seen him like that before. His eyes were completely empty and deserted and glazed over. And it was like he wasn't even seeing me and I wasn't seeing him. It was—I felt like he was a different person." When she later showed Jason the bruises on her arms and rib cage, she said, "It wasn't registering to him and it just blew my mind that he didn't care. No remorse whatsoever."

Unlike in the first trial, Holt made sure to have Cargol share with this jury details of Jason's other violent outbursts. His former fiancée testified the first incident occurred in the parking lot of an outdoor amphitheater following a Barenaked Ladies concert. She was sitting in the driver's seat of her car with Jason in the passenger seat. They were chatting while waiting to get in line to leave the parking lot.

Cargol made a point of telling the jury what a great time they had been having up until then. But that changed, she said, almost in an instant. While she and Jason were talking, she casually mentioned she had a mutual, male friend walk her back to her apartment a week or so before the concert. Jason "became so enraged that he punched out my windshield," she testified. "He took his bare fist and punched right through my windshield and shattered it."

The second incident occurred at Jason's apartment in Charlotte, Cargol told jurors. She had just arrived from Raleigh and was using the bathroom. While there, she noticed a letter sitting out on the sink from Jason's camp friend, Carol Anne.

Cargol had never met her before but understood from Jason that she was younger than him and that they were "good buddies," not romantic partners. But when she skimmed through the letter, she was surprised to see Carol Anne "pouring her heart out to him and saying how much she loved him and had always loved him. And she knew that he was serious with me but that she would wait for him if things didn't work out."

When she showed the letter to Jason, Cargol testified, she expected him to tell her he had no idea his friend felt that way about him. Instead, he became "absolutely irate with me, and I was very confused because I thought, 'If somebody is supposed to be upset here, shouldn't it be me?' And I couldn't figure out why he was so angry with me for reading it." Jason became so angry, Cargol told jurors, he punched a hole right through the drywall of his apartment. She found it "bizarre that he was so angry about this letter."

Holt ended her direct examination by showing her witness the September 12, 2006, email Jason had sent her, in which he professed his eternal love. Though she didn't publish it to the jury then, the Assistant DA did so the following day, during testimony about the forensic examination of Jason's laptop computer.

Klinkosum's cross-examination was very short, aimed only at confirming Jason had been drinking before the incident in their Texas hotel room and that Cargol had remained in a dating relationship with him for about a year even after she broke off the engagement — despite his violent outbursts.

Carol Anne Sowerby took the witness stand next. As in the first trial, she was an emotional wreck. It took her some twenty seconds to gather herself sufficiently to even state her name. Her testimony was nearly identical to the first trial, including her hanging her head in shame as she admitted to having sex with Jason on the couch while Cassidy was asleep upstairs.

Her direct examination ended rather oddly, though. Cummings suggested to her that she woke up naked the following morning.

Bewildered, Sowerby responded, "That didn't occur."

Michelle Money's testimony was also mostly a carbon copy of her testimony at the first trial. She testified Jason told her, prior to coming to Orlando on October 7, he was going to tell his wife he was going on a business trip to Florida that weekend. Holt asked her, "What happened during the course of that weekend?"

"We just spent a lot of time talking and hanging out at the house. We ended up having an intimate relationship while he was there," Money responded, once again leaving out the R-rated details.

"So at that point, were you actually engaged in an affair with the defendant?" Holt asked.

"Yes, ma'am," she replied. In contrast to Sowerby, she didn't appear embarrassed or ashamed.

"We also talked about us and how we couldn't do what we did," Money continued, noting that they "didn't have a future, and that we needed to go back to being friends."

But she also admitted she and Jason were trying to meet in Orlando a second time—the weekend of November 4, when her husband would next be out of town—but it didn't work out because of Jason's business meeting on November 3 and the football game the following day.

Money testified she and Jason spoke multiple times a day from October 7 until Michelle's death, including during Jason's drive to Hillsville, Virginia on November 2, on his way to his business meeting on November 3, and later that afternoon on his way to his mother's home in Brevard.

She also told jurors about their meeting in Myrtle Beach in June 2007. They sat on the beach together, Money testified, "and talked for a long time. And we talked about—I remember we talked about the media and how they blew a lot of things out and we talked about how there was a lot of lies said about us and hurtful things that weren't true."

During cross-examination, she told the jury that following their tryst in Orlando, she and Jason both agreed their relationship couldn't go on any further. And that their relationship was more than physical anyway—they had developed a friendship and felt comfortable talking to each other about a wide range of things, in particular their children. Jason talked about Cassidy "all the time," she testified.

Then, out of nowhere, Klinkosum asked, "Ms. Money, this question has to be asked: Did you have anything to do with Ms. Young's death?"

"No," she replied, somewhat surprised by the question.

.....

Toward the end of its case, the State called Fiona (Ginter)

Childs to the stand—another witness who hadn't testified at the first trial. Though she wasn't a member of the McBroads, Childs was already a member of ADPi when Michelle rushed the sorority as a sophomore. She liked Michelle so much, she became her big sister. The following year, Childs moved into the condo Linda had purchased for her elder daughter and lived there for three years, the last two while working as a legal secretary. She later went to law school and became a practicing attorney.

The prosecution witness testified she first met Jason at the Youngs' engagement party. She made a point to tell the jury though she arrived late, Jason wasn't even there yet. When he finally arrived, he was sweaty and wearing running clothes, as he had been out jogging around the neighborhood. She found that "a little bit unusual."

Childs came to the hospital to visit her "little sister" after Cassidy was born, she testified. While there, she had a rather odd interaction with Jason. The new father seemed very intrigued with the C-section, Childs told jurors, and mentioned he was able to see over the curtain during the operation. Jason told her that he was able to see Michelle's body opened up, including "her organs and stuff and that the doctor just pulled her uterus out 'like it was a dirty dish and was scrubbing it, and then put it back in.' And he seemed rather fascinated with that."

Cummings asked Childs to describe her observations of the couple's relationship. She responded, "Right from the very first time I met him, they didn't appear to be very similar ... Michelle, she was a very fun person, but also was, you know, responsible and behaved like an adult ... Jason appeared to me to be the kind of person where just the world was like a playground to him and fun came before responsibilities."

In July 2005, Childs testified, she prepared wills, a health care power of attorney, and a living will for Jason and Michelle. That fall, Michelle contacted her to let her know she and Jason were considering purchasing life insurance. Her husband, Michelle said, wanted to get a $1 million policy for each of them "and that seemed to be excessive to her, that she didn't think they needed that much, and kind of just asked my opinion on that."

The prosecutor asked her if she knew what Michelle ended up doing about life insurance. "I do," Childs responded, "because oddly she brought it up about three to five times over that year preceding her death. She brought it up just saying she was concerned it was too much … that a million dollars just, you know, 'Why does he need to have a million dollars? It's just so much.'"

Cummings also asked the witness about Michelle's miscarriage. She testified she sent her friend flowers because she was so distraught. When they were talking about a week later, Childs continued, Michelle said she "was just so sad and she said that what was making it worse was Jason's just very nonchalant attitude about it. And she indicated to me that he told her she needed to 'just get over it.'"

When she arrived for Ryan's and Shelly's wedding, Childs told the jury, she heard that Jason and Michelle had been fighting—like "World War III." She sat with Michelle, just the two of them, a distance from everyone else. She was concerned about her friend. As they talked, Michelle told her she wanted Childs "to be there for the birth of her new child. She just didn't trust Jason to be there with her," the witness explained.

Cummings asked her if she had learned Michelle was planning to reduce her work schedule once Rylan was born. Childs was aware that was Michelle's plan, but was concerned about it. Asked to explain her concerns, she testified, "It was very apparent to me that her marriage was not good and that it was not working out and from what I could see was heading in the direction of perhaps separation or divorce, potentially." She felt it would be harder for Michelle to leave the marriage if she weren't financially independent.

During his cross-examination, Collins clarified with Childs she had learned following Michelle's death—from the police— that Michelle had acquired not just $1 million in life insurance, but $2 million in basic insurance and an additional $2 million in accidental life insurance. The defense lawyer suggested she had told detectives that was "nice."

Childs strongly disagreed, telling the jury she was in "complete and utter shock" when she heard that.

Collins next suggested Childs had told detectives the amount of insurance Jason was insisting on didn't raise any red flags for her. The amount of insurance, she clarified, "did not cause me any red flags when Michelle was alive, no."

Finally, Jason's attorney asked the witness if she had any personal knowledge of violence between Jason and Michelle. Childs replied she was aware of only one incident that might fit into that category—in which Michelle had acted violently toward Jason.

During his redirect examination, Cummings followed up on Collins' question about the amount of life insurance not raising any red flags. "When you say that it did not raise any red flags to you at the time she was alive, what do you mean by that?" he asked.

"I do remember that she brought it up several times throughout the year preceding her death," she responded. "And while we would have, you know, in-depth conversations about all kinds of things, it did raise a red flag to me after her death that she brought up specifically her life insurance multiple times throughout that year."

Cummings then asked the prosecution witness about an observation her husband had made at Ryan's and Shelly's wedding. Jason was "extremely intoxicated" at the wedding, Childs recalled. While observing his behavior, her husband said to her, "Something is wrong with that guy. He is just not well."

Asked to clarify what her husband was referring to, Childs told the jury that while she was talking to Michelle off to the side, her husband observed Jason doing what he referred to as his "dick tricks."

"At the time of this wedding when Jason is, as your husband described, doing his 'dick tricks' around people, he has a two-and-a-half year-old daughter, is that correct?" Cummings asked incredulously.

"Correct," she responded.

"And he is at [his wife's] best friend's wedding doing 'dick tricks?'"

"Correct," Childs replied, with evident disdain.

Though Linda, Cargol, Sowerby, and Money certainly painted a negative picture of Jason, as they had at the first trial, the State's new witnesses—particularly Powers, Sargent, and Childs—inflicted significant damage on the defense. They gave this new jury much more to think about as it considered whether Jason had the evil mind and depraved heart necessary to have committed such a heinous, brutal crime.

# 21

## KITCHEN SINK

Howard Cummings and Becky Holt had several more surprises in store for the defense team. On February 20, they called to the stand Brooke Bass and Ashley Palmatier, Cassidy's former daycare teachers at the Country Sunshine Children's Center in Raleigh. They testified Cassidy returned to daycare the Monday after Michelle's murder.

Both told the jury Cassidy was withdrawn and keeping to herself, rather than interacting with the other children as she normally did.

That Thursday—the last day Cassidy attended the Raleigh daycare before being moved to Brevard—both Bass and Palmatier noticed something very unusual outside on the back porch of their classroom. Cassidy had taken two dolls out of a bucket. She held one of them, whom she referred to as "Mommy," in one of her hands.

The mommy doll had long brown hair and a pony tail. In her other hand, the toddler held another female doll with short, gray hair and a purple jumpsuit. Cassidy also held a toy chair in that hand.

Over Mike Klinkosum's objection, Palmatier testified she noticed Cassidy had the gray-haired doll strike the mommy doll repeatedly with the chair. Palmatier tapped Bass on the shoulder and pointed toward Cassidy. As they both looked on, Cassidy placed the mommy doll facedown on the bed on the second floor of the nearby doll house.

Cummings then handed Palmatier the two dolls and asked her to demonstrate the toddler's actions. As she showed the jury, the witness stated that just before Cassidy placed the mommy doll facedown on the bed, she said, "Mommy's getting a spanking for biting." After placing the mommy doll down, Palmatier testified, Cassidy told her, "Mommy's got boo-boos all over. Mommy has red stuff all over."

The Assistant DA also asked Bass about an interaction she observed one of her coworkers having with Jason when he came to pick up Cassidy prior to Michelle's death. The coworker asked Jason if he was excited to be having a baby boy, Bass said. Jason replied bluntly, "that was the only way that he could get Michelle to have sex with him."

.....

Tom Riha, the product specialist from Hush Puppies, had testified at the first trial, mainly to tie up some loose ends in Agent Morrow's shoe-impression analysis. During his direct examination in the second trial, Holt asked him some additional questions.

She first asked how many size 12, brown Hush Puppies Orbital shoes had ever been manufactured. Riha responded the company made less than 200 in that size and color combination.

Holt then had him examine the shoes Jason was wearing in a still photo made from the security camera video footage at the Greensboro Cracker Barrel. She asked him if there was sufficient detail in the photo for him to positively identify the shoes.

"Specifically, I mean, I could identify some characteristics of the shoe," Riha responded. He testified the shoes appeared to be dark, slip-on shoes.

The prosecutor followed up, asking, "Is there anything that you observed in that photo that's inconsistent with the Hush Puppy Orbitals?"

"No," Riha replied. "I would say this would be consistent from a visual of this photo to be similar to the Orbital product."

"But simply, it's not enough detail for you to say specifically that is the Hush Puppy Orbital based on the photo?"

"No," he agreed.

"But there's nothing inconsistent?" Holt asked again.

"No," Riha responded.

Curiously, during his cross-examination, Collins neglected to ask Riha how many other shoes sold in the United States might also appear similar to the shoes Jason had on in the Cracker Barrel photo. Nor did Jason's lawyer ask whether the Kenneth Cole slip-on shoes found in Jason's Explorer were similar to the Orbitals.

. . . . .

That same day, the State called Sergeant Spivey to the witness stand. After discussing several aspects of the investigation with him, Cummings asked Judge Stephens for permission to play for the jury the entire video of Jason's testimony from the first trial.

Through a large TV monitor centered in front of the jury box, the jury was able to see and hear every word Jason told the first jury—all four hours of his direct and cross-examination. Once again, jurors were riveted as they watched and listened, hearing Jason's voice for the very first time.

When the video had finished playing, Sergeant Spivey resumed his seat on the witness stand. With Cummings, the most seasoned Assistant DA in the office at counsel table, prosecutors would now attempt to discredit Jason and demonstrate his testimony was nothing more than a tangled web of lies.

One of the questions Holt had asked the defendant during her cross-examination was what had upset Michelle the evening of the couple's belated anniversary dinner.

Jason had responded he "was on the phone with a coworker, my previous employer, and when I picked her up I was still on the phone with my previous employer, and so I was finishing that conversation … all the way to Bella Monica, to the restaurant."

That is what started the argument with Michelle, he had testified in June.

With the luxury of seven months to scrutinize Jason's phone records, however, investigators discovered something quite different. Sergeant Spivey told the jury Jason did indeed begin a telephone call that day at 5:17 p.m.—about the time he would have picked up Michelle from Progress Energy—and remained on the phone for nearly 25 minutes.

But the person at the other end was not a coworker—it was Michelle Money. Worse still, Jason continued to text and speak with Money incessantly throughout that evening, until 1:08 a.m. the next morning, the detective testified.

After handing Sergeant Spivey the official transcript of Jason's trial testimony, Cummings had him read aloud the series of questions and answers about the two times Jason said he had left his hotel room—the first to retrieve a laptop charger and the second to get a newspaper from the front desk and to go outside to smoke a cigar.

Using still images from the hotel's surveillance video, Sergeant Spivey showed the jury that at the time Jason approached the front desk near midnight, he was holding a water bottle in one hand and another item in his other hand. Another still image, taken fourteen seconds later as Jason was walking down the hallway toward the exit door, showed him holding the same two items, the detective told the jury. If that were true, Jason's claim that he got a newspaper from the front desk couldn't be.

Cummings pivoted to Jason's testimony about smoking a cigar in the parking lot. Sergeant Spivey told the jury that other than a suit jacket, no outerwear of any type was found among the items Jason took with him on his business trip.

The prosecutor showed him weather data for that evening from Hillsville, Virginia, which revealed a temperature just before midnight of about thirty degrees, with the wind blowing at 21 miles per hour and gusting to thirty. Though the detective didn't say those conditions made smoking a cigar impossible, they made it appear highly improbable.

The Assistant DA next asked Sergeant Spivey to read aloud

Jason's testimony about eating breakfast in the Hampton Inn's breakfast area the morning of November 3. The prosecution witness told the jury he reviewed all the hotel's video footage of the breakfast area starting at 6:30 a.m. that morning.

Cummings asked him if the defendant appeared anywhere in that footage. Though Sergeant Spivey responded that Jason couldn't be seen in the video footage, he qualified his answer by acknowledging there wasn't enough detail in the footage "to really make out who people are."

Cummings then shifted his questioning to the photo of Cassidy's third birthday party in which Jason was wearing a shirt with a thin white stripe across the chest. His defense counsel had left the subtle impression during the first trial that their client was wearing the same shirt in the birthday photo as he had been seen wearing at the front desk of the hotel shortly before midnight. The seven months between trials had given the detective the chance to put the two images side-by-side to compare the shirts.

Judge Stephens let Sergeant Spivey step down in front of the jury box to show jurors the side-by-side comparison. The detective pointed out the similarities in the shirts—their color and the stripe across the chest—as well as the key difference: their necklines. The shirt in the birthday party photo had a crew neckline. The shirt Jason was wearing at the hotel's front desk was a zip-up V-neck. They were clearly different shirts.

The next area of Jason's testimony the Assistant DA and Sergeant Spivey tried to rebut was that he couldn't afford to fight for custody of Cassidy. One by one, Cummings had the detective walk through the various sources of funds Jason could have tapped into to fight for custody. There was a home equity line from which he had advanced $12,000 to pay money to his sister Heather and his mother; an IRA that held $20,000; and a 401(k) account that held nearly $24,000—roughly $60,000 in all.

They also attacked Jason's testimony he had "lost everything. I've lost—I've lost family, friends, jobs. I've lost everything." Cummings asked Sergeant Spivey, "Are there any words left out of that like 'I've lost my wife too?'"

"Yes, sir, there are," the detective answered.

"I mean, nothing he said on that video or said last summer is left out of that transcript; is that correct?" Cummings asked.

"That's correct. This is a true transcript."

The Assistant DA also asked Sergeant Spivey about Jason's last phone call with his wife the evening of November 2—which Jason testified not being able to recall in detail because it was such an ordinary good-night call.

That call was just before 11:00 p.m., the detective testified, and lasted just shy of five minutes. He told the jury that after that call, the records revealed Jason had *five* conversations with Money before midnight. Perhaps that was why, Cummings hoped jurors would conclude, the defendant couldn't recall any details of the last conversation he ever had with his wife.

Klinkosum's cross-examination barely touched on his client's testimony at the first trial. He did, however, push back on Jason's purported ability to afford a custody battle over Cassidy. As compared to the $60,000 Jason allegedly had available to him, the defense lawyer asked Sergeant Spivey if he knew how much it would have cost for Jason to have hired attorneys to contest custody. The detective confessed he didn't.

Klink also asked him whether he knew how much Jason had to pay to retain Roger Smith, Jr.

Once again, Sergeant Spivey acknowledged he didn't know. He agreed with the defense lawyer the appointment of Bryan Collins—the Public Defender—signified Jason had been declared indigent by the court.

Hearing this line of cross-examination, Cummings decided, during his redirect examination, to release one arrow he had deliberately left in his quiver.

"Mr. Klinkosum asked you about the defendant's finances and about whether you knew how much it would cost to hire a lawyer for various things?" he asked.

"Correct," Sergeant Spivey replied.

"Do you know how much this defendant is out on today?"

"Yes, sir. I do."

"How much?"

"900,000," the detective replied.

Content with that answer, Cummings announced, "That's all the questions I have."

.....

Part of the prosecution's shift in strategy in the second trial was to focus more intently on Jason's status as the primary beneficiary under Michelle's life insurance policy. If his deteriorating marriage and affair with Michelle Money didn't supply sufficient evidence of motive, Cummings and Holt believed his hope of becoming an instant millionaire would.

To help make these points, the State called two witnesses who hadn't testified at the first trial. Jennifer Ray worked for Progress Energy in the department that handled employee benefits. Mark Thomas worked for AON, the international insurance brokerage firm that assisted the American Institute of CPAs in procuring insurance for its members, including Michelle.

Ray helped process life insurance claims for deceased Progress Energy employees. She testified that following Michelle's death, she sent a notification to Jason as the beneficiary under Michelle's life insurance policy from Prudential, instructing him how to submit a claim.

Cummings showed her the claim form Jason completed and asked what had happened after the claim was submitted. She responded she received a letter from Prudential indicating the company was unable to pay the claim "because they cannot pay to a beneficiary if they are considered a potential suspect." Ray added she continued to receive updates from Prudential—who was not willing to pay the claim because it couldn't rule out Jason's involvement in his wife's death. She told the jury the life insurance proceeds were ultimately paid to Linda Fisher, as Cassidy's guardian, instead of Jason.

Mark Thomas personally handled Michelle's application for coverage in November 2005. He testified Michelle's life insurance with Prudential went into effect on February 1, 2006. The coverage on her life was $2 million, plus an additional $2 million if her death were accidental, meaning it hadn't resulted from natural causes.

Thomas told jurors Jason had also obtained a policy, which became effective on March 1, 2006. The application he signed on November 28, 2005, asked whether he had "smoked cigarettes, cigars, or a pipe within the last year." Jason's response was "no." Thomas also testified the account had been "under investigation" by both the Department of Insurance and Prudential, and the entire $4 million under Michelle's policy was ultimately paid, not to Jason, the designated beneficiary, but rather to Michelle's estate.

Curiously, Jason's attorneys didn't lodge a single objection to the relevance—or prejudicial effect—of Ray's or Thomas's testimony. Nor did they ask either witness any questions.

．．．．．

The most significant adjustment the prosecutors had planned for the retrial was yet to come. They intended to share with the jury details of the civil wrongful death case Linda had filed against Jason, including the judgment—signed by Judge Stephens himself—that declared Jason to be Michelle's slayer. Not a word about the wrongful death case, or the slayer declaration, was uttered during the entire first trial. Following the near acquittal, the prosecution team had decided this new jury needed to know all about it.

After Mark Thomas stepped down from the witness stand, and while the jury was outside the courtroom on a break, Cummings announced his next witness would be Lorrin Freeman, the duly elected Clerk of Superior Court of Wake County. He previewed she would be testifying about facts related to the defendant's appearance bond, the wrongful death case, and Judge Stephens' declaration that Jason was Michelle's killer.

Collins jumped to his feet. "Your Honor, we object to the entire line of questioning about the wrongful death case," he said. He argued it would be confusing, misleading, and unduly prejudicial to his client. Rather than fleshing out this argument, though, Jason's lawyer stated he didn't wish to be heard any further.

Judge Stephens had clearly anticipated this objection and had given it considerable thought. In overruling the objection, the judge stated, "The fact that the primary beneficiary elected to be defaulted in response to the wrongful death action and permitted the court to enter a judgment disqualifying him from benefiting from the death of Michelle Young … might be relevant to any number of matters that the jury has already heard and will hear and are considering, and so I do believe it's relevant and I do believe that the probative value outweighs any prejudicial effect."

He told the lawyers he would provide the jurors with further instructions limiting their use of such evidence.

When the jury returned to the courtroom, Freeman took the witness stand. Cummings first asked her how the defendant had been able to post a $900,000 bond.

The prosecution witness testified Pat Young had issued a deed of trust to the State of North Carolina for five separate tracts of land, two in her home county, Transylvania, and three in Buncombe County, where Asheville is located.

The combined tax value of the five tracts was more than $1.1 million. Against that value, the Clerk stated, there was less than $70,000 in mortgage debt—thus, over $1 million in equity. If Sergeant Spivey's testimony hadn't convinced the jury Jason had access to plenty of money for a custody battle, Freeman's testimony left little doubt on the matter.

The Assistant DA then shifted gears to the wrongful death case. After his first question, Collins lodged an objection, which was quickly overruled by Judge Stephens.

Freeman explained the purpose of North Carolina's slayer statute. She told the jury the law is intended to prevent someone who causes another person's death from benefiting through life insurance or other sources.

The Clerk explained Linda's wrongful death suit sought a finding from the court that Jason was Michelle's "slayer." Quoting from the complaint, she stated the lawsuit had alleged, "'In the early morning hours of November 3, 2006, Jason Young brutally murdered Michelle Young at their residence.'"

Because there was no response to the complaint, Freeman told the jury, she, as the Clerk of Court, entered a "default" against Jason—which meant he wouldn't be permitted to dispute the complaint's allegations, she explained.

Freeman told jurors that following the entry of a default, the next step in the process is for the plaintiff to move for a default judgment—which requires a hearing before a judge. A hearing on Linda's motion for a default judgment, she testified, was held on December 5, 2008.

Cummings then had the Clerk read aloud from the judgment entered that day, making especially sure to highlight it had been signed by none other than Judge Stephens. He asked her if the judgment specified Jason had "unlawfully killed Michelle Marie Fisher Young" within the meaning of the slayer statute. Before Klinkosum could get his objection out, Freeman responded it did.

The jurors, who had been dutifully watching the evidence unfold for weeks, now knew the judge who had been guiding them—and who was their sole authority on the law—had ruled three years earlier that Jason killed Michelle. If they weren't already convinced of his guilt, this new revelation certainly increased the odds they ultimately would be.

Cummings then turned to the second default judgment, the one signed by Judge Osmond Smith. Freeman told the jury Judge Smith had entered a wrongful death judgment against Jason for more than $15 million.

Klinkosum's cross-examination was aimed at convincing the jury the wrongful death case had been nothing more than a money grab by greedy lawyers.

He had Freeman focus on Michelle's estate file, which showed that, despite Prudential paying over $4.25 million in life insurance proceeds, only $3.19 million was actually paid into the coffers of the estate.

The Clerk acknowledged that was because more than $1 million was paid to Paul and Jack Michaels, Linda's attorneys. Freeman also confirmed that Linda, as the executrix, received $156,000 as a commission.

On redirect examination, Cummings asked the witness if

Jack Michaels had stated in an affidavit that, after reviewing the extensive criminal files, he was of the opinion Jason had brutally murdered Michelle.

Freeman responded Michaels had made that statement in his affidavit and, further, Judge Stephens had that affidavit before him at the time he entered his judgment. She further testified both Judge Stephens and Judge Smith had before them—in the civil file—search warrants describing the investigation and the autopsy results.

For some reason that wasn't very clear at the time, Klinkosum underscored these very points during his cross-examination by reading aloud from Jack Michaels' affidavit, telling the jury Michaels had stated he had reviewed hundreds of pages of law enforcement and SBI reports prior to filing suit.

Based on that review, Michaels stated in his affidavit, "It is my firm belief and opinion that the allegations of plaintiff's complaint in this matter are true, including the allegation that in the early morning hours of November 3, 2006, Jason Young brutally murdered Michelle Young at their residence."

.....

The State had only two witnesses left to call before resting its case: Josh Dalton and Mike Schilawski. Though Dalton had testified for the defense in the first trial, Holt's cross-examination had scored so many points she decided to call him during the State's case in the retrial.

His testimony was essentially the same, including the part about Jason telling him at a tailgate party he was having an affair with Money.

This time, Holt had him include the additional detail that Michelle was also at that same tailgate, though not by their side during that discussion.

She also asked the witness about a new topic—cigar smoking.

Dalton testified he had never seen Jason smoke a single cigar during their golf trips or any of the numerous times they were together.

Schilawski's testimony was also nearly identical to the first trial. But there was one notable difference. Cummings handed the divorce lawyer a copy of the child custody complaint he had filed on Meredith's and Linda's behalf, which was admitted into evidence without any objection from the defense.

Schilawski read aloud from paragraph six: "'In the early morning hours of November 3, 2006, the defendant brutally murdered Michelle Marie Fisher Young (Michelle) at their residence. Michelle was pregnant with defendant's son at the time of her murder. Upon information and belief, Cassidy was in the residence at the time the defendant murdered her mother.'"

Cummings then had the divorce lawyer read aloud from paragraph twenty: "It says," Schilawski told jurors, "'On December 5, 2008, a judgment was entered against the defendant in Wake County Superior Court under the caption 08 CVS 18831, which declared that the defendant "willfully and unlawfully killed" Michelle, and as a result of that judgment the defendant is barred from collecting any insurance proceeds payable on Michelle's life or from inheriting any property from Michelle's estate.'"

Schilawski also testified about the temporary visitation schedule Meredith and Linda had proposed to Jason before the custody suit had ever been filed. Had he simply agreed to their request, the divorce lawyer told the jury, there never would have been a custody battle for Jason to fight—or fund.

"And so, this idea of a full-blown custody battle and how expensive that was," Cummings asked, "that could have been avoided if he had just signed that one document right there so that the visitation schedule could have been in written—"

"That's true," the witness interrupted.

"So this cost that's going to be involved in all this," the prosecutor continued, driving home his point, "that is because of his lack of agreement, isn't it, lack of consent to what was proposed for visitation?"

"We tried to do it the easy and the economical way," Schilawski responded. "Yes."

Satisfied with that response, Cummings stated he had

no further questions, which prompted Holt to stand up and announce the State had completed its presentation of evidence.

# 22

## DEFENSE REDUX

When it came time for them to put on their evidence, Bryan Collins and Mike Klinkosum found themselves in a somewhat different place than at the same juncture in the first trial.

Though they scored many of the same points in their cross-examination of prosecution witnesses, exposing deep holes in the crime scene and forensic evidence, they needed to adjust to the prosecution team's increased emphasis on Jason's mindset and motive—and to the fact their client's truthfulness from the witness stand had been seriously challenged.

The first witness they called was yet another person who hadn't testified at the first trial. Trooper David Dicks worked for the North Carolina State Highway Patrol in western North Carolina. He investigated the May 29, 2006, accident in which Jason's SUV had plunged into the French Broad River.

Because the prosecution team had implied that the vehicle's plummet was no accident at all, Jason's attorneys wanted the jury to hear a very different perspective.

When Trooper Dicks arrived at the accident scene at about 8:30 a.m. that morning, Jason's Mitsubishi Endeavor was "nose forward into the French Broad River," he testified. Both Jason and Michelle had already been taken to the hospital.

Collins asked the officer what he did to investigate the accident. Trooper Dicks testified he looked at the tire impressions, which showed clearly, "The vehicle had run off the roadway to the right, overcorrected, and then gone down the embankment into the river."

After they were released from the hospital, Jason and Michelle returned to the accident scene and spoke with the officer. In contrast to Meredith's and Valerie Bolick's testimony, he recounted that Michelle told him she had been wearing her seatbelt when the vehicle ran off the road. He also told the jury that Jason's description of the accident was perfectly consistent with the physical evidence. Trooper Dicks didn't investigate the accident further, he testified, because "there didn't seem to be any more investigation warranted."

Collins asked him if he saw anything at the scene that led him to believe the accident had been caused intentionally.

"No," the officer answered, telling the jury the accident was a "typical wreck," consistent with what "we see on a routine basis as a trooper in doing motor vehicle investigations."

.....

As in the first trial, the defense presented testimony from Pat Young, Gerald McIntyre, and Heather and Joe McCracken. During his cross-examination of McIntyre, Cummings focused on Jason's reaction to learning of Michelle's death—in an attempt to demonstrate that it was contrived. He asked McIntyre, "And he immediately started crying?"

"Right. Just fell. If I hadn't have gotten hold of him, he would have [fallen] plumb to the ground. He just broke out crying."

"He didn't say anything at all—just started crying?" the prosecutor asked.

"No, he didn't say nothing," McIntyre confirmed.

Cummings also asked about the search of Pat Young's home in February 2008.

"They come up and looked and stomped through the place and had a couple of women with them, and they never did find anything that I know of," McIntyre said of the law enforcement officers who turned his place upside down.

Jason's stepdad also described an O.J. Simpson-like moment

when investigators went with Pat, search warrant in hand, to meet up with Jason. "They tried to put his shoe on his foot," he testified. "It wouldn't fit."

Cummings asked the defense witness if he ever asked his stepson about the circumstances surrounding Michelle's death.

"No. I didn't ask him nothing," he replied. "Didn't want to know nothing. Least said about it the better off you are."

During Heather's direct examination, Collins handed her a T-shaped, heavy-duty metal object and asked her to identify it. The black object was a little larger than her hand. She told the jury it was a tool one could use to break open a car window or cut a seatbelt if they became trapped in a car. The tool she was holding seemed to fit the description of what Meredith testified Michelle had purchased for Jason for Father's Day. The prosecution had elicited that testimony from Meredith hoping the jury would conclude the Father's Day gift was the missing murder weapon.

Collins asked Jason's sister how she had gotten ahold of the tool. She responded it was in the console of Michelle's Lexus SUV when the vehicle became hers following her sister-in-law's death. She told jurors the metal object didn't have any blood on it. Upon Collins' request, Judge Stephens permitted the bailiff to bring the tool to the jury box for jurors to see and handle for themselves.

During Pat Young's lengthy testimony—largely the same as in the first trial—Collins asked her what she recalled about Jason's reaction when McIntyre told him that Michelle was dead. Her recollection was somewhat more nuanced than her husband's.

"He just, I think he said, 'What? What? That can't be right.' And he just—you saw the color just drain from his face. He started just going down and I thought he was going to just fall down. He started crying. He asked about Cassidy, 'What about Cassidy?' And Gerald and I, of course, were on each side of him, and Gerald was, you know, we were trying to hold him up."

Collins also questioned the former schoolteacher about

one of her visits to the Birchleaf Drive home to get it ready to sell after the murder. While at the house, Pat told the jury, she found "a humidor, I believe is what they're called, that you put cigars in to keep them climatized, or whatever." The defense shared this discovery to bat back the suggestion that Jason would never have been outside smoking a cigar in the Hampton Inn's parking lot.

The Public Defender approached the witness and handed her a black and gold cylinder with a "Kwikset" label on the outside. Pat confirmed the cylinder was the humidor she found while packing up the house and explained that Kwikset was a brand named of locks sold by one of Jason's former employers, DeWalt. She unscrewed the top at Collins' request, looked inside, and showed the jury the cylinder was empty. Though this discovery didn't directly support her son's testimony that he smoked a cigar in the hotel parking lot, it did make that possibility seem a bit more plausible.

.....

Next to take the witness stand were two of Jason's and Michelle's neighbors—Fay Hinsley and Cindy Beaver. Though Hinsley didn't testify at the first trial, the two sides had stipulated to what her testimony would be and handed that stipulation to the jury. This time, the defense decided the jury needed to see and hear her live and in person. And she made quite the impression.

Hinsley, a woman in her seventies full of vim and vigor, had lived by herself in the home directly behind 5108 Birchleaf Drive for more than twenty years. Before she even began to testify, she had the jury in stitches. As she was getting settled into her seat at the witness stand, Klinkosum told her, "We appreciate you being here."

Without missing a beat, she responded, "You better!" The judge, jury, lawyers, and spectators erupted in laughter.

Hinsley said the Friday morning of the murder was her day to get her hair "fixed." She left her home, she said, between 6:00 and 6:30 a.m. While she was driving down the street, she explained, "all of a sudden there was this little car sitting there right on the edge where the crack of the cement and the driveway connects. I mean, like it's someone said, 'Oh, I'm going to jump right out in front of you,' and it caught my attention." Though she described herself as "not a car person," Hinsley was pretty sure the vehicle was an SUV and that it was gray. She said it was "right on the edge of the driveway, like it was ready to go, boy!"

Klinkosum asked the witness whether she had met with Sergeant Spivey during the summer of 2011. With a wry smile, she responded, "No, he met *with me*," which evoked uproarious laughter throughout the courtroom once again. The detective, she explained, had parked his vehicle in a driveway and took pictures to try to match the position of the car Hinsley was describing.

Some five minutes into his questioning, Jason's lawyer abruptly announced he had no further questions.

"You're through with me? Hinsley asked incredulously. "You brought me all the way up here for *that*?" That retort caused even Jason to chuckle.

In response to Holt's questions, the Youngs' good-humored neighbor explained the car she saw that morning was right on the very edge of the driveway, like it was at a starting line in a race. The Assistant DA asked if she could tell whether anyone was in the car.

"There was no one in the car," Hinsley replied, "because I was scared it was going to run over me and I looked at that."

Holt ended her cross-examination by showing the defense witness a photo to orient her to Birchleaf Drive. To everyone's amazement, Hinsley told the prosecutor that the SUV she saw that morning "wasn't on Birchleaf," but rather, was on Enchanted Oaks Drive—a nearby street. Finding that answer much to her liking, the Assistant DA announced she had no further questions.

In contrast to Hinsley, Cindy Beaver was more certain about what she saw the morning of November 3 and where she saw it. She testified to seeing someone in a vehicle at the edge of the Youngs' driveway. Two people, in fact. That made her the only eyewitness in the entire case—and even more important than Gracie Calhoun.

Beaver, a 29-year employee with the Postal Service, was the defense team's foil to Gracie Calhoun, whose brain injury, memory problems, and questionable identification raised huge obstacles for the prosecutors. And whereas Calhoun testified in barely decipherable, monotone answers, Beaver's testimony was full-throated and filled with emotion and animated gesticulations. Hoping her testimony would prove crucial in the end, the defense team had her testify in much greater depth than in the first trial.

Beaver lived about ten houses down from 5108 Birchleaf Drive. For at least a dozen or so years, she had passed by that house every day on her way to work. On November 3, 2006, she told jurors, she was driving down Birchleaf Drive at about twenty miles per hour—with the Youngs' house on her left—between 5:20 and 5:25 a.m.

"That particular night, as I approached that address," she testified, "there was a car in the driveway at that address and the pillar lights were on at the end of that driveway, and the lights of the car—the car was coming out of the driveway facing forward—it wasn't like somebody was backing into the street. It was as if they were going to pull out face forward."

Beaver stated that as she rounded a curve, "my bright lights hit the car and there was two people in the car, a driver and a passenger. The passenger, I assumed, was a woman. I don't know. When my bright lights hit the passenger that person quickly jerked their head away. It was, you know, very obvious, and my first concern was, 'Oh, gosh, I've just blinded this person.'"

Though she wasn't able to see the passenger's face, she assumed it was a woman judging by the hairstyle, which she described as "thicker, you know, about like mine." The passenger seemed to be talking to the driver, she said.

She was "embarrassed about what had happened," the defense witness told jurors, "so I purposely looked over to the end of the driveway where they are. I didn't know whether I should apologize or wave or say something, 'good morning,' or, you know, whatever, or what I might be met with either, but I looked and there the driver was a white male, and I remember very vividly he had his hands on the steering wheel," using her own hands to demonstrate a "10-2" position.

The postal worker also recounted passing by a boxy-type, working van to her right, parked on Blue Sage Drive. She recalled a man in the driver's seat with some newspapers spread out across the steering wheel. She assumed he was a newspaper carrier.

That same afternoon, between 3:15 and 3:20 p.m., she was heading home on Birchleaf Drive, Beaver told the jury, with the Youngs' home now on her right. She noticed several cars lining the street and people in suits walking around. She also saw "a woman there holding a small child with blond hair" — presumably Meredith and Cassidy — "and they were crying," she testified.

Because she didn't ordinarily watch or listen to the news and seldom read the newspaper, Beaver explained, several days passed by before she heard about the violence inside the Youngs' home. She eventually learned law enforcement was asking anyone who might have seen something between midnight and 5:00 a.m. on November 3 to contact the Sheriff's Office. She didn't reach out initially, she testified, because she passed by the house in question after the 5:00 a.m. cutoff.

"The very next telecast," the postal worker told jurors, "we were at work and it said they had extended it from midnight to six a.m. and I went, 'Yikes!'" She told her supervisor, a former police officer, what was going on. He called the Sheriff's Office for her and two investigators came to the post office to meet with her.

"To the best of your recollection," Klinkosum asked, "what you saw in the early morning hours around 5:20, 5:30, was it the same day that when you came back you saw all the cars out front of 5108 Birchleaf?"

"Yes," Beaver replied with confidence.

"It was the same day you saw the woman holding the child with blond hair?" he asked.

"And the same day," she answered, "the paper guy was …"

"Okay, okay. All right," Jason's lawyer interrupted.

"A lot of activity in one day that normally I don't see," she continued, finishing her thought.

Cummings handled Beaver's cross-examination. To obtain a conviction against Jason, he knew it was imperative to diminish her credibility—or to at least make the jury question whether she was talking about the same day as Michelle's murder. He asked her to confirm she had called law enforcement at some point "and indicated that you wanted to withdraw your statement, didn't you?"

Beaver responded she had an unpleasant interaction with someone from the SBI, as the result of which, "I was getting weary with it all. But it was not a retraction. I just said, 'I'm getting tired of dealing with this.'"

Cummings recounted her testimony from the first trial, when Beaver stated that her account of what happened that morning would be corroborated by the newspaper carrier who was in the van on Blue Sage Road. He asked her if she knew the delivery person for the *News & Observer* did, in fact, testify in the first trial and didn't corroborate her observations. She responded, "That would mean the person in the van with those papers weren't carrying *News & Observer*s, I assume."

The Assistant DA also pointed out Beaver told Sergeant Spivey, in February 2008 she was worried and having trouble sleeping. She said, "Yes, of course. This was heavy on you."

Cummings then told the defense witness Sergeant Spivey's notes indicated she wasn't sure of the date she made her observations—that though she knew it was on a Friday, she couldn't recall which Friday.

Her hesitation was caused by the SBI agent, Beaver testified, "who started putting all these scenarios in front of me, and after that, when they left the office, that's when I called and said, 'Look, guys, I'm, you know, I've got other things on my plate right now.'"

The Youngs's neighbor ended her testimony by telling the jury she had "studied it over, and, you know, I drive by that driveway every day of my life, just about, and there is no doubt ... And it's been five and six years and it's definitely something you're desperately trying to forget. Again, I don't know what else to say."

.....

Jason's friend Brian Ambrose took the stand next. His direct examination mirrored that of the first trial. During cross-examination, however, Holt unearthed a few new details he hadn't been asked about at the first trial.

The first was about Jason's interactions with Michelle Money the day of the N.C. State-Boston College game in September 2006. Ambrose and his wife stayed at 5108 Birchleaf Drive that weekend along with several members of the McBroads. He testified there had been "a lot of drinking" when they tailgated that afternoon and after getting back to the Youngs' home, there was "a lot of flirtation" between Jason and Money.

Holt also had Ambrose confirm he had told detectives Jason was a "manipulator." He explained Jason "has that personality where he can convince, you know, convince people to do things that might not necessarily be what they want to do."

As an example, he stated Jason "can be late to something, you can plan everything around him, he can be late to it but, you know, he'll somehow or another convince you that there's a reason he's late and it's not a problem."

The prosecutor also questioned Ambrose about his knowledge of his friend's relationship with Carol Anne Sowerby. She asked whether he had told law enforcement, though Jason and Sowerby were never officially dating, they "hooked up" from time to time.

"I don't know if I ever knew that they truly hooked up," he replied, "but I think it was kind of just a foregone conclusion with all of us that they had."

Demetrius Barrett was next to take the stand. His testimony was also very similar to the first trial. One new detail he added, though, was about Jason's behavior at the funeral. Barrett testified his friend "was in a state I've never seen him before." He told jurors he asked Josh Dalton if he had ever seen Jason like that. Dalton responded, "No, he's taking it pretty tough.

He's on a lot of drugs." To Barrett, he "just seemed out of sorts."

During his cross-examination, Cummings asked the defense witness about the tailgates in which he and Jason participated.

Barrett told jurors the tailgates were "pretty massive," often involving as many as 100 people. "Actually, before Michelle came into the picture," he explained, "our tailgates were more or less, 'All right, who's getting the keg?' basically. There was no food or anything or anything kind of. It was just like, 'All right, let's basically get hammered.' So Michelle came into the picture and she brought order, and she—actually, I think I told you this—she made us adults."

Cummings also established with Barrett that Jason gambled enough to have a bookie, or at least someone Barrett assumed was a bookie. He also described Jason as a "horndog—he was quite flirty. I'm trying to be delicate. Yeah, he was."

The prosecutor pushed Jason's friend to elaborate on his definition of "horndog."

"Well, he had a lot of hookups in college," Barrett explained.

.....

Unlike in the first trial, the defense team called two of its own investigators to the witness stand to testify in the second—Steve Hale and Marty Ludas. Hale, a private investigator, was appointed by the court to assist Collins and Klinkosum with Jason's defense. Hale had worked as a PI since retiring from the Wake County Sheriff's Office in 2003. He had been seated at or near the defense counsel table throughout both trials.

Hale informed the jury he had gone to the Hillsville, Virginia Hampton Inn in May 2011 and rented Room 421, the same room assigned to Jason the evening before the murder. He did several experiments to determine whether the room door could be closed without actually locking. He discovered it could.

The defense investigator testified if the door were closed from a distance of less than six inches, it wouldn't always lock—and could easily be pushed open without a keycard.

The defense team then showed the jury a video of Hale's experiment.

Hale also conducted a similar experiment with the emergency exit door. Just as Jason testified he did, the defense investigator found a stick in some shrubbery near the door and used it to prop it open. He showed the jury photos documenting his findings.

During her cross-examination, Holt intimated Jason had cooked up his story about propping open both doors only after he had received discovery information the State provided his lawyers. But her questions backfired.

Hale testified it was actually in one of his first interviews with Jason after his December 2009 arrest when Jason told him his hotel room door wasn't locked—long before his lawyers were provided with any discovery.

Holt did score some points, however, when she asked Hale about the stick he used to prop open the emergency exit door. In response to her questions, he acknowledged the stick would hold the door open only if he placed it right where the latch was, midway up the edge of the door.

On redirect examination, the defense investigator told the jury he had no problem holding the exit door open with one hand and grabbing a stick from the shrubbery with his other— just as Jason testified he did.

Marty Ludas had spent nearly his entire forty-year career as a fingerprint expert, with stints at the FBI, SBI, and CCBI. He had provided expert testimony some 450 times as a prosecution witness. Only twice before, he said, had he testified for the defense.

Ludas's testimony was highly technical and jargon-filled, stuffed with information that can baffle weary juries. His primary point was that the CCBI had obtained palm prints from Jason's closet door that matched neither Jason nor Michelle, although the jury may well have missed that point amid the fog of his complicated descriptions.

Klinkosum also briefly called Sergeant Spivey back to the stand. He had the detective confirm that, in April 2007, the Sheriff's Office had received a call stating a mallet, or large hammer, had been found in the front yard at 5108 Birchleaf Drive by a neighbor who had been mowing the lawn. Investigators sent the hammer off for testing to determine if any blood could be detected. But none was. Nor were any fingerprints.

Jason's lawyer also had Sergeant Spivey authenticate the voicemail Jason had left for Michelle on the home answering machine on November 3. But the quality of the recording was so poor, one juror raised his hand to report, "Your Honor, we couldn't understand a word of that."

Finally, Klinkosum handed the detective a stack of credit card statements for a Visa Signature card that was actually in Michelle's name. The statements dated back to February 2004. Klink had Sergeant Spivey confirm that a purchase had been made on that credit card in early 2004 at Cigars by Antonio in Tampa, Florida. Again, the defense team wanted to make sure jurors knew there was evidence supporting Jason's testimony he had smoked a cigar in the Hampton Inn parking lot.

Cummings picked right up on that point in his cross-examination, noting the credit card records spanned over four years, and that only one single transaction appeared to have anything to do with cigars.

The Assistant DA also elicited a curious exchange Sergeant Spivey had with Pat Young in February 2008, while they were riding together to meet Jason to search his SUV for the Hush Puppies Orbitals. During that drive, Pat shared with him a discussion she had with Jason shortly after an SBI agent had been permitted to take a swab from Cassidy's cheek.

Jason told his mom, the detective testified, "We would probably find his DNA on the dropper because he had given Cassidy the adult Tylenol, but he had diluted it with water."

Klinkosum returned to this subject during his redirect examination. By this point in the trial, it had become clear the prosecution team had abandoned the theory Jason had drugged his daughter with Tylenol and/or Pancof PD, likely because the fingerprint on the medicine cup atop the Tylenol bottle didn't match Jason's.

Klink wanted the jury to know this idea had been Sergeant

Spivey's theory all along.

In response to his questions, the detective confirmed he did, initially, believe Jason had drugged Cassidy. He also confirmed they were never able to identify whose fingerprint was on that medicine cup.

.....

On Wednesday, February 29—without even taking a pause to discuss whether to call Jason to the stand again—the defense rested its case. The State then called three rebuttal witnesses to cast doubt on Cindy Beaver's testimony—Travis Branch, Jimmy Arrington, and Sergeant Spivey.

Branch was the regular *News & Observer* delivery person for the Enchanted Oaks subdivision. He delivered the Raleigh paper to nearly 300 subscribers in his white minivan. Branch told the jury he delivered papers on Birchleaf Drive the morning of the murder and noticed nothing out of the ordinary—in contrast to Beaver. Yet his timing didn't match her testimony, as he testified he would have made his deliveries on that street between 4:00 and 4:30 a.m., long before Beaver spotted the newspaper delivery van she described.

Arrington was Beaver's supervisor at the Postal Service, who had retired in 2008 after 23 years. He had previously worked eight years as an officer for the Raleigh Police Department and five years in alcohol law enforcement. He had supervised Beaver for more than ten years before retiring. Arrington told the jury he called the Wake County Sheriff's Office on her behalf because she was reluctant to get involved. Later on, investigators spoke with him as well. At that time, he apparently described Beaver as being "nosy." Holt asked him what he meant by that.

"Cindy, knowing her for the period of years I worked with her," her former boss replied, "had a tendency to get involved with other employees' affairs, and it was a constant thing going on with people. You were putting out fires every day. He said/she said type thing, scenario, and she would get involved with somebody's affair when she really shouldn't have ever got involved in it. And then the personnel clash would come about and I'd have to get involved to try to smooth things over. And it was a constant battle every day almost."

Sergeant Spivey took the witness stand—for the third time— to describe a phone call he had with Beaver in February 2008, after she had left him a message to call her. On that occasion, he testified, the postal worker told him she was having trouble sleeping at night because she was unsure of the exact date on which she observed the SUV in the Youngs' driveway—she was certain it was on a Friday, but beyond that, wasn't sure which Friday.

The detective also told the jury that, after she met with an SBI agent, Beaver told him she wanted to withdraw every statement she had previously made.

Just before wrapping up their rebuttal case, the prosecutors called to the witness stand a Nationwide Insurance manager, Robin Jones, whose unit fielded a homeowner's insurance claim apparently filed by Jason's sister Kim.

Jones told the jury that, on November 20, 2006, a call center adjuster had received a call indicating there had been a murder in the Youngs' home that resulted in blood in the master bedroom and the need to replace carpet, do some painting, and perform some other repairs.

Cummings asked him if there had also been a claim made for the theft of property—"jewelry or rings or anything like that"—which had been covered under the same insurance policy. No claim had been made for the theft of jewelry, cash, or any other property, Jones testified.

The testimony wrapped up that Leap Day afternoon. Jurors had heard from 65 witnesses. Over the course of more than three weeks, they had been provided a tremendous amount of information. It was now up to the lawyers to help them make sense of it all.

# 23

## GRAND FINALE

On March 1, 2012, jurors sat at the edges of their seats, eagerly awaiting the arguments in which the prosecutors and defense lawyers would stitch together the evidence into more coherent narratives. The courtroom's gallery was filled to capacity, with family members, friends, and spectators anxious to hear the lawyers' closing remarks.

Mike Klinkosum was first to speak. Much as he did in his closing in the first trial, he focused relentlessly on the physical evidence, asking the jury to consider ten circumstances "that show you that Jason Young did not kill Michelle Young." He started with the fight in the bedroom, the attempted strangulation, and scratch marks on Michelle's neck, evidence that "she was trying to pry those hands away."

If Jason had been her attacker, he insisted, there would have been scratches somewhere on his hands.

He spent considerable time discussing Michelle's blood—how much of it was found in the house, and how none of it had been detected in Jason's Explorer, the Hampton Inn, or any of her husband's belongings.

While discussing Cassidy's shockingly clean appearance, Klink interjected an entirely new defense theory. The only way she could have been cleaned up so meticulously, he suggested—without any evidence of blood in any sinks or bathtubs—is if she had been removed from the house altogether and cleaned up somewhere else.

Yet Jason didn't have enough time, his lawyer argued, to commit the murder, remove Cassidy from the house, clean her up, and then get as far as Wytheville, Virginia by 7:40 a.m. that morning. He pointed out that even Sergeant Spivey, in one of his search warrants, had asserted his belief the toddler had been removed from the house.

If the State's theory were to be believed, Klinkosum continued, his client killed Michelle "in the bloodiest way possible and is under enough time pressure to do that but still has enough time to clean himself up, find his daughter in the blood, put her in the bathroom, leave her in there long enough for her to smear blood all over the walls and all over the floor, and then somehow get her cleaned up and put her back in his bed near his dead wife."

"If he took her away, he took her away to get the blood off of her, and he cleans her up, why," Klink asked, "would he take her back to the master bedroom and put her in there? That makes no sense."

He next discussed the lack of fiber transfer between the Hampton Inn and the crime scene as well as the DNA evidence. Unlike in the first trial, however, Klinkosum was unable to argue about the cigarette butts that contained DNA from two unknown males, or the hair on the picture frame whose DNA didn't match Jason's or Michelle's. Judge Stephens hadn't allowed the defense attorneys to present that evidence in this trial because they couldn't properly establish where the cigarette butts, or that hair, came from.

Klink focused instead on the unknown DNA found on the jewelry box, arguing that the master bedroom, "almost like an inner sanctum of a home," wouldn't contain DNA from friends or other visitors. "That's where you and your spouse or people in your immediate family are allowed to go," he argued, "and there was DNA on the jewelry box in this master bedroom that doesn't match either of the adults that lived in this house. There is something not right with this crime scene, ladies and gentlemen."

He then pivoted to the fingerprints found in the master

bedroom. "It's the inner sanctum of a home and you have fingerprints that cannot be identified to anyone. The fingerprints that CCBI compared—they found unidentified prints on Michelle Young, around Michelle Young's closet and inside Jason Young's closet on the shoe box, on the shoe-shine box—and these prints," Klinkosum continued, "were compared to over 160 different people. Family members, close friends of the Youngs, acquaintances of the Youngs." But not a single one matched.

He also focused on the unidentified prints found on the eBay printouts Jason sent Meredith to retrieve. He suggested the prosecutors would contend the prints belonged to law enforcement officers. "If you have law enforcement officers' prints on file," Klink asked, "why don't you just compare them and then eliminate them?" The failure to take that logical step couldn't be so casually excused.

"That's not right," he argued. That's not proof beyond a reasonable doubt. That's not uncovering every stone, and, ladies and gentlemen, in a case where a man's very liberty is on the line, where he could go to prison for the rest of his life, that's very little to ask."

Klinkosum then pointed to the fingerprints and palm prints on Jason's closet door frame—from which Jason had been excluded. "You have palm prints within three or four feet of Michelle Young's body and yet that question mark hangs out there in the air about who they belong to. It doesn't make sense, ladies and gentlemen."

Circumstance six, he stated, involved Jason's telephone calls the night before the murder. According to Michelle Money and Demetrius Barrett, it was "same old Jason," he reminded jurors, rather than "the mind of a man that is trying to plot out a murder and get away with it."

The Hampton Inn was circumstance seven. The phone records established that Jason was in his room speaking with Barrett until 11:11 p.m. The western stairwell camera went black at 11:20 p.m. "How did he, in the span of nine minutes in a hotel he'd never been in," Klinkosum asked, "go throughout that entire bottom floor, figure out exactly which camera to unplug and then do it in the span of nine minutes without even being seen downstairs? There's cameras all over the first floor and yet there's not one picture of him walking anywhere down there until midnight."

The defense lawyer then transitioned to the shoeprint evidence, circumstance eight, suggesting it left two possibilities other than those posited by the prosecutors. The first was that two different people were involved in the murder, one of whom was wearing a pair of Hush Puppies just like Jason's. The second possibility—a radical departure from Jason's testimony Michelle must have donated his Hush Puppies—was that the Hush Puppies shoeprints may have been made by Jason's shoes, but with other feet wearing them.

Klink reminded jurors that Jason's and Michelle's closets had been "pillaged and rummaged through," with clothes strewn everywhere and shoe boxes torn open. Unlike the dark and distinct prints left by the Franklin athletic shoes, the prints from the Hush Puppies were so faint they had to be enhanced with chemicals in order to discern any details. What that meant, Jason's lawyer contended, was Michelle's assailant had been wearing the athletic shoes—pressing them hard against the floor while beating her repeatedly.

Realizing he had blood all over his shoes, Klinkosum theorized, the assailant may have thought, "'I can't track blood out of here; it might lead back to me,' and so what do they do?" He suggested the killer rummaged through Jason's closet, found the Hush Puppies, and put them on so additional prints weren't made as he exited the house.

The closets were circumstance nine. If Jason had been Michelle's assailant, Klink asked, why would he have rummaged through both closets to find whatever he was looking for? "Why would Jason Young's closet have been pillaged like that unless it was someone who was not Jason and was not—didn't know where things were in Michelle's closet either?"

The tenth and final circumstance, the defense lawyer stated, was the "investigation itself" and how investigators "focused like a laser on Jason Young."

To underscore that point, he reminded jurors how differently two of the most critical witnesses—Gracie Calhoun and Cindy Beaver—had been treated. Calhoun, he argued, "was just welcomed with open arms by law enforcement and the prosecution." They "didn't do one thing to test her memory."

"But yet Cindy Beaver, okay, Cindy Beaver, who saw a car in that driveway at around 5:30 in the morning, 'Oh, she's not credible.' … A twenty-plus year employee, federal employee, who's driven that route every morning for the last twenty years has something stand out to her and all of a sudden she's not credible."

As he began wrapping up, Klinkosum implored the jury to find that the physical evidence "points to someone else and that they were trying to get you mad at him for the way he treated Michelle, for having an affair on her, for everything he's done that's wrong."

He granted the jury permission to be mad at Jason. "Hate him if you want to. I don't blame you. But what you feel about him in terms of him as a person, that anger that you feel, put it in context, ladies and gentlemen. Put that in context, because when you look at the physical evidence in this case, it does not match up. It does not match up to Jason having killed his wife and unborn son."

Bryan Collins stood up to present Jason's final argument. He repeated several of the themes he relied on in the first trial—including the analogy of a highlight reel of Michael Jordan's worst moments on the basketball court. He showed the jury the same PowerPoint presentation to illustrate Jason's testimony about his travels had to be accurate—and the State's theory couldn't be.

A new theme he presented was about the prevalence of electronic information in the modern world—from cell phones, computers, surveillance cameras, electronic keycards, credit card swipes, and so forth—all of which had been admitted into evidence.

Jason was leaving "electronic traces of himself everywhere he is," Collins told jurors. "And the thing about that is that every single one of those electronic traces that he left of himself are exactly where he says he was and exactly when he says he was there and he's doing for the most part what he says he's doing in those electronic traces." But not a single electronic trace of Jason existed between midnight and 7:40 a.m. the morning of the murder.

"And do you know why that is?" Collins asked. "When you're in your hotel room asleep, you're not generating electronic evidence. You're not driving. You're not talking on your cell phone. You're not using your computer. You're asleep."

The Public Defender suggested the wrongful death case was irrelevant, noting Jason simply decided "not to participate. He wasn't going to play that game." As a result, "Cassidy gets all of Jason's money and Cassidy gets all of Michelle's life insurance, and that's the way it should be. That's the way Jason wanted it. It makes you wonder a little bit what Linda's lawyers did to earn a million dollars in that case," Collins mused, "and it makes you wonder a little bit what she did to earn $150,000 in that case, but that would be pure speculation and that doesn't help you decide this case."

He next pivoted to the custody case, telling jurors, "Jason didn't give Cassidy away. Jason is still Cassidy's father" and could reclaim custody of her at any time he proved that to be in her best interests.

He asked them to consider the timing of the custody case: "At that time Jason was still a suspect. He hadn't been charged with anything. The media was hounding him. He didn't have a job because of that. He didn't have a house. He was being sued for $15 million. He was sitting around wondering when or if law enforcement officers were going to come and take him to jail."

Jason had consulted a really good family-law attorney, Collins reminded the jury, "and what do you think she told him his chances were of winning a child custody case? Think about that." At the hour-long hearing that had been scheduled, "Do you really think a judge is going to let him have custody of his child?" he asked rhetorically. "So he agreed that Meredith could have her, that she could take custody of her and take care of her … He did the best thing he could do for Cassidy at that time. But the point of that is none of that helps you decide this case."

Turning to Roger Smith, Jr.'s advice to Jason not to cooperate with the investigation, Collins suggested that was actually "good advice to give to an innocent man." That's because "if you tell the police a story that doesn't fit their theory, they are relentless in going after you … You saw how that worked with Cindy Beaver. This poor innocent woman, who's just driving through her neighborhood, trying to be a good citizen and tell the police what she saw. They grilled that poor woman."

Had his client submitted to an interview and gotten "the most minor, insignificant detail wrong," the Public Defender argued, "then trained, experienced law enforcement officers or trained, experienced prosecutors are going to seize on that and they're going to claim that you're lying and then they're going to use that claim that you're lying to argue that you're lying about everything and that you can't be believed about anything."

Jason's lawyer then grabbed the Hampton Inn check-out receipt from his counsel table and held it up before the jury to stress its significance. That receipt would have been placed under Jason's hotel room door between 3:00 and 5:00 a.m., he reminded jurors. "He had this," Collins asserted, clutching the receipt. That means he was in that hotel room after this was slid under the door, so we know he was in the hotel room."

And if Jason's hotel room door had been propped open all night as the prosecution team suggested, he argued, Keith Hicks would have noticed it either when he slid the receipt under the door or when he hung the *USA Today* on the door handle.

"Keith Hicks, the man who can see a little rock in the door. Keith Hicks, who's worried about security because he's the only person there at night. Keith Hicks would have seen that, and if he didn't see it when he went to hang the paper on the door, it would have opened and he would have noticed it then. That door wasn't propped open all night long. Jason was there asleep," he insisted.

As he neared the end of his argument, Collins focused on a vacuum cleaner investigators had found plugged into an outlet in the second-floor home office. Pointing to a photo, he showed the jury a footprint made in dirt on the very bottom step of the staircase leading upstairs from the kitchen; the same photo didn't reveal dirt on any other step.

"How is that possible?" he asked. "Well, was somebody using that vacuum cleaner to vacuum those steps? We'll never know because they didn't seize the vacuum cleaner. Might we want to know whose fingerprints were on that vacuum cleaner? If there were unidentified fingerprints on that vacuum cleaner, wouldn't that really tell you something? How can there just be dirt on that step, and none of those, and yet we've got a vacuum cleaner out in the middle of a crime scene and nobody bothers to look?"

At that moment, Collins began choking up with emotion. "And they want to put this man in prison for the rest of his life," he said, voice quavering, "and they *didn't even bother to look.*"

As he began wrapping up, the Public Defender reminded jurors about Beaver's observations the morning of the murder. "Her testimony cripples the State's case and they know that," he argued, unable to contain his frustration. "The law enforcement officers knew that from the very beginning. The State knows that, the prosecutors know that, and what they have done to her is wrong. Just like what they're doing to Jason Young is wrong."

Collins concluded with familiar words from the first trial: "We're not ever going to know what happened in that house that night. We just can't. It's too late. The case is not solved. The evidence is not clear. It's not beyond a reasonable doubt. Please do your duty and find Jason Young not guilty."

Following a lunch break, Becky Holt picked up right where Collins left off, telling jurors, "This case *is* solved. Jason Young brutally murdered Michelle Young in the early morning hours of November the 3rd of 2006, in the bedroom that they shared at 5108 Birchleaf Drive. He is guilty of first-degree murder beyond a reasonable doubt."

Michelle, Holt said, found herself "married to a man who wouldn't grow up, didn't want the same things that she wanted, who didn't want to be married to her, who abused her verbally, enough that she went to seek help." And she told her therapist that, though Jason was complaining about the lack of sex in the marriage, she felt like he was forcing himself on her.

Meanwhile, the Assistant DA continued, "Jason had had it with Linda Fisher. Her visits were too long, her visits were too often, and he absolutely was not going to have her move in the house with him."

The defendant had confided in his friend Josh Dalton that he didn't think he could divorce Michelle "because she will move to New York and she'll take Cassidy," Holt reminded jurors. He also told Dalton he thought he might be in love with Money and talked about getting her pregnant. At nearly the same time, the prosecutor added, he had sexual intercourse with Carol Anne Sowerby in his home and had written to Genevieve Cargol that she was the "love of his life."

Why was any of that important? Holt asked. She explained the State wasn't asking the jury to convict Jason because he engaged in extramarital sex or because he was a jerk to his wife. Rather, she contended, when the defendant finally made a statement—from the witness stand—"1,693 days after Michelle's murder," and said he loved his wife, the evidence of his blatant infidelity "should make you question his honesty."

In view of the sorry state of his relationship with Michelle, the prosecutor asked jurors whether it made any sense that he was shopping for a belated anniversary present before leaving the house on November 2. Or that he left with the MapQuest directions, but not the eBay printouts he had printed off the very same printer.

"The defendant, who had sent a card for the anniversary and not purchased a gift now, almost a month later, has decided before he leaves for a business trip that he's going to shop for an anniversary gift. Does that make sense?" Holt asked incredulously. "Or in light of what you now know, is that part of the plan, the plan to leave those papers so that he could later have an excuse to have Meredith go over to the house?"

She next discussed the photo of Jason at the Cracker Barrel, reminding jurors Tom Riha had testified the shoes Jason was seen wearing were consistent with the appearance of Hush Puppies Orbitals. And it just so happened that Jason owned a size 12 pair of those very shoes, only 195 of which existed in the entire world.

The Assistant DA also focused on Jason's testimony about his activities at the Hampton Inn, asking jurors if it made sense to them that he would leave his computer and all of his belongings in his hotel room with the door propped open. Or that he needed to get the *USA Today* from the front desk to look at sports scores, even though his room had a TV and wireless internet access—which he was actually using to access sports websites.

Equally incredible, she suggested, was the defendant's testimony he went to the parking lot to smoke a cigar. Not only did the evidence reveal Jason hated to be around anyone who was smoking, his friend Josh Dalton had never seen him smoke a cigar, despite all of their activities together over several years. On top of all that, it was thirty degrees outside that night with the wind blowing twenty miles an hour.

"Your reason and common sense should call 'foul,'" she asserted.

Holt reminded jurors about the three voicemails Jason left, designed to get Meredith into the house to retrieve the eBay printouts—two to her and one to his mother. "You know from those three phone calls he wants Meredith to hurry up and get over there. Is it because the surprise is important?" she asked in disbelief. "Is it because there really, really is going to be a purchase of a purse and he doesn't want Michelle to find out about that? Or is it because he knows that somebody needs to get over there and get Cassidy?"

Reminding the jury of Brian Ambrose's testimony that Jason was a "manipulator," Holt began wrapping up, telling jurors, "Don't let yourselves be manipulated in this case. When you go back to deliberate, consider all the circumstances in this case.

Consider how it is that the defendant could have been so lucky to be trapped in a situation and that his wife just happened to be murdered, that the things that happened at this hotel would happen on that very night, that Gracie Calhoun would see him and recognize him, that the wedding rings would be the only thing missing."

The situation, the prosecutor explained, "was not tolerable for the defendant. He wanted out, and while he may have loved Cassidy, Jason Young loved himself more. He's a salesman by trade. Do not buy that statement that you heard ... Tell Jason Young by your verdict that you know that these circumstances are important, that you see through the story that he tried to concoct four years later. Tell Jason Young that your reason and common sense dictate a verdict of guilty of first-degree murder of Michelle Young."

Howard Cummings stood up to address the jury. Though he wasn't directly involved in the first trial, he had served as the lead prosecutor in the case since the day Michelle had been murdered. Particularly after the first trial ended in a hung jury, the first Assistant DA felt an immense sense of responsibility to deliver justice for Linda and Meredith, for the dozens of law enforcement officers who had devoted so much time and energy to the case, and, most importantly, for Michelle Young.

He began his closing by articulating a theme he would return to repeatedly: "It is not a stranger that did this," he said. "This is not a stranger crime. This is an act of domestic violence that had been coming on for a while."

Cummings tried to explain away some of the forensic evidence on which Klinkosum had so heavily relied. There was no blood anywhere downstairs, he noted, so why would there have been any in Jason's Explorer? The Youngs had recently had a house "full of people" for the N.C. State-Boston College game, many of whom stayed several nights. Law enforcement officers hadn't been able to obtain prints of everyone who had been there. Naturally, the prosecutor explained, there were unidentified prints and DNA in the house.

The only unexplained fingerprint evidence that would have been significant, he argued, would have been a fingerprint made in blood. "That would tell you that that person was there that had that fingerprint after the bleeding started, but that doesn't exist anywhere in the house."

Bewildered, Cummings asked why the defense, all of a sudden, seemed to be rejecting Jason's own testimony that Michelle had donated his Hush Puppies—and was now suggesting someone else had worn those shoes the night of the murder.

The Assistant DA held up still images taken from security cameras at the Hampton Inn. The first showed Jason at the front desk at about midnight. He suggested Jason wanted to be seen to establish his alibi.

The object in his hand, as he walked toward the exit, had to be the road atlas found in his Explorer, not a newspaper, Cummings argued, as he was holding that same item when he approached the front desk. He then held up the road atlas that had been entered into evidence and pointed to Meredith's telephone number, insisting Jason had written it down "because he had to call Meredith to go over there to take care of Cassidy."

He asked the jury where the shirt was that Jason was seen wearing at the Hampton Inn's front desk and where his Hush Puppies shoes were. When he arrived at Meredith's home the night of the murder, Cummings reminded jurors, Jason wasn't wearing either and neither was in his car or in his luggage.

"You know, sometimes people don't tell the truth. Sometimes people tell lies. Sometimes people live a lie," the prosecutor snarled with scorn and derision.

That statement led him inexorably to the topic of Jason's infidelity. "Why would a married man whose wife is pregnant have condoms in his luggage?" he asked. "Not just one. Why would he do that unless he was doing something that is dishonest. Adultery is dishonest. That's what he's doing. And I'm not asking you to pass judgment on him because of the adultery. I'm asking you to pass judgment on him because of his honesty in his life or his dishonesty in his life."

Cummings next turned to Klinkosum's contention that Jason's closet had been "pillaged." The Assistant DA argued the disarray could have resulted from the defendant's time crunch. Another possibility was that Jason had deliberately staged the scene to make it look like a robbery. Michelle's missing wedding and engagement rings—for which no insurance claim was ever filed—might also have been part of the staging, he suggested.

The prosecutor asserted that the manner in which Michelle had been killed didn't fit with the notion of a stranger having been her assailant: "A stranger comes into your house, and all he is going to do is strangle you, and that doesn't work—how many times is he going to hit you afterwards?"

Holding up a gruesome photo of Michelle's bloody and disfigured face, he asked: "Is it going to be like *this*? Is this what a stranger does?" There was only one word to describe the beating inflicted on Michelle, he continued, "Overkill," which would not have resulted from a confrontation with a stranger.

Cummings also pointed to Jason's reaction when his stepfather told him Michelle was dead. "No reaction or disbelief ... He does not say, 'I need to call and find out about this.' It's because he knows what happened."

The Assistant DA puzzled over the oddity of Jason's statement to his mother, during their long drive to Meredith's home, that he would surely lose the house. Cummings noted Jason stood to receive $4 million in life insurance proceeds. "The only way he's going to lose the house is if because, as he killed his wife, he will not be able to claim the life insurance. He will never get it. That's why. That's the only way he can lose that house."

Neither Klinkosum nor Collins had addressed the testimony of Cassidy's daycare teachers. Not only did Cummings remind jurors of their testimony, he used the actual dolls Cassidy held that day to recreate the beating she had one doll inflict on the other.

He told jurors, "You can consider what they reported to determine whether or not that is evidence that Cassidy actually observed what happened."

He mocked Jason's testimony—that he loved Michelle, even

though he wasn't a proper husband, and he was a good father to Cassidy. "Cheating on her mother in the same household, talking about your sex life to your daycare workers, public humiliation of this child's mother—is that being a good father to this child?" he asked derisively.

Shifting to the custody lawsuit, Cummings emphasized that Linda and Meredith hadn't even asked Jason to grant them custody—merely to have regular visitation with Cassidy. They sued him only after he wouldn't agree, he reminded jurors.

"He had every opportunity in the world, both in family-law court and in regular civil court," the prosecutor argued, "to say to a judge or a jury the same thing that he said on that video, the same thing he said last summer. He could have said that at any time he wanted to, but he never would do that. They would have been happy with just visitation. That's all they wanted, but he couldn't do that, and then he got sued and he couldn't stand to answer the questions either in civil court or in domestic court."

Those references to "civil court" were as close as the prosecution team came to mentioning the wrongful death case. Neither Cummings nor Holt reminded the jury Jason had been declared Michelle's slayer—by Judge Stephens himself— or that he had been found liable for her wrongful death and ordered to pay more than $15 million.

As he neared the end of his argument, Cummings returned to the topic of domestic violence, which he told jurors "takes shape in many different ways. It is about control. It is as much about verbal abuse and mental abuse as it is physical abuse."

He pointed out that a "history of prior acts of physical violence doesn't always come before the first serious act. Thirty blows. Thirty blows. That's not from a stranger," he argued. "That is a mad, mad domestic abuser who is mad about the place he's found himself in."

Standing beside a flip chart near the lectern, he began filling the blank page with all of the circumstances he contended left no doubt that Jason had been Michelle's killer: strangulation, thirty plus blows to her body, no forced entry, no theft, no harm to Cassidy, Jason's ownership of size 12 Hush Puppies, strange camera events at the Hampton Inn, in-law problems, $4 million in life insurance, an affair, and the way he testified at the first trial.

"When all those things come together," the prosecutor asserted, "and there may be more, but you think about the fact that he's going to be able to, if it works like it's supposed to, he's going to be able to get the life insurance, he's not going to have to deal with his in-laws anymore, no harm is done to his child. She's obviously over-killed and there's no forced entry. All of those things come together to say that this is not a stranger that did this."

Cummings acknowledged Jason may have had help, possibly to clean up Cassidy. And that the second set of shoeprints did suggest an accomplice may have been involved. None of that mattered to the jury's decision, he explained, because Jason had clearly committed this murder.

The first Assistant DA ended his argument using a puzzle as a metaphor. "Sometimes when you're with your family on a rainy day," he mused, "you all get around a breakfast room table and get a big box out that has a puzzle in it. You don't always get to look at the outside and know what it's going to be when you get through."

Like missing puzzle pieces, he suggested to jurors, there were facts in this case no one would ever be able to explain—the unidentified fingerprints and two sets of shoeprints, as examples. "What I'm going to say to you is that the State has given you enough pieces, enough pieces to that puzzle" to be able to clearly see the picture, even without the missing pieces.

The jury didn't need every last piece, Cummings argued, to be "convinced to a moral certainty and beyond a reasonable doubt of what this picture is. And in this case, when you go back there and you begin deliberating—take all the pieces that the State has given you and put them the way that they do fit together. And at the end, the picture will be quite clear that this defendant murdered his wife, Michelle Fisher Young, on November the 3rd of 2006. It will be quite clear, and the State asks you to find him guilty of murder in the first degree."

With those final words, Cummings resumed his seat next

to Holt, hopeful that jurors now had all they needed to reach a unanimous guilty verdict.

Though the prosecution team's arguments covered a wide swath of the evidence presented, there was one glaring omission: Cindy Beaver. Despite the emphasis both Klinkosum and Collins had placed on her testimony—and the way she had been treated by law enforcement personnel—Cummings and Holt apparently decided their best strategy was to ignore her testimony altogether, gambling that jurors would conclude on their own that she was either misguided or mistaken.

Whether their gamble had paid off would be known soon enough.

.....

Jurors returned to begin their deliberations on Friday, March 2. After deliberating for more than five hours, they left for the weekend without reaching a verdict. Having waited more than five years for justice, Linda and Meredith would have to wait another three days. At the very least.

The following Monday, the jury returned, eager to complete its mission. At about 10:00 a.m., the foreperson had a note delivered to Judge Stephens.

She asked permission for the jury to review numerous items of evidence, including the still frame of Jason inside the Cracker Barrel, the jeans and *USA Today* newspaper found in his Explorer, the autopsy report, photos taken of the master bedroom before the crime scene was processed, Cassidy's pajamas, photos of Cassidy's hutch, the shoe impressions Agent Morrow made of the Hush Puppies Orbitals, the enlarged roadmap of Virginia and North Carolina, a diagram of the first floor of the Hampton Inn, and a photo showing the back of Jason's Explorer before it was processed.

With the assistance of the Clerk, the lawyers assembled the requested items on a table. After jurors returned to their seats, Judge Stephens had the bailiff begin passing several of the items through the jury box. He then allowed jurors to step into the well of the courtroom to examine Jason's jeans and

Cassidy's pajamas. They then returned to the jury room to continue their deliberations.

At 3:15 p.m., another note from the foreperson indicated jurors needed a twenty-minute break. And further, they intended to retire for the day at 4:45 p.m. It was becoming increasingly apparent, like the first jury, these jurors were also having a difficult time reaching a verdict. It now seemed inevitable deliberations would spill into a third day. For those waiting on the verdict—members of the Fisher and Young families in particular—anxiety and frustration were escalating with each passing minute.

The jury returned from its break just after 3:30 p.m. Less than ten minutes later, however, the foreperson knocked on the jury room door and handed the bailiff yet another note. Judge Stephens summoned the lawyers as the bailiff walked the note toward the bench. With mild trepidation, they began to examine the note together, fearful its contents might reveal that this jury was also "immovably hung."

But to their collective surprise and intense relief, the note indicated the jury had reached a unanimous verdict. More than two years after Jason's arrest. Nearly five and a half years since Michelle's murder. Finality was now just moments away.

. . . . .

The packed courtroom was filled with nervous anticipation as the eight women and four men emerged from the jury room and filed into the jury box one final time. Judge Stephens asked the foreperson if the jury had reached a unanimous verdict. She confirmed it had and handed the bailiff the manila envelope containing the verdict form. The entire courtroom fell eerily silent as the bailiff walked the envelope from the jury box to the bench. Time crawled almost to a halt, the suspense almost too much to bear.

With a poker face, Judge Stephens stared down at the verdict form for what seemed like an eternity.

He then announced the verdict: "We the jury, by unanimous verdict, find the defendant, Jason Lynn Young, to be *guilty* of first-degree murder of Michelle Fisher Young."

As the judge read the verdict, Jason stared straight ahead, devoid of any expression or emotion. The same could not be said for Linda and Meredith who from their seats just behind the prosecution table, quietly hugged one another, tears streaming down their faces. Finally. Justice. They were overwhelmed with emotion. Howard Cummings leaned over and grabbed Linda's hand, a broad smile washing over his face.

After thanking jurors for their service and excusing them from the courtroom, the judge asked if the defendant would be moving to set aside the verdict. After Collins responded that his client would, Judge Stephens began what turned into a five-minute soliloquy.

In a tone mixed with exasperation and sadness, the judge stated, "The Court's assessment of the evidence in the case is actually pretty simple. This is a domestic violence homicide case." He found "fingerprints of the domestic violence" throughout the case, stemming from a relationship that "escalated from disagreements to irreconcilable differences in which the defendant had pretty much declared he was done with the marriage." It appeared, he lamented, "to be a relationship in which some traumatic event was not only predictable, but almost inevitable."

As he continued, Judge Stephens periodically glanced directly at Jason, making sure the now-convicted defendant knew he was the intended audience.

The judge suggested if Michelle had called the police on November 2, 2006, and reported her husband had beaten her, and the police had found her "with missing teeth, a broken nose, and black eyes, no one that this couple knew, including their closest friends, would have been surprised. They would not, in my opinion, have been a bit surprised. So why would anyone be surprised when Michelle Young was found beaten to death?" he asked rhetorically. "The pattern is the same. The case is similar to every other case of domestic violence that has been played out in this courtroom in years' past."

Michelle "wasn't just murdered," Judge Stephens lamented.

"She suffered a beating the likes of which we seldom see. This woman was *punished*. The assailant struck her over thirty times with a weapon of some sort and she was undoubtedly unconscious after the second or third blow."

He said, "Overcome by anger and rage," Jason "continued to beat her until he was exhausted. Only then did he stop beating her, because he didn't have the strength to strike her any more."

Even then, the judge continued, disgust and derision now dominating his tone, "he had the energy to strip her of her engagement and wedding rings, perhaps because in his mind she was unworthy to wear them." He noted how Jason had also violently stripped his former fiancée of her engagement ring "when she had challenged him or somehow proven herself unworthy" to wear it.

Wake County's senior-most judge expressed his opinion Jason had significant mental health and anger-management issues, "and significant issues involving women." Not only did he have the motive and opportunity to commit this crime, he continued, "the circumstances of the crime scene point directly to him. I have no quarrel with this jury verdict."

His soliloquy complete, Judge Stephens asked Collins if his client wished to address the court before being sentenced. The Public Defender responded Jason didn't wish to do so.

"Very well," the judge replied. "Jason Young, stand please." In full compliance, Jason, Collins, and Klinkosum rose from their seats.

Judge Stephens then announced the only sentence permitted under the law: "The jury, having returned a verdict of guilty of murder in the first degree of Michelle Young, as by law required, it is the judgment of the court that the defendant be sentenced to life imprisonment in the North Carolina Department of Corrections without the benefit of parole. Jason Young, you're in the custody of the Sheriff to begin serving that sentence."

With that pronouncement, the freedom Jason had enjoyed for more than seven months came to a sudden—and permanent—end. Two uniformed Sheriff's deputies whisked him away through a side door. This time, there would be no last hug for his mom. Not even a wave goodbye. The next time Pat Young would get to see her son, there would be a thick glass window separating them.

.....

Interviewed outside the courthouse, Cummings told reporters Linda and Meredith had "been seeking justice for Michelle for almost six years. And now they feel like they have that. They feel like the jury has spoken the truth, and they are relieved." It had been "a long, hard path for the family of Michelle Young," Holt chimed in. "What sometimes gets lost in the coverage is that this is a real life that was lost."

Sheriff Donnie Harrison, reflecting on the hard work of his officers, added, "I wouldn't be able to tell you how many hours we spent on this case." Noting the absence of any "smoking gun," he expressed pride his office had "brought some closure to this family." He reminded reporters, "It was a brutal killing."

Tracey Raksnis, a 31-year-old healthcare worker who had relocated to Wake County from Delaware the year after the murder, served ably as the jury's foreperson. In an interview the day after the verdict, she provided a glimpse inside the jury room. "Going into the weekend," she said, "we were at seven guilty and five undecided." She hadn't yet made up her own mind.

The guilty verdict, she said, boiled down to a few key facts: "The lack of the shirt, the lack of the shoes, the fact that he didn't talk. This is a man who is on trial for his life, and didn't even say, 'I am not guilty.'"

Also critical to the jury's decision was the fact Cassidy had been cleaned up, the foreperson explained. "I don't see anyone else doing that. If this was random, if this was just a robbery, I don't think you pay that kind of attention."

Raksnis noted she had slept easy "knowing that I made the right decision."

# 24

## APPEAL

Less than five seconds after Judge Stephens sentenced Jason to life in prison, Bryan Collins—still on his feet—announced his client would appeal the jury's verdict.

In response to that oral notice of appeal, the judge appointed the North Carolina Appellate Defender's office to serve as Jason's appellate counsel. Soon, lawyers from that office began poring over more than 8,500 pages of trial transcripts, in search of an issue that would compel the Court of Appeals to overturn their new client's guilty verdict. It didn't take them long to find one.

In their view, Jason had been deprived of a fair trial because the criminal jury had been informed Judge Stephens had also been involved in the civil, wrongful death case against Jason, had reviewed the evidence, and had declared that he was Michelle's killer.

His appellate lawyers had never heard of a judge in a criminal case permitting a civil judgment of any kind—let alone one that had been pronounced by the criminal trial judge himself—to be admitted against a criminal defendant. Surely, they believed, there were precedents in court cases that prohibited civil judgments from being used in this manner.

Not only did they quickly find court cases along those very lines, those cases led them directly to the Holy Grail they were confident would set Jason free—or at least grant him a new trial. Buried deep within the tens of thousands of laws comprising the North Carolina General Statutes, Jason's new lawyers found a single sentence that read like music to their legal ears.

Section 1-149 of the General Statutes—which in one iteration or another had been on the books since 1868—stated, quite simply: *No pleading can be used in a criminal prosecution against a party as proof of a fact admitted or alleged in it.*

But that is exactly what Judge Stephens had permitted the prosecutors to do, they believed, when Clerk of Court Lorrin Freeman recited chapter and verse from the wrongful death complaint and the default judgment he had entered. And, once again, when the child custody complaint referring to that judgment was admitted into evidence during Mike Schilawski's testimony.

In their 52-page brief to the Court of Appeals, Jason's appellate lawyers made the violation of section 1-149 the centerpiece of his appeal.

.....

On December 12, 2013, just three city blocks from where the second jury had convicted Jason of first-degree murder, a packed courtroom anxiously awaited yet another battle in Jason's case—this time at the North Carolina Court of Appeals.

Linda and Meredith Fisher sat together with Jack Michaels, the lawyer who five years earlier had filed the wrongful death case that would be the featured topic of the oral argument that day. Pat Young sat on the opposite side of the gallery, surrounded by friends.

Howard Cummings and Becky Holt were in the front row, seated directly behind lawyers from the North Carolina Attorney General's office who would be arguing for the State.

Conspicuously absent from the day's proceedings was Jason Young himself—by then better known as Prisoner 1309245. He was hundreds of miles away at the Alexander Correctional Institution in the North Carolina mountains—his new home.

As the Clerk gaveled the courtroom to order, the three

judges assigned to the case made their entrance and assumed their seats. Judge Donna Stroud — the most senior of the three — called the case of *State v. Jason Lynn Young* on for argument.

Assistant Appellate Defender Barbara Blackman — Jason's new lawyer — walked up to the lectern dividing the two counsel tables and prepared to deliver her argument. The rules provided her all of thirty minutes to make her points and answer whatever questions the judges might pose.

Blackman began by quoting from Becky Holt's closing argument, which Holt herself had begun, "This case is solved. Jason Young brutally murdered Michelle Young in the early morning hours of November the 3rd, 2006, in the bedroom they shared at 5108 Birchleaf Drive." Blackman told the judges that those words "should sound familiar to you, because it's the language that appears in the wrongful death and child custody complaints."

"When the State's circumstantial case only got it a hung jury favoring acquittal," she argued, "the State turned to this inadmissible evidence in its attempt to gain a conviction. And if this type of evidence is admitted — for what will apparently be the first time in the country in a homicide prosecution — I think that it's simply going to open the door to the pursuit of civil litigation before indictment in order to manufacture evidence for use at an eventual criminal trial."

Before Blackman could get another word out, Judge Robert N. Hunter, Jr. interrupted, asking why no objection had been lodged based specifically on section 1-149. She agreed a more specific objection should have been made and lamented Jason's trial counsel had failed to conduct the necessary research to become aware of the statute's existence. But no specific objection was required, she argued, because Judge Stephens needed to comply with section 1-149's statutory "mandate" irrespective of whether an objection had been made.

The prejudice to Jason resulting from the admission of evidence related to the wrongful death case, Blackman argued, was easy to see, noting that in the first trial — when no such evidence was admitted — the jury voted 8-4 in favor of acquittal. But when that evidence was presented in the second trial, the jury reached a unanimous guilty verdict. "So I think we can say with confidence," she argued, "that this evidence did have a probable impact on the jury."

Jason's new lawyer contended it was "fundamentally unfair for the jury to be advised" a judgment had been entered declaring her client to be the killer and that his failure to answer the wrongful death complaint constituted an admission he was, in fact, the killer.

Assistant Attorney General Dan O'Brien made the primary argument for the State. Jason's lawyers were "simply wrong," he argued, in their position that section 1-149 "bars civil matters from being used in criminal cases. That's just not so." The statute, he told the judges, merely prevents prosecutors from using evidence of civil proceedings to tell the jury, "'See … this has already been adjudicated.' That's what's improper."

Judge Chris Dillon pressed O'Brien to explain why the State sought to have the wrongful death case brought to the jury's attention if it wasn't to suggest the defendant's guilt. O'Brien replied, in view of everything Jason had on the line when he failed to answer the wrongful death complaint—more than $4 million in life insurance proceeds and custody of Cassidy—his decision to remain silent, and not respond with the same information he shared with the first jury, helped establish his testimony had been fabricated.

Judge Hunter seemed perplexed by that response, asking why Jason's default "is of interest, or relevance, to a criminal jury trying to make a determination of who killed Mrs. Young? I mean, so what if he allows a default judgment to go in. How does that fact, one way or the other, have any impact on whether he killed his wife?" Pressing the Assistant Attorney General further, he asked, "Isn't the purpose of it for the State to say that he has admitted liability in the civil case and that he is guilty in the criminal case?"

"Absolutely not," O'Brien responded. "The State never admitted it for that purpose and never argued that." Rather, he contended, Jason had given this "simple explanation" during his testimony in the first trial related to his stay at the Hampton Inn. "If that was all he had to say, if that was his explanation for why he was really somewhere else, he would have said that when $4.2 million and custody of his child was on the line. And so it discredits his statement."

Judging by his bewildered expression, however, Judge Hunter didn't seem impressed by that explanation.

In less than an hour, the entire argument was over. Interviewed outside the courthouse, Cummings didn't appear the slightest bit concerned about what he had just observed—or the likely outcome.

"I believe that the case against Jason Young was tried free from error," he told reporters, "and our office and the Attorney General's Office is confident that the Court of Appeals will affirm his conviction."

As it turned out, however, that confidence was misplaced.

.....

On April 1, 2014, the Court of Appeals issued a unanimous, 58-page opinion. To Linda and Meredith Fisher, it read like a bad April Fool's joke—only it was no joke. The headline on the WRAL News website succinctly captured its significance: *NC Appeals Court Orders Third Murder Trial for Jason Young.* It was as devastating to Linda and Meredith—and the prosecution team—as the hung jury had been three years before. Yet another startling turn of events.

Not surprisingly, the opinion was authored by Judge Hunter, whose skepticism of the State's position had permeated the oral argument. That same skepticism was on full display in the opinion, which noted the State "did not offer an explicit purpose for offering evidence of the default judgment nor did the State offer a purpose for admitting the child custody complaint."

The opinion rejected the State's contention this evidence had been offered to impeach Jason's testimony by showing Jason's "silence in not responding to the lawsuits cast doubt on his subsequent testimony at his first trial."

The State's position seemed to be, Judge Hunter wrote, Jason had "great incentives to answer the civil matters and explain the evidence." But that purpose, he reasoned, revealed the State's true intention of introducing evidence of the civil matters—"to show proof of Defendant's guilt, in violation of N.C. Gen. Stat. § 1-149."

It also wasn't permissible for the State to impeach Jason's testimony, the opinion continued, because it was the State—not Jason—who introduced that testimony at the second trial. Because Jason hadn't testified at the retrial, there was nothing to impeach. It was also noteworthy, Judge Hunter wrote, that the State was unable to point to a single precedent "where a trial court has attempted to gain admission of a default judgment and a slayer determination in a homicide prosecution."

The three judges unanimously concluded Judge Stephens had improperly disregarded section 1-149 and abused his discretion in admitting evidence of the civil proceedings, resulting in Jason's presumption of innocence being "irreparably diminished." Admission of this evidence, the court held, "severely impacted" Jason's "ability to receive a fair trial."

The three-judge panel therefore ordered that Jason receive a *third* trial.

The ink on the opinion was barely dry when the North Carolina Attorney General's Office announced—the very next day—it would seek review by the North Carolina Supreme Court. Which would mean another round of briefing and yet another oral argument—before the entire, seven-member Supreme Court—a process that would likely last another year.

Justice for Linda and Meredith—having already been delayed for over seven years—would have to wait that much longer. Their only saving grace was that, this time, Jason would spend that entire time in prison.

·····

On May 19, 2015, Jason's case came on for argument before the North Carolina Supreme Court. Once again, the Fishers and Pat Young sat on opposite sides of the gallery, each with very different hopes and expectations. Linda and Meredith, for their part, were hopeful the Supreme Court would undo the Court of Appeals' decision and finally put an end to their long, arduous quest for justice.

Pat, on the other hand, was equally hopeful the decision would be affirmed, and her son would have the opportunity to convince a third jury that the State—relying only on proper evidence—couldn't prove his guilt beyond a reasonable doubt.

The seven justices sat in rapt attention as Dan O'Brien— representing the State, now as the appellant—delivered his argument. He began by suggesting the Court of Appeals had failed to appreciate it was *Jason's counsel* who interjected the civil pleadings into the second trial, specifically, during Bryan Collins' cross-examination of Meredith.

During that cross-examination, the Assistant AG told the justices, Meredith was asked directly about the custody complaint's allegation that Jason had brutally murdered Michelle. Thereafter, O'Brien pointed out, the defense team never objected to any evidence regarding the custody case. Any appellate review of the introduction of the custody case, he asserted, was therefore waived.

He then focused on the wrongful death complaint and judgment, reminding the court that Jason had testified he gave up custody of Cassidy because he had no money left to fight the custody case. That is the very reason why, O'Brien contended, his failure to respond to the wrongful death complaint was so significant: after all, by failing to respond to that complaint, he gave up the right to claim more than $4 million in life insurance proceeds "and let his assets be seized without even an answer."

O'Brien argued section 1-149 was merely a "common-sense principle" that proof of a fact in civil court is not proof of that same fact by the "beyond a reasonable doubt standard" required in criminal court.

At that point, Justice Robin Hudson jumped in, expressing her concern Lorrin Freeman had been permitted to testify at some length about the slayer statute and that Jason had been declared the slayer. She asked the Assistant AG if Judge Stephens had adequately explained to jurors they couldn't use that determination in assessing his guilt.

Though O'Brien responded Judge Stephens had, in fact, properly guided the jury how to use this evidence, Justice Hudson didn't appear convinced. She also seemed very troubled Judge Stephens, who had made the slayer declaration, "was also the very judge who presided over the criminal trial."

"So the jury then knew," she stated with apparent disapproval, "that the judge who was sitting there had already decided that this defendant was the one" who murdered Michelle.

As O'Brien's time neared its end, Justice Sam "Jimmy" Ervin—the grandson of the late United States Senator of the same name, and of Watergate fame—offered a helping hand. He suggested the State's position was that section 1-149 merely prevented the prosecution from using a civil pleading for the *sole purpose* of proving the matter alleged in the pleading. And further, that so long as a civil pleading is offered into evidence for a different purpose, "you could admit it for anything else."

O'Brien agreed, firmly grabbing the lifeline thrown by Justice Ervin. He also highlighted the failure of Jason's attorneys to object to that evidence on the basis of section 1-149.

Barbara Blackman began her argument by reminding the court the first jury had hung 8-4 in favor of acquittal. The State, she insisted, had resorted to the introduction of the civil complaints, Jason's default, the wrongful death judgment, and the slayer declaration in its zeal "to change the outcome at the new trial."

"This evidence," she asserted, "made molehills out of the mountains of problems in the State's circumstantial evidence case." But it also led to a "diminution in the defendant's presumption of innocence," Blackman argued, "as great as this court has ever reviewed."

Justice Hudson asked the Assistant Appellate Defender for her perspective on Judge Stephens' jury instructions. Blackman insisted the instructions were defective because they failed to inform the jury it couldn't use the civil pleadings and wrongful death judgment as proof of Jason's guilt.

Justice Ervin asked her whether Jason's defense counsel

had even objected to the content of the judge's instructions. Blackman conceded they hadn't, but contended it was nevertheless incumbent upon Judge Stephens—even without an objection—to instruct the jury it couldn't utilize this evidence to determine Jason's guilt.

Justice Robert Edmunds then chimed in, noting the Supreme Court—some 75 years earlier—had held a defendant's failure to object to the introduction of civil pleadings operated as a waiver of the defendant's right to assert the violation of section 1-149 on appeal.

"It seems to me in that instance," he told Blackman, "we did put the burden on the defendant to make the objection."

She disagreed, voicing her view, "The lack of an objection here didn't waive the 1-149 problem," because evidence of the default judgment was being used for an improper purpose.

Blackman ended her argument by asserting that one of the "biggest holes" in the State's case was establishing the time of Michelle's death. The only evidence admitted related to time of death, she noted, was from a paramedic who examined Michelle the afternoon of November 3, 2006, and concluded she "had been dead for some time." That left open the possibility she had been killed on November 2, rather than November 3. Yet the wrongful death complaint had to assert she was murdered on November 3, she told the justices, as Jason had an airtight alibi in Virginia on November 2.

Thus, in filing the wrongful death complaint, Blackman explained, the civil lawyers merely speculated Michelle had been murdered on November 3, which then "became *enshrined* in the civil judgment." The prosecution team's repeated references to November 3 as the date of death, she argued, hadn't been supported by any evidence beyond the allegations and findings of the civil pleadings and wrongful death judgment. In her view, that proved the State had indeed relied on the civil pleadings and wrongful death judgment to prove that Jason had killed Michelle on November 3.

Following the oral argument, Lorrin Freeman was interviewed outside the Supreme Court building. Her involvement in the case had grown significantly since her 2012 testimony about the wrongful death pleadings and judgment, upon which the now-completed arguments had focused. In November 2014, she had been elected as Wake County's new District Attorney.

"We are hopeful that based on the arguments today," Freeman told reporters, the Supreme Court justices "will make a determination that is different from that of the Court of Appeals. We will continue to fight for justice for Michelle Young."

. . . . .

August 21, 2015, would serve as yet another critical turning point in what had evolved into Linda's and Meredith's marathon for justice. On that date, the Supreme Court released a unanimous 44-page opinion that reversed the Court of Appeals' decision.

Writing for the court, Justice Ervin expressed agreement with the basic proposition Dan O'Brien had articulated during his argument: A trial court could admit evidence of civil pleadings in a criminal trial—despite the language of section 1-149—if "relevant for some purpose other than proving the same facts found, admitted, or alleged in the civil proceeding in question."

Consequently, section 1-149 didn't constitute a statutory mandate, as Barbara Blackman had argued, that required Judge Stephens—even without an objection—to exclude the evidence of the wrongful death complaint and judgment and child custody complaint.

Rather, as Justice Edmunds seemed to be suggesting during the oral argument, Jason's trial lawyers *were* required to cite the statute as the specific basis for their objection.

Because they had failed to do so, the justices ruled, Jason was precluded from asserting this argument—for the first time—on appeal.

They also held Judge Stephens didn't abuse his discretion in deciding to admit that evidence—particularly in view of the careful, limiting instruction he provided to the jury, to which

Jason's lawyers had also failed to object.

The final paragraph of the Supreme Court opinion contained two sentences intended to direct the case forward. In the first, the court ruled that the Court of Appeals "erred by awarding defendant a new trial."

In the second, it remanded the case back to the lower courts to permit Jason to argue that his trial lawyers' failure to cite section 1-149 as the basis for their objection to the admission of the civil pleadings and judgments resulted in him receiving "ineffective assistance of counsel"—legal parlance in the criminal arena essentially equivalent to the concept of malpractice in the civil arena.

Under the law, however, the hurdle a criminal defendant must clear to establish "ineffective assistance of counsel" is extremely high. Were it otherwise, criminal defendants dissatisfied with their guilty verdicts would pursue this avenue in virtually every case.

Thus, in contrast to the Court of Appeals—which had awarded Jason a third trial without qualification—the Supreme Court erected an extremely high bar Jason would need to surmount to obtain one. And to surmount that bar, he would need to put his own lawyers—Bryan Collins and Mike Klinkosum—on trial.

# 25

## OVERTIME

On the morning of June 15, 2017, those involved in the Jason Young case assembled in a Wake County courtroom for a final time, including family members, lawyers, Sheriff Donnie Harrison, and Sergeant Spivey. Though many of the faces were familiar, much had changed over the more than five years since Jason's last courtroom appearance.

For starters, the eleven-story, $184 million Wake County Justice Center in which the day's proceedings were being conducted was barely under construction in March 2012. Bryan Collins was no longer serving as Wake County's Public Defender, having parlayed his public exposure in Jason's case into his election to a Superior Court judgeship in November 2012. He now presided over murder trials from his perch on the bench, rather from a seat adjacent to the accused.

Collins wasn't the only lawyer involved in Jason's case now donning a black robe. In November 2016, Becky Holt won her own election and was Wake County's newest superior court judge. For his part, the County's longest-serving judge— Donald Stephens—was nearing the end of his illustrious 33-year tenure on the bench, which, under North Carolina law, would conclude in October 2017, following his 72nd birthday.

One lawyer notably absent that June morning was Mike Klinkosum. Though only in his mid-forties, Klink had suffered a massive stroke in July 2016 and was no longer a practicing lawyer, the stroke having robbed him of his short-term memory and some of the cognitive ability that had made him such an excellent courtroom lawyer. The day's proceedings had actually been delayed for nearly a year with the hope Jason's former counsel might regain enough mental acuity to be able to testify—a hope that, sadly, didn't come to pass.

Judge Paul Ridgeway presided over the "evidentiary hearing." Only 57, Judge Ridgeway was the most senior judge on the County's superior court bench after Judge Stephens. Upon Judge Stephens' retirement, he would assume the position of senior resident judge.

The Jason Young who Deputy Sheriffs ushered into the courtroom that morning couldn't have looked more different than he had during the two trials. His five and a half years in prison had aged him considerably. He appeared gaunt—almost malnourished—his suit jacket swimming across his shoulders and torso as if he were a child wearing an adult garment. It appeared as if his hair hadn't been cut a single time since the last trial, as it now hung well below his shoulders. During the lunch recess, he actually tied it into a tight pony tail.

Bob Trenkle, a criminal defense attorney from neighboring Chatham County, had been appointed to represent Jason at this special proceeding that had been necessitated by the Supreme Court's decision. He would serve as the fourth lawyer furnished to Jason at taxpayer expense—preceded by Collins, Klinkosum, and Blackman.

Trenkle's sole mission was to establish—to Judge Ridgeway's satisfaction—that Collins and Klinkosum had provided Jason with ineffective assistance during the second trial. And in particular, that their failure to bring section 1-149 to Judge Stephens' attention as a basis for excluding the wrongful death and custody complaints, default judgment, slayer determination, and $15 million wrongful death judgment had deprived their client of his Constitutional right to be afforded effective counsel.

As his first witness, Trenkle called Judge Bryan Collins, who rose from his seat in the back row of the gallery and began striding toward the front of the courtroom. As he walked by the defense counsel table, the former Public Defender gently patted Jason on the back—twice—as if to say, "I'm still here for you." For his part, Collins looked a good bit older than at his last appearance for Jason, his hair considerably grayer and hairline more elevated.

It became clear early in his testimony that Collins was more than willing to fall on his own sword. If admitting to failures in his representation of Jason would help his former client win a third trial, he was more than happy to oblige.

Collins testified he learned the prosecution team might seek to introduce evidence from the wrongful death case when it provided the defense team portions of the civil case file in discovery between the first and second trials. His biggest concern about the possible admission of that evidence, he said, "was that Judge Stephens had entered an order declaring Mr. Young to be the slayer."

That concern increased significantly at a December 16, 2011, hearing, a little more than a month before the second trial began. At that hearing, when Howard Cummings announced the State intended to offer evidence about the wrongful death proceedings, Judge Stephens responded there was nothing "'that would preclude an inquiry about that matter,'" Collins testified.

Trenkle asked what the defense team did after realizing Judge Stephens appeared inclined to allow that evidence to be admitted at the second trial. The witness responded that even though he and Klinkosum agreed it would be Collins' job to try to keep this evidence from being admitted, he neglected to conduct any legal research in his effort to keep this evidence out—admitting to not reviewing any cases or statutes. Instead, Collins testified, he had merely "thought about it a lot."

Trenkle then fast-forwarded to the trial, just before Lorrin Freeman took the witness stand to testify about the wrongful death proceedings. Judge Stephens called the lawyers into his chambers to discuss the matter, Collins testified. He said, "I did the best I could to convince Judge Stephens to exclude this testimony." The essence of his argument was, "This just isn't fair." But he wasn't able to cite any cases or statutes because he hadn't performed the necessary legal research.

During the chambers conference, Jason's former lawyer testified, Judge Stephens made it clear he was going to allow the evidence in. "He had a limiting instruction already prepared. Wasn't anything we asked for or had any input into. And my memory is that he told me he was going to let this into evidence and that I could go outside and make my objection, [saying] 'Let's move on.' That's what we did."

Getting to the heart of the matter, Trenkle asked, "You did not object under North Carolina General Statute 1-149?"

"I did not," Collins readily conceded. "I didn't know any other way to keep it out. If you want to call that my failure to do research, then that's what it was." Again, if admitting to this failure gave Jason a path to a third trial, he had no qualms about doing so.

But that wasn't the only failure Trenkle established during the former Public Defender's testimony. He asked Collins to confirm no specific objection had been made to Cummings' question which revealed that Judge Stephens himself had signed the judgment declaring that Jason had unlawfully killed Michelle.

"That's correct," Collins answered.

"Were you concerned that this jury might take the testimony that Judge Stephens had found Mr. Young to be the slayer as an expression of Judge Stephens' opinion?" Trenkle inquired.

"Not overtly," Collins responded, "but I think it was, I know it was very concerning that that would be a factor that they would consider."

"But yet you made no objection to that, other than the general objection?"

"Not specifically. No, I did not," Collins acknowledged. He also conceded he had failed to lodge any objection to testimony that Judge Osmond Smith had entered a wrongful death judgment against Jason for $15 million.

It wasn't every day Howard Cummings got to cross-examine a sitting superior court judge, but this was no ordinary day. Oddly, during this Kabuki dance that had Collins denigrating his own performance, Cummings' questioning was designed to make his former adversary appear to be Perry Mason. Or Ben Matlock. He had very little success doing so, however, and eventually passed the witness back to Trenkle for redirect examination.

Trenkle ended by asking the former Public Defender, "Did either you or Mr. Klinkosum want this evidence to come in?"

"No," Collins responded emphatically.

"Did either one of you think it would be a good idea for this evidence to come in?"

"No," Collins answered, putting a fine point on his testimony.

Trenkle tendered Joe Zeszotarski, a Raleigh criminal defense lawyer, as an expert witness in criminal defense trial representation. Zeszotarski had tried dozens of cases in Wake County since completing a clerkship for a federal judge in 1995. He testified that, upon his review of materials from Jason's second trial, the two areas that "jumped out" at him were the slayer declaration by Judge Stephens and the wrongful death judgment in the amount of $15 million, both of which he believed "would be very prejudicial for the jury to hear in a criminal case."

Zeszotarski explained that the normal course of action for a defense attorney confronted with the possibility of the prosecution seeking to admit this type of evidence would have been to conduct basic legal research. When he personally conducted computer-assisted legal research to determine if that type of evidence is admissible in a criminal trial, Trenkle's expert witness testified, it took him less than ten minutes to locate relevant case law and section 1-149 of the General Statutes.

In his opinion, Zeszotarski told Judge Ridgeway, it would have been the "prevailing norm of practice" for Collins and Klinkosum to have conducted that type of legal research and to have then filed a pre-trial motion—called a "motion *in limine*"—to try to exclude or limit this evidence at Jason's second trial. And further, to have objected when Cummings alerted the jury that Judge Stephens was the judge who made the slayer declaration, and to introduction of evidence about the $15 million wrongful death judgment and custody complaint.

Because Trenkle had the burden of proof to demonstrate Jason had received ineffective assistance of counsel, he was permitted to make the last argument.

Arguing first, Cummings focused nearly exclusively on establishing that whatever failures had occurred in Jason's representation, they didn't matter because the other, admissible evidence against him was so overwhelming. He reprised much of his and Becky Holt's closing arguments from the second trial for Judge Ridgeway—a newcomer to the case—arguing that "there was overwhelming evidence of this defendant's guilt beyond" the civil pleadings.

Trenkle began his argument by focusing on the deficiencies in Jason's legal representation. "Bryan Collins and Mike Klinkosum are both excellent lawyers and worked very hard in this case," he acknowledged, "but their failure to do legal research, failure to file motions in limine, and failure to object properly both to the wrongful death and the slayer declaration and the custody complaint … was deficient."

He suggested if a student on a first-year law school exam had failed to answer, "conduct legal research," in the situation that confronted Jason's attorneys, he or she would have failed. "There is no excuse for not conducting legal research," he asserted. "These are excellent attorneys, but they messed up here."

Trenkle contended Judge Ridgeway couldn't logically conclude the other evidence against Jason was overwhelming, because there had already been "a test case. We had the first trial. Eight people voted not guilty; four people voted guilty. And the only substantive evidence … that changed in the second trial," he argued, somewhat disingenuously, "was the wrongful death slayer evidence and the child custody complaint. And the verdict went from 8-4" in Jason's favor to 12-0 against him.

If the evidence at issue had been excluded, Trenkle continued, "I think there is a reasonable probability it would have been different." Recounting the gaps and holes in the forensic evidence around which Klinkosum had framed his closing argument, Jason's new lawyer pushed back hard on Cummings' assertion there was "overwhelming evidence" of Jason's guilt apart from the civil pleadings. "This case was far from overwhelming evidence," he contended.

With the evidence and arguments concluded, Judge Ridgeway told the lawyers he would take the matter "under advisement" and issue a ruling after he had a chance to "dig into" the issues further. Yet more waiting for everyone involved.

.....

On August 29, 2017, Judge Ridgeway released a meticulously detailed 51-page order. It signaled the likely end of Jason's path to a third trial.

Judge Ridgeway agreed with Trenkle that there was "no doubt that counsel for defendant failed to make themselves aware through research or consultation with other experienced practitioners in the field, of several pertinent legal grounds to challenge the admission of the contents of the civil wrongful death action or the child custody action."

"Among other things," he wrote, "defendant's counsel failed to make themselves aware of N.C. Gen. Stat. 1-149."

"By not making themselves aware of this law," he continued, "counsel did not assert timely objections to the admission of this evidence, and consequently, did not preserve certain arguments for appeal."

But Judge Ridgeway chose not to address whether those failures "amount to errors so fundamental that counsel was not functioning as the counsel guaranteed by the Sixth Amendment." Instead, he focused on whether Jason had suffered any prejudice as the result of Collins' and Klinkosum's failures—and concluded he hadn't.

First of all, the judge noted, the Supreme Court had made clear civil pleadings could, in some instances, be admitted into evidence in a criminal trial without violating section

1-149.

The admission of those pleadings in Jason's case, he ruled, was permissible as "probative for impeachment purposes of defendant's testimony at his first trial, to discredit his alibi, and to raise questions regarding defendant's conduct in the several years following the murder."

Therefore, he reasoned, even had Collins and Klinkosum "properly and thoroughly researched the admissibility of the civil pleadings in this criminal proceeding," and "noted more complete and comprehensive objections thereto, those objections would be properly denied because the civil pleadings were admissible for proper purposes other than to prove merely the facts alleged therein."

Judge Ridgeway flatly rejected Trenkle's argument that admission of the civil pleadings in the second trial was the only material difference between the two trials—and the logical reason why the second jury had unanimously voted to convict Jason though the first jury had nearly acquitted him.

That argument conveniently omitted, his order stated, how Jason's own testimony at the first trial "became a centerpiece of the State's case in the second trial. Because defendant testified at the first trial (and not at the second), the State was able to develop compelling evidence that defendant's first public statement, made 1,693 days after the murder and after he had reviewed all of the State's evidence against him through discovery and trial, was one of a guilty man who murdered his wife rather than a man who loved his wife. It was a statement that the State could impeach and to use to raise doubt about defendant's alibi."

Thus, considering the "totality of the circumstances," Judge Ridgeway concluded, there was no reasonable probability more proficient representation by Jason's defense lawyers would have resulted in a different outcome. "His claim of ineffective assistance of counsel fails," he ruled, "and the relief he seeks of a new trial is therefore denied."

.....

November 30, 2018, marked the end of the distinguished careers of two public servants who played central roles in Jason's case: Sheriff Donnie Harrison and Howard Cummings.

Harrison, now 72, had emerged victorious in every election since 2002 by comfortable margins. It had been widely assumed 2018 would be no different. But not only did he lose his re-election bid by a wide margin, he was beaten by one of his former deputies. His defeat marked the end of an illustrious 50-plus-year career in law enforcement.

For his part, Cummings left on his own terms, having decided 29 years was just enough service in the Wake County DA's Office. Ironically, he joined the law firm of Tharrington Smith, where his new partners would include Roger Smith, Jr. and Alice Stubbs, both of whom had represented Jason prior to his arrest. And the firm at which Bryan Collins began his career.

Fittingly, the Court of Appeals handed down its opinion resolving Jason's case—once and for all—as Sheriff Harrison and Cummings were cleaning out their respective desks and removing the pictures from their office walls. Sheriff Harrison grew wistful as he held the picture of Michelle Young and Cassidy that had sat on his desk for nearly twelve years.

After considering Judge Ridgeway's ruling, the appellate court issued a unanimous 33-page opinion. This time around, Judges Hunter, Stroud, and Dillon concluded Jason was *not* entitled to a third trial, holding Judge Ridgeway had correctly resolved the issues before him.

Though they expressed concern regarding "irregularities" exhibited by Collins and Klinkosum, they held Judge Ridgeway had ample evidence before him that demonstrated the defense lawyers' "subpar conduct" hadn't prejudiced Jason. For all intents and purposes, their decision marked the final chapter in Jason's seven-year appellate journey.

.....

Twelve years had passed since that fateful November day. Twelve agonizing years that irrevocably—and profoundly—

changed the life of every member of the Fisher and Young families.

A mother, daughter, and sister had been forever lost, as had hopes for a grandson, son, and nephew—whose life ended before it even began. A father, son, and brother had been sucked through the criminal justice system like a piece of meat through a grinder, finally succumbing to its mighty power.

A daughter had been left to grow up without either mother or father, surely aware by now her father was serving a life sentence for savagely killing her mother. Like cancer, these battle scars would gradually eat away at all surviving members of these two families.

But at the end of the day, the criminal justice system—as imperfect as this case demonstrated it is—served its purpose and worked precisely as designed. Dozens of professionals had labored tirelessly to achieve the correct result. As best they could, law enforcement officers thoroughly investigated a heinous crime. As best they could, prosecutors and defense lawyers marshalled mountains of evidence and made compelling arguments.

Two juries sifted through the evidence and arguments and ferreted out the truth, fulfilling one of the greatest responsibilities of citizenship. And ten appellate judges and one trial judge carefully reviewed the significant issues presented on appeal, faithfully applied the law, and ultimately resolved them.

When all was said and done, a man accused of a vicious crime had his day in court—not once, but twice. He and he alone had decided when, how, and with whom to share his story.

More than anything else, it was that story—and when and how he first told it—that best explains why the second jury concluded he had, in fact, brutally murdered his wife at the home they shared on Birchleaf Drive—and why, barring a turn of events of a magnitude far greater than the hung jury or the first Court of Appeals' decision, Jason Lynn Young will spend the rest of his life in prison.

# ACKNOWLEDGEMENTS

Unfortunately, even all these years later, the events described in the foregoing pages left virtually everyone involved too wrought with emotion to sit down with me for interviews—including Jason and Michelle Young's family members, prosecutors, defense lawyers, family-law attorneys, detectives, and jurors. With the one exception noted below, my efforts to interview them and obtain their feedback on my drafts were unsuccessful.

To my good fortune, however, I was able to stumble upon the full transcripts of both trials and virtually every hearing. And thanks to WRAL never taking down from its website its daily, gavel-to-gavel video footage of both trials, I was able to watch—on my laptop and at my leisure—nearly everything that happened in the courtroom as if I had been there. That allowed me to convey the emotions displayed by the lawyers and witnesses—and even the judge—in ways that would have been impossible solely with the written transcripts at my disposal.

Amanda Lamb, who covered both trials for WRAL-TV and who is herself a published true crime author (as well as novelist), was gracious enough to sit with me as I started this project and persuade me that, despite this being my maiden voyage, I could actually do it. I greatly appreciate her time, encouragement, mentoring, and thoughtful feedback on my early drafts.

I am grateful to Jack Michaels, with whom I attended the same church for many years, who provided valuable information and insights about his and his brother Paul's representation of Linda and Meredith Fisher in the wrongful death case that loomed so large over the criminal and appellate proceedings.

My managing partner at the Poyner Spruill law firm, Dan Cahill, was aware of my work on this project and could have steered me away from it. Instead, he encouraged me, even if it, from time to time, distracted me from my day job. My amazing personal assistant at the firm, Sandy Chrisawn, couldn't have been more encouraging, reading every chapter hot off the press and making me believe she loved it. Whether she did or didn't, her enthusiasm and support kept me going.

My mom, Evelyn Epstein, grammar police officer that she is, relished her job ferreting out typos and grammatical errors, which she did with aplomb. She encouraged me the way only a mother truly can—and I sincerely appreciate her support.

My beautiful and talented South African tutu-designing bride, Aletia Ferreira, couldn't have been more supportive, despite me beginning this project barely a year after we exchanged vows on our back deck. Her support didn't waver even when I would go dark for days on end in my attempts to polish the many rough edges that hopefully disappeared before these pages saw the light of day.

Though I purposefully kept our kids, Benjamin, Madeline, Enzo, Tucker, and Thomas blissfully unaware of what I was doing until Black Lyon Publishing came calling, they nonetheless served as an inspiration to me, and always will be.

As I neared the end of my first draft, I decided to contact another reporter who covered this story for years, Anne Blythe, who had the courtroom beat at the *News & Observer*, Raleigh's long-time daily newspaper. Not only did Anne agree to read the draft, her initial comments convinced me it was nowhere near ready for "prime time."

At my request, she labored tirelessly to help me edit and revise each chapter into something much better than it was before. Without Anne's help, this book would never have been ready for prime time. I am enormously grateful for her able assistance.

Finally, I would be remiss if I didn't acknowledge a certain treadmill at the gym I frequent, upon which I had many epiphanies that led directly to words and passages found on the foregoing pages. To the extent credit is due for any particularly insightful thoughts or elegant or pithy turns of phrase (including this one), that credit rightly belongs to that treadmill, rather than to me.

CPSIA information can be obtained
at www.ICGtesting.com
Printed in the USA
LVHW041239120520
655430LV00003B/81